The Logic of Regional Inte

MW00444516

Europe and Beyond

In the late 1980s regional integration emerged as one of the most important developments in world politics. It is not a new phenomenon, however, and this book presents the first analysis of integration across time, and across regions. Walter Mattli examines projects in nineteenth- and twentieth-century Europe, but also in Latin America, North America, and Asia since the 1950s. Using the tools of political economy, he considers why some integration schemes have succeeded while many others have failed; what forces drive the process of integration; and under what circumstances outside countries seek to join regional groups. Unlike traditional political-science approaches, the book stresses the importance of market forces in determining the outcome of integration; but unlike purely economic analyses, it also highlights the importance of institutional factors. The book will provide students of political science, economics, and European studies with a new framework for the study of regional integration.

WALTER MATTLI is Assistant Professor in the Department of Political Science and a member of the Institute on Western Europe and the Institute of War and Peace Studies at Columbia University.

The Logic of
Regional Integration

Europe and Beyond

Walter Mattli

CAMBRIDGE
UNIVERSITY PRESS

PUBLISHED BY THE PRESS SYNDICATE OF THE UNIVERSITY OF CAMBRIDGE
The Pitt Building, Trumpington Street, Cambridge CB2 1RP, United Kingdom

CAMBRIDGE UNIVERSITY PRESS
The Edinburgh Building, Cambridge, CB2 2RU, UK http://www.cup.cam.sc.uk
40 West 20th Street, New York, NY 10011–4211, USA   http://www.cup.org
10 Stamford Road, Oakleigh, Melbourne 3166, Australia

First published 1999

Printed in the United Kingdom at the University Press, Cambridge

Typeset in 10/12pt Plantin   [CE]

A catalogue record for this book is available from the British Library

Library of Congress Cataloguing in Publication data
Mattli, Walter.
The logic of regional integration: Europe and beyond / Walter Mattli.
     p.   cm.
Includes bibliographical references.
ISBN 0 521 63227 7 (hardback). – ISBN 0 521 63536 5 (paperback)
1. International economic integration.
2. Europe – Economic integration.
3. Regionalism (International organization)
4. European federation.   I. Title.
HF1418.5.M39   1998   337.1′4–dc21   98–11655   CIP

ISBN 0 521 63227 7 hardback
ISBN 0 521 63536 5 paperback

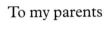
To my parents

Contents

Acknowledgements

I have incurred many debts in writing this book. The University of Chicago, the Mellon Foundation, the Swiss National Foundation for Research, the Janggen Pöhn Foundation, and the European University Institute have supported me financially at various stages of my research. Columbia University also provided me with leave time, research support, and an intellectually stimulating environment.

My deepest debt is to the University of Chicago where I had the great fortune to be a graduate student in the first half of the 1990s. Chicago's truly interdisciplinary spirit and long tradition of critical thought provided me with the ideal environment in which to grow intellectually. One Chicago workshop, the Program on International Politics, Economics, and Security (PIPES), played a particularly important role as a testing ground of my ideas on regional integration, and more generally as a forum in which I learned to think analytically about international relations. In weekly PIPES sessions, faculty and graduate students would meet to analyze new work on the various facets of international relations and to debate vigorously the latest trends in world affairs. The two PIPES directors, Charles Lipson and Duncan Snidal, have served on my dissertation committee, along with Russell Hardin. The three have constantly supported me in my research and have generously given of their time to read and thoughtfully comment on my various chapter drafts. I owe them an immense debt of gratitude. Other PIPES fellows I would like to thank warmly for their constructive criticism of my work are Daniel Verdier, Hein Goemans, Jim Fearon, Atsushi Ishida, Barbara Koremenos, Andy Kydd, and Brian Portnoy. At Columbia University, where I started to teach in the Fall of 1995, I received helpful comments from my colleagues David Baldwin, Robert Jervis, Helen Milner, Edward Mansfield, Hendrik Spruyt, and from doctoral students Marc Austin, Tim Büthe, Shanker Satyanath, Leslie Vinjamuri Wright, and Katja Werlich. Scholars from other universities to whom I am grateful for insightful comments on drafts or for helpful discussion on integration issues are Christopher Ansell, Peter Barsoom, Pieter Bouwen, Steve

Brams, Dirk DeBrievre, Richard Doner, George Downs, Karl-Orfeo Fioretos, Geoff Garrett, Philipp Genschel, Kate McNamara, David Lake, David Lazer, Nathan Lucas, John Odell, Robert Pastor, Thomas Risse, Manfred Rist, Philippe Schmitter, Wayne Sandholtz, Alec Stone, as well as the participants of seminars at the University of Chicago, Columbia University, the University of California, Irvine, Emory University, the European University Institute, Princeton University, the University of Rochester, Stanford University, and Tulane University. Debbie Davenport deserves special thanks. She perused the entire manuscript and suggested countless improvements of the text. Gregory Weisler, Ashley Leeds, and Tim Büthe provided invaluable research assistance. At Cambridge University Press, I would like to express my gratitude to John Haslam, the commissioning editor for the social sciences, for his most expert handling of my manuscript at the various stages of production, to Jean Field, my copy-editor, for carefully reading and correcting the entire text, and to two anonymous reviewers for excellent comments.

Finally, I am very grateful to Yves Mény, the director of the Robert Schuman Center of the European University Institute in Florence, for having invited me to spend the 1997–1998 academic year as a Jean Monnet Fellow at his Center. It was there that I put the finishing touches to the manuscript. I will forever cherish the memory of the spectacular view from my office at the Center of the cypress-tree lined hill of Fiesole and the large olive-tree grove of the *convento* San Domenico.

1 Introduction

1 The phenomenon of regional integration

Regional integration schemes have multiplied in the past few years and the importance of regional groups in trade, money, and politics is increasing dramatically. Regional integration, however, is no new phenomenon. Examples of *Staatenbünde, Bundesstaaten, Eidgenossenschaften*, leagues, commonwealths, unions, associations, pacts, confederacies, councils and their like are spread throughout history. Many were established for defensive purposes, and not all of them were based on voluntary assent. This book looks at a particular set of regional integration schemes. The analysis covers cases that involve the *voluntary* linking in the economic and political domains of two or more formerly independent states to the extent that authority over key areas of national policy is shifted towards the supranational level.

The first major voluntary regional integration initiatives appeared in the nineteenth century. In 1828, for example, Prussia established a customs union with Hesse-Darmstadt. This was followed successively by the Bavaria Württemberg Customs Union, the Middle German Commercial Union, the German Zollverein, the North German Tax Union, the German Monetary Union, and finally the German Reich. This wave of integration spilled over into what was to become Switzerland when an integrated Swiss market and political union were created in 1848. It also brought economic and political union to Italy in the *risorgimento* movement. Integration fever again struck Europe in the last decade of the nineteenth century, when numerous and now long-forgotten projects for European integration were concocted. In France, Count Paul de Leusse advocated the establishment of a customs union in agriculture between Germany and France, with a common tariff bureau in Frankfurt.[1] Other countries considered for membership were Belgium, Switzerland, Holland, Austria-Hungary, Italy, and Spain. In

---

[1] See Paul de Leusse, "L'Union Douanière Européenne," *Revue d'Economie Politique* 4 (1890), 393–401.

1

Austria, the economist and politician Alexander Peez forged plans for a Middle European Zollverein that included France.[2] And Count Goluchowski, the Minister of Foreign Affairs of Austria-Hungary, passionately advocated the idea of a united Europe in his public speeches. Many other politicians, economists, and journalists made proposals for European union which circulated through the European capitals during that decade.[3] Ultimately, all the projects came to naught.

Half a century later, the idea of European integration was re-invented and the process of merging European nation-states into one prosperous economy and stable polity began. The first step was taken with the creation of the European Coal and Steel Community (ECSC) in 1952. In 1957, Germany, France, Italy, Belgium, Luxemburg, and the Netherlands signed the Treaty of Rome establishing the European Community (EC).[4] The first enlargement of the EC occurred in 1973, with the accession of the United Kingdom, Denmark, and Ireland. Greece joined in 1981, Spain and Portugal in 1986. Nine years later, Austria, Finland, and Sweden became the Community's newest members. In the meantime, European integration had moved beyond trade. In 1979, the European Monetary System was established. And in 1992 the Community adopted the Maastricht Treaty on European Monetary and Political Union. By November 1993, the Community had changed its name to the European Union (EU) to mark the deep level of integration attained.[5]

Integration is not an exclusively European phenomenon, of course. In the 1960s the Latin American Free Trade Association, the Andean Pact, and the Central American Common Market were launched. In the early 1990s, more than half a dozen new integration projects were started in Latin America, the most notable being the Mercado Común del Sur

---

[2] Alexandre Peez, "A Propos de la Situation Douanière en Europe," *Revue d'Economie Politique* 5 (February, 1891), 121–139; see also his *Zur Neuesten Handelspolitik* (Vienna: Commissionsverlag v. G. Szelinski, 1895).

[3] See, for example, Paul Leroy-Beaulieu, "De la Nécessité de Préparer une Fédération Européenne," *L'Economiste Français* 2 (September, 1898), 305–307; Gustave De Molinari, "A Zollverein in Central Europe," *Gunton's Magazine* 12 (January 1897), 38–46; Handelskammersekretär Wermert, "Einige Betrachtungen über einen Mitteleuropäischen Zollverein," *Annalen des Deutschen Reichs für Gesetzgebung, Verwaltung und Statistik* 12 (1888), 943–954. For a good survey, see Ernst Francke, "Zollpolitische Einigungsbestrebungen in Mitteleuropa während des letzten Jahrzehnts," *Schriften des Vereins für Socialpolitik* 90 (Leipzig, 1900), 187–272.

[4] The Treaty of Rome established two new communities: the European Economic Community (EEC) and the European Atomic Energy Community. The EEC has been referred to as the European Community (EC) for many years. I will follow this convention throughout the book.

[5] I use the terms European Community and European Union interchangeably throughout the book.

(MERCOSUR) comprising Argentina, Brazil, Paraguay, and Uruguay. In North America, a Free Trade Agreement between the United States and Canada was signed in 1989. This agreement grew into the North American Free Trade Agreement (NAFTA) when Mexico joined in 1994. In Asia, the most notable regional grouping is the Association of Southeast Asian Nations (ASEAN), formed in 1967. In 1992 members agreed to establish gradually an ASEAN Free Trade Area. One of the most rapidly expanding groups is the Asia Pacific Economic Cooperation forum (APEC). It was launched in 1989 by Australia, New Zealand, Japan, South Korea, Canada, the United States, and the ASEAN countries. Today it comprises eighteen members. Malaysia also recently promoted the idea of a Japan-centered Asian bloc, the East Asian Economic Grouping (EAEG).

Tables 1.1 to 1.3 provide a sample of the most important regional integration schemes around the world, past and present.

2   Explaining regional integration

This book seeks to introduce analytical order to this multitude of integration schemes and to address the general question of what forces drive the process of voluntary integration. The study is motivated by the belief that there is a general logic to regional integration, or – in the words of Milton Friedman – "that there is a way of looking at or interpreting or organizing the evidence that will reveal superficially disconnected and diverse phenomena to be manifestations of a more fundamental and relatively simple structure."[6] To claim that there are recurring regularities, however, is not to deny the complexity of the phenomenon under study, nor to belittle the importance of differences that remain unexplained by my approach. Regional integration is a product of many and varied forces. This book offers no full account of the phenomenon, neither descriptively nor analytically. It simply seeks to answer a few important questions about regional integration which have remained unaddressed, by incorporating hitherto much neglected factors into the explanation of a complex reality.

This book is also an invitation to the reader to think scientifically about integration and to be wary of so-called explanations that fail basic tests of scientific inference. Unfortunately, these explanations are many. In the context of recent European integration, three popular accounts of the forces driving integration are frequently encountered. First, it is said that politicians, haunted by the horrors of the Second World War, were

[6] Milton Friedman, *Essays in Positive Economics* (Chicago: University of Chicago Press, 1953), p. 33.

Table 1.1. *Selected regional integration schemes in Europe*

Name of integration scheme	Objective
Bavaria–Württemberg Customs Union 1828–1833	Common tariff. Each state retains own customs administration.
Middle German Commercial Union 1828–1831	Closer commercial ties. To keep commercial expansion of Prussia in check. No common tariff.
German Zollverein 1834	Developed from customs union of 1828 between Prussia and Hesse-Darmstadt; all German states eventually joined; laid down the economic foundation for political unification of Germany.
Tax Union (Steuerverein) 1834–1854	Established by Hanover and Brunswick; Oldenburg joined in 1836; Lippe Schaumburg in 1838. Genuine customs union with common tariff, common excises, joint customs administration.
German Monetary Union (Deutscher Münzverein) 1838	Fixed rates (based on the Cologne mark of fine silver) between the thaler of Prussia, Hanover, and other North German states and the florin currency in the South German states.
Moldovian-Wallachian Customs Union 1847	Led to the foundation of Romania in 1878.
Swiss Confederation 1848 (completed in 1874)	Economic and political unification of Switzerland.
German Monetary Convention 1857	Attempt to secure fixed rates between Prussian thaler, South German florin, and the Austrian monetary system; a Union thaler (*Vereinsthaler*) was introduced (equal in value to one Prussian thaler).
Latin Monetary Union 1865	The basis of this union was the French franc (established in 1803 as a metric coin on a bi-metallic base). Belgium based their franc on French coin in 1832; Switzerland in 1850; Italy in 1865 (year of conference establishing LMU); Greece joined in 1867.
Scandinavian Monetary Union 1875	Based on crown of 100 ore; included Sweden, Denmark, Norway.
Benelux 1944	Customs convention between the Netherlands and the Belgian–Luxemburg Economic Union of 1921.
European Community (EC) 1958	By 1968 removal of tariffs and quotas; common external tariff; common policies in agriculture, regional development, research and development, education, economic cohesion etc. Powerful supranational institutions.

	Single European Act (1987): Plan to establish free movement of goods, services, factors of production by 1992. Maastricht Treaty (1993): seeks monetary union (EMU) and closer political union. Members: Austria (1995), Belgium, Denmark (1973), Finland (1995), France, Germany, Greece (1981), Ireland (1973), Italy, Luxemburg, Netherlands, Portugal (1986), Spain (1986), Sweden (1995), UK (1973).
European Free Trade Agreement (EFTA) 1960	Elimination of all tariffs on manufactures by mid-1967; special rules for agricultural trade; various EFTA members sought free-trade agreements (FTAs) with the EC in 1972–1973. Members: Iceland (1970), Liechtenstein (1991), Norway, Switzerland. The UK and Denmark left in the early 1970s. Austria, Finland, and Sweden left in 1994 to join the EU. *European Economic Area* (EEA) (1992): Extended EC law provisions of "EC92" to EFTA. (Switzerland rejects the EEA in 1992.)
European Monetary System (EMS) 1979	Established by members of the EC to coordinate and stabilize exchange rates of member countries. Membership is voluntary.

naturally driven to devise a novel structure of European governance capable of eradicating the very roots of intra-European conflicts. The creation of the European Coal and Steel Community served this purpose directly. It established supranational control over resources that render warfare possible. The concern about securing peace may also have contributed to the set-up of the European Community, and there is evidence that this concern lingered on into the 1980s. But is it the *main* force that has driven European integration? Why then was a rival regional community set up, the European Free Trade Association, given the tendency of rival commercial unions to exacerbate conflicts? Why did not all European countries participate in the peace-building effort from the beginning? Did the United Kingdom, Denmark, and Ireland join the European Community in 1973 because of concerns about peace?

A second set of explanations centers around the notion of leadership. Insightful, charismatic leaders, it is alleged, managed to transcend the narrow-mindedness and selfishness of domestic pressure groups hostile to integration and European unity. But this account is flawed by its inability to explain numerous failures of these leaders and long phases of stagnation in the process of community building.

Table 1.2. *Selected regional integration schemes on the American continent*

Name of integration scheme	Objective
Gran Colombia 1948	Plan to establish a Greater Colombia Economic and Customs Union (members: Colombia, Ecuador, Panama, Venezuela).
Central American Common Market (CACM) 1960	Objective: customs union and joint industrial planning (import substitution industrialization). By 1966, tariffs were removed on 94% of intraregional trade, and 80% of extraregional imports were covered by a common external tariff. Intraregional trade increased from 5.9% in 1958 to 24.2% in 1968. CACM's success story ends with the "Soccer War" of 1969 between El Salvador and Honduras. *1991*: Renewed effort to implement free-trade agreement. (Adoption of timetable for trade liberalization. Members, however, fail to agree on common external tariff by 1992.) *1993*: CACM and Panama sign the Central American Economic Integration Treaty. Members: Costa Rica (1963), El Salvador, Guatemala, Honduras, Nicaragua. *1993*: CACM signs free-trade agreement with Colombia and Venezuela. *1994*: CACM signs free-trade agreement with Mexico.
Latin American Free Trade Association (LAFTA) 1960	Objective: free trade association with joint industrial planning. Common list of products to be liberalized by 1972. Partial implementation in the 1960s. Common list not liberalized on schedule. LAFTA was replaced by Latin American Integration Association (LAIA) in 1980. *1990*: Announcement of renewed tariff reductions and trade liberalization. Members: Mexico and all South American countries, except Guyana, French Guiana, Suriname.
Andean Pact (AP) 1969	Objective: Customs Union and joint industrial planning. Postponed several times. *1989*: AP targets 1995 for the establishment of a free-trade area and 1997 for the establishment of a common market. *1996*: The Trujillo Act changes the group's name to Andean Community and lays down proposals for the strengthening of the political aspects of the bloc through the creation of a secretary general and an Andean Parliament. Members: Bolivia, Ecuador, Colombia, Peru, Venezuela (Chile withdrew in 1976).

Caribbean Community (CARICOM) 1973	Objective: customs union and joint industrial planning. Little progress. *1990*: New schedule outlined establishing a common external tariff. A subgroup of CARICOM, the Organization of East Caribbean States (OECS) agreed to implement CARICOM's external tariff ahead of schedule and to implement a phased removal of quantitative restrictions on all intraregional imports. Members: Antigua and Barbuda, Bahamas (1983), Barbados, Belize (1974), Dominica (1974), Grenada (1974), Guyana, Jamaica, Montserrat (1974), St. Kitts and Nevis, St. Lucia (1974), St. Vincent and the Grenadines, Trinidad and Tobago, Suriname (1995).
Mercado Común del Sur (MERCOSUR) 1991	Objective: Creation of a single market in goods, capital, and people by January 1995, but the treaty was amended by the Protocol of Ouro Preto in December 1994 with the member states agreeing on an imperfect customs union by January 1995. *1995*: MERCOSUR agrees to a five-year program under which it hopes to perfect the customs union. Members: Argentina, Brazil, Paraguay, and Uruguay.
Canada–US Free Trade Agreement (1989) North American Free Trade Agreement (NAFTA) 1994	Obective: Removal of all tariffs and most quantitative restrictions by 1999. Liberalization of trade in services, government procurement, and investment. Objective: NAFTA is a new, improved, and expanded version of the US–Canada FTA. It provides for phased elimination of tariffs and most non-tariff barriers on regional trade within ten years. A few import-sensitive products will have a fifteen-year transition period. NAFTA extends the dispute settlement of the US–Canada FTA to Mexico.

[handwritten margin note: Changed Pref – not proven]

An ever-popular third explanation refers to changed preferences. The timing of a new application for membership, it is claimed, is attributable to the pressure from growing segments of society desirous of being connected to the larger "Euro-culture." These accounts based on *ad hoc* shifts in preferences seem little more than thinly veiled acknowledgements of theoretical ignorance. They shift the causal impetus to the social level, but then leave it unexplained.

The problem with explanations of this kind is not necessarily that they are wrong but that they are insufficient. The fact that a country or a region has a particular historical, political, or geographical trait provides no justification for the inference that there is a causal connection unless it identifies an attribute that can also explain a number of other cases or

Table 1.3. *Selected regional integration schemes in Africa, Asia, the Pacific, and Middle East*

Name of integration scheme	Objective
Southern African Customs Union (SACU) 1969	Based on customs union dating back to 1910. Goods and factor markets are well integrated. Common external tariff is operational. Members: Botswana, Lesotho, South Africa, Swaziland. Namibia joined in 1990.
Communauté Economique de l'Afrique de l'Ouest (CEAO) 1972	Objective: free-trade area. Members belong to the Western African Monetary Union (WAMU) and to the Economic Community of West African States (ECOWAS). Community Development Fund to compensate members for loss of tariff revenue. Members: Benin, Burkina Faso, Côte d'Ivoire, Mali, Mauritania, Niger, and Senegal.
Union Dounière et Economique de l'Afrique Centrale (UDEAC) 1973	Objective: Customs union. Little progress. Common external tariff was abolished *de facto*; intra-union trade in manufactures restricted to those produced by firms enjoying the status of *Taxe Unique* system. Members: Cameroon, Central African Republic, Congo, Gabon, Chad, Equatorial Guinea.
Economic Community of West African States (ECOWAS) 1975	Objective: full economic integration in fifteen years (customs union, development, and policy harmonization). Progress negligible. Includes members of CEAO and the Mano River Union (Guinea, Liberia, Sierra Leone). New project to eliminate non-tariff barriers (NTBs) by 1995. Members: Benin, Burkina Faso, Cape Verde, Côte d'Ivoire, Gambia, Ghana, Guinea, Guinea-Bissau, Liberia, Mali, Mauritania, Niger, Nigeria, Senegal, Sierra Leone, Togo.
Southern African Development Coordination Conference (SADCC) 1980	Objective: reduce economic dependence on South Africa through cooperation on projects to foster balanced regional development. Members: Angola, Botswana, Lesotho, Malawi, Mozambique, Namibia (1990), Swaziland, Tanzania, Zambia, Zimbabwe.
Preferential Trade Area for Eastern and Southern Africa 1984	Objective: elimination of tariffs on all goods by 2000. Harmonization of policies. Some progress in tariffs (difficulties due to macroeconomic imbalances and the equitable distribution of costs and benefits). Members: Angola, Burundi, Comoros, Djibouti, Ethiopia, Kenya, Lesotho, Malawi, Mauritius, Mozambique, Rwanda, Somalia, Sudan, Swaziland, Tanzania, Uganda, Zambia, Zimbabwe.

Association of South East Asian Nations (ASEAN) 1967	Objective: free-trade area and common industrial projects. Minimal intra-trade liberalization achieved. Industrial cooperation scarcely implemented. Effective in promoting regional political stability. Recent proposals by Thailand to create an ASEAN Free Trade Area (AFTA) within fifteen years. Plan endorsed in 1992 by ASEAN ministers. Members: Indonesia, Malaysia, the Philippines, Singapore, Thailand, Brunei, Vietnam. *1997*: ASEAN decides to extend membership to Burma, Cambodia, and Laos.
Australia–New Zealand Closer Economic Relations Trade Agreement (ANZCERTA) 1983	Objective: elimination of all tariffs by 1988 and all quantitative restrictions by 1995. In 1988, agreement for liberalization of trade in services and harmonization of regulatory practices. The agreement was slightly expanded in 1992.
Gulf Cooperation Council (GCC) 1981	Objective: customs union and political cooperation. Harmonization of policies, and customs unions. A common external tariff has not yet been implemented. Members: Bahrain, Kuwait, Oman, Quatar, Saudi Arabia, United Arab Emirates.
Asia Pacific Economic Cooperation forum (APEC) 1989	Started as a consultative body for trade issues. Members signed in 1994 an APEC "free -trade" agreement that is nonbinding and fails to define the scope of free trade. Members: ASEAN countries, Canada, United States, Australia, New Zealand, Japan, South Korea, China (1991), Taiwan (1991), Hong Kong (1991), Mexico (1993), Papua New Guinea (1993), Chile (1994). Vietnam has applied for membership.

Sources (Tables 1.1 to 1.3): Jacob Viner, *The Customs Union Issue* (New York: Carnegie Endowment for International Peace, 1950); Pierre Benaerts, *Les Origines de la Grande Industrie Allemande* (Paris: F. H. Turot, 1933); L. Bosc, *Union Douanières et Projets d'Union Douanières* (Paris: Librairie Nouvelle de Droit et de Jurisprudence, 1904); Sidney Pollard, *European Economic Integration 1815–1970* (London: Harcourt Brace Jovanovich, 1974); Augusto de la Torre and Margaret Kelly, *Regional Trade Arrangements*, occasional paper 93 (Washington: International Monetary Fund, March 1992); Jaime de Melo and Arvind Panagariya (eds.), *New Dimensions in Regional Integration* (Cambridge: Cambridge University Press, 1993); *Latin America Monitor – Central America* 10, no. 12 (December 1993). Jeffrey Frankel, *Regional Trading Blocs in the World Economic System* (Washington: Institute for International Economics, 1997).

phenomena or is logically derived from a theory that has wide explanatory power. It is almost always possible to provide an "explanation"
after the event if any amount or type of information about a sufficiently
complex single case can be used in constructing the explanation.[7]

At various times, social scientists have searched for more rigorous
explanations of economic and political integration. In political science,
one major analytical framework for understanding integration is neofunctionalism. It clarifies and refines many of the ideas developed by its
predecessor theory, functionalism. It begins with the assumption that
supranationality is the only method available to states to secure
maximum welfare and then proceeds to provide an insightful account of
how integration evolves using concepts such as functional spillover,
updating of common interests, and subnational and supranational
group dynamics. Neofunctionalism is an important building-block of a
comprehensive account of integration. But it is not enough. By its very
assumption it fails to give an explanation of the link between welfare
maximization and regional integration. It seeks to account for the
institutional arrangements within a region in which economic transactions take place, but it leaves these transactions unexamined. Another
weakness is that it never fully specifies the conditions under which
subnational demands for integration become accepted at the national
level. As a result, neofunctionalism fails to answer several important
questions: what exactly are the forces that render the nation-state
obsolescent? Why is decision-making at the supranational level more
efficient? Why have some integration schemes failed? Why does a
country seek to join an already existing community and what explains
the timing of such a request for membership? Other questions that
neofunctionalism fails to address are: what role do external events play
in regional integration? What is the impact of community-building on
non-members?

Intergovernmentalism is an alternative approach to integration in
political science. Unlike neofunctionalism, it assigns a central role to
heads of states. It argues that regional integration can be best understood as a series of bargains among the political leaders of the major
states in a region. These bargains are the result of converging preferences among these leaders. Small states are often bought off with side-
payments offered by the leading states. The emphasis on power-related
variables does enable intergovernmentalists to elucidate important fea-
tures of regional agreements that elude neofunctionalists. Nevertheless,
as a theory of integration, intergovernmentalism suffers from several

---

[7] Mancur Olson, *The Rise and Decline of Nations* (New Haven: Yale University Press,
1982), pp. 10–11.

shortcomings. For example, by focusing solely on episodes of interstate bargains, the theory cuts into on-going economic, legal, and social processes and presents a picture of integration that ignores, discounts, or treats in an *ad hoc* fashion defining events that precede or follow interstate bargains. Further, if progress towards integration through interstate bargains is the result of converging preferences on the part of the leaders of major states, then the stopping or slow-down of the process of integration must, by implication, also reflect such preferences. However, a theory that "explains" the varying course of integration in terms of shifting preferences offers little to assess the theory's validity.

Economists who study regional integration look primarily at market relationships among goods and factors of production within a region and assume away the relevance of institutional and political forces. They are interested in the welfare effects of integration. For example, one classic economic account of integration, customs union theory, seeks to understand the welfare implications of integration in terms of trade creation, trade diversion, and terms of trade. More broadly, economic explanations are positive theories of welfare gains and losses associated with regional integration, not explanations of the political choices that produce such areas. The weakness of these explanations is evident. By narrowly focusing on markets, these theories overlook a key aspect of integration, namely the provision of common rules, regulations, and policies that govern regional economic areas. The failure to consider this institutional dimension renders economic theories of integration ill-equipped to tackle questions that pertain to the deepening and broadening of integration.

The analytical framework presented in this book seeks to remedy some of the weaknesses of traditional approaches by bridging political science and economics. Such an analysis is based on the conviction that market integration cannot be explained without reference to institutions, and that institutional analysis that fails to refer to market transactions risks being empty. This framework also incorporates factors, such as new technologies, that have been overlooked in many analyses of integration despite their obvious importance to the process of integration. Finally, this book pays particular attention to the external causes and effects of integration.

3   Themes and organization of the book

After a brief review of existing theories of integration in chapter 2, the book turns to two related puzzles in chapter 3, one implicating the insider countries in an integration process, the other, the outsiders. First, why have so many attempts at integration failed while a few have been crowned with success? Failure and success are primarily measured by the extent to which integration groups manage to match their stated integration goals with subsequent achievements. Second, what explains when outsiders become insiders? Outsiders can become insiders either by joining an existing economic union or by launching their own regional group.

The analysis of the first puzzle is primarily concerned with identifying the conditions under which implementation of an integration scheme is likely to succeed or to fail. It takes the decision to adopt an integration treaty as a given. The signing of such a treaty does not establish integration. It only signifies a promise by the leaders of several states to engage in a particular course of action over a period of time towards the aim of tying the economies of their countries closer together. True integration is achieved through the implementation of this promise, which entails a lengthy process of establishing common rules, regulations, and policies. It is these rules, regulations, and policies, based either on specific treaty provisions or derived over time from the general principles and objectives written into integration treaties, which will translate the aspiration for regional prosperity into reality.

Treaty implementation, that is, the attainment of a treaty's stated integration goals, is far from easy and automatic, as a glance at the history of regional integration schemes reveals. Indeed, the majority of integration schemes have failed at the implementation stage, including the Middle German Commercial Union, the Latin American Free Trade Association, the Andean Pact, and the Economic Community of West African States. Some projects, on the other hand, have been extremely successful, notably the European Union and the German Zollverein. Between these polar cases are a few integration projects with mixed results. What explains this variation of outcomes?

Chapter 3 argues that two sets of conditions must be satisfied if integration is to succeed, namely, demand-side and supply-side conditions. The demand-side condition is derived from insights provided by economic institutional theories, such as property rights theory, economic history, and new institutional economics. These theories seek to explain the evolution of domestic institutional arrangements in terms of changes in the extent and structure of markets. Chapter 3 extrapolates their insights to an account of the demand-side condition for integration. In short, the argument is that regional institution-building may be viewed as an attempt to internalize externalities that cross borders within a group of countries.[8] Externalities affecting cross-border trade and investment arise from economic and political uncertainty as well as a wide range of financial risks that market actors face when dealing with foreign firms and governments. The cost of these externalities increases as new technologies raise the potential for gain from market exchange, thus increasing the payoff to regional rules, regulations, and policies which alleviate these costs.

However, demand is not enough for integration to succeed. Economic institutional theories have rightly been criticized as "naive" for assuming that demand alone would miraculously generate institutional change. What they have overlooked are supply conditions. These are the conditions under which political leaders are willing and able to accommodate demands for deeper integration at each step of the integration process. Willingness depends on the payoff of integration to political leaders. Chapter 3 assumes that these leaders value political autonomy and power, and that their success in holding on to power depends on their relative success in managing the economy. It follows that leaders may be unwilling to deepen integration if their economies are relatively prosperous. Why sacrifice national sovereignty if the economy is growing relatively quickly and the people are thus content? Put differently, economically successful leaders may not see the need to pursue deeper integration because their expected marginal benefit from further integration in terms of retaining political power is minimal and thus not worth the cost of integration. However, in times of economic difficulties, political leaders will be more concerned with securing their own survival and will thus be more willing to accommodate demands by market players for regional rules, regulations, and policies.

But even willing political leaders may be unable to supply regional rules, regulations, and policies because of collective action problems such as the Prisoners' Dilemma (PD) and, even more importantly, the Coordination Dilemma (CD). The PD problem is one of free-riding.[9] It is mitigated if the integration agreement provides for the establishment of "commitment institutions," such as centralized monitoring and third-

---

[8] The meaning of the terms "internalization" and "externalities" in the context of regional integration is explained in section 3 of chapter 3. Externalities involve an interdependence of utility or production functions. A negative externality lowers the utility or production of an affected party. For example, the upstream pulp mill which discharges effluent in the river thus reducing the scope for fishing downstream is said to impose an externality on the fishermen. Internalization describes the process of taking into account an externality and reducing the output of the offending good to its optimal level, i.e., the level at which the cost of reducing the externality (by a further unit) is equal to the benefit from such a reduction.

[9] "Free-riding" here means defecting from the obligation to contribute to the building of an integrated economy while enjoying the fruits of the joint effort by others.

party enforcement. The provision of such institutions is one supply condition for successful integration, but it is a weak one. In its absence, cooperation may still be possible on the basis of repeat-play, issue-linkage, and reputation. Nevertheless, "commitment institutions" can catalyze the process of regional integration, particularly if they offer direct access to those actors with the greatest vested interest in seeing integration completed.

The problem in the Coordination Dilemma is not one of free-riding but of agreeing on one of several possible courses of action in a situation in which the states have opposing interests. Coordination problems are particularly salient in integration, because most regional integration schemes, including free-trade areas, customs unions, or economic unions go beyond the removal of border barriers. They may include efforts to adopt common rules of origin, common commercial policies, common investment codes, common health and safety standards, or common macroeconomic policies. Coordination also gives rise to distributional issues, as a chosen course of action benefits some states within the group more than others. Questions of fairness and equitable distribution of the gains from cooperation will need to be addressed to prevent discontent from derailing the integration process. These observations lead to a key supply condition for successful integration, namely the presence of an undisputed leader among the group of countries seeking closer ties. Such a state serves as a focal point in the coordination of rules, regulations, and policies; it may also help to ease distributional tensions by acting as regional "paymaster". In sum, regional groups that satisfy both demand and supply conditions stand the greatest chance of succeeding, whereas groups that fulfill neither set of conditions are least likely to attain any significant level of integration.

Chapter 3 also considers the effect of regional integration on outsider states and examines outsiders' responses to integration. In a nutshell, the argument is as follows: countries that are negatively affected by regional integration can pursue one of two strategies. They can either seek to merge with the group generating the external effects (I call this the "first integrative response") or they can respond by creating their own regional group (this I call the "second integrative response"). The first integrative response is possible only if the existing group is willing to accept newcomers. However, if an outsider is not a desirable candidate in the sense of being able to make a net positive contribution to the union, the union is generally unlikely to accept it. If an outsider is rejected, or knows it is likely to be rejected if it were to apply, or is unwilling to accept the terms of membership in a given group, it may opt for the "second integrative response." Like any integration scheme, to be successful counter-unions must satisfy both demand and supply conditions.

Chapter 4 illustrates and tests the analytical framework of chapter 3 on integration schemes from nineteenth and twentieth-century Europe. It begins with an examination of a particularly successful integration scheme, the European Union, tracing the EU's achievement to the existence of demand and supply conditions. Discussion of the demand side focuses on the role played by market actors in promoting legal integration (i.e., the constitutionalization of the Treaty of Rome) and in the revitalization of the integration process in the 1980s which led to the Single European Act. The discussion of the supply side of European integration highlights the importance of two "commitment institutions," the Commission and the European Court of Justice, as well as Germany's critical role as an institutional leader and regional paymaster. The German Zollverein is the second successful integration scheme analyzed in chapter 4. A key factor on the demand side of the Zollverein was the German Commercial and Industrial League which untiringly pushed for integration. Prussia, the largest and wealthiest state in the region, played a critical role on the supply side, assuming the role of regional paymaster, and serving as institutional focal point and coordinator in the deepening process of German integration.

Chapter 4 also examines the responses of outsiders to integration. A striking regularity that emerges from the analysis of the enlargement of the European Union and the Zollverein is that the outsiders sought no integration when there was no performance gap with the regional group, and that sustained performance gaps always eventually triggered moves toward integration. Countries that failed to experience such a gap saw no reason to pay the price of integration and thus opted to stay out. More specifically, the finding is that eighteen out of twenty applications for EU membership by eleven West European states were submitted after one or – more typically – several years of economic growth rates that fell well below the Community average. Similarly, the results from the Zollverein show that the rulers of the many German kingdoms, electorates, and duchies clung to their sovereign rights and obstructed proposals for economic unification till economic crisis and empty treasuries forced them to seek membership of the Zollverein. Chapter 4 concludes with a discussion of several failed European integration schemes. The focus is on projects for a "United States of Europe" in the 1890s. Failure can be explained in terms of absence of demand and supply conditions.

Chapter 5 examines the logic of integration beyond Europe. It argues that most integration projects in the Americas and in Asia were triggered by external events that threatened economic prosperity. The predominant external causes were integration in Europe and, more recently, in North America. Thus many of the integration schemes in Latin America and Asia can be understood as examples of the second integrative response. Most developing countries depend heavily on the markets of industrialized countries for their exports. Potential trade diversion is viewed with great alarm. The reaction by the President of Uruguay to the creation of the European Community is typical: "[T]he formation of a European Common Market ... constitutes a state of near-war against Latin American exports. Therefore, we must reply to one integration with another one, to one increase of acquisitive power by internal enrichment by another, to inter-European cooperation by inter-Latin American cooperation."[10] The main analytical concern of chapter 5 is to explain the varying outcomes of these "counter-unions" outside Europe. The argument is that, in all cases, the fate of these regional integration projects can be explained parsimoniously within the demand and supply framework presented in chapter 3. The chapter also uses the framework to predict the likely outcomes of the most recent integration schemes, including MERCOSUR, APEC, the ASEAN Free Trade Area, and NAFTA.

Chapter 6 summarizes the main findings of the book and considers the implications of these findings for the development of the world economic order over the next decade.

4   Caveats

Before proceeding, I would like to preempt some possible criticism. First, the analytical framework of the book seems to attribute a strong form of rationality to decision-makers. It may be objected that this is not realistic. Rightly so. I do not make the assumption that political or economic actors *consciously* calculate costs and benefits of alternative courses of actions, any more than the modern consumer engages in utility maximization when buying one good instead of another. The rationality I attribute to actors is primarily a matter of consequences, not states of mind or intentions. Some readers may still take offense at the self-consciously rationalist perspective of the book and argue that non-rational motives are equally or more important to understand integration. My response is not to deny this possibility but to ask: how can we know? The answer I suggest is that by starting with the assumption of narrowly rational motivation we may obtain predictions that serve as

---

[10] *The Observer* (London, July 30, 1961), 1.

useful benchmarks by which to assess the extent and impact of other motivations.[11]

Second, in focusing on characteristics common to many integration schemes, I play down the many significant differences among regions. I do this by design. The purpose of an analytical framework is not to deny the variety of a phenomenon or to provide a full and realistic description of a particular case, but to capture general tendencies and explain those fundamental traits that are common to most cases. Such an approach, I feel, is necessary to get at some important questions that have been neglected by earlier studies.

Third, the book does not seek to offer a comprehensive explanation of regional integration. Its purpose is to shed light on certain facets of integration. As a result, the scope of the framework is limited in several ways. Coercion, for example, is left out, even though its role in building certain types of communities is well known. However, to reduce the complexity in a manageable way, I have defined my object of study as *voluntary* integration. Thus coerced integration does not fall within the scope of my study. The mechanisms, for example, by which Nazi Germany swallowed Austria are altogether different from those by which Austria became a member of the European Union. The framework of this study is contractarian and focuses on welfare, not on military aggrandizement or mergers by intimidation.

The scope of the framework is also limited by the research questions. For example, the second puzzle concerns "What explains when outsiders become insiders? Outsiders can become insiders either by joining an already existing economic union or by creating their own regional group." It follows that I do not seek to explain the creation of all regional groups but only those set up in response to an original group. The explanation of the formation of the original group is beyond the scope of the book. Nevertheless, the framework does claim to offer a broadly applicable explanation of the outcomes of regional integration schemes – that is, success or failure – for both original groups and groups which correspond to the "second integrative response".

The analysis focuses primarily on economic factors. On the demand side, the explanatory variable is economic gains from market exchange; on the supply side, it is national economic growth, even though the role of power is also considered. Some readers may find such a focus too narrow and the framework too parsimonious. They may ask that other variables be incorporated into the model, notably the quest for national security and the role of military alliances. Security issues are far from

[11] Russell Hardin, *Collective Action* (Baltimore, Md.: Johns Hopkins University Press, 1982), p. 11.

irrelevant in integration, but they shed little light on the specific questions asked in this book. For example: why did the UK, Norway, Denmark, and Ireland opt to remain outside the European Community in the 1950s but not in the 1960s? It is not plausible to assume that their assessments of the security implications of membership changed. There are many questions about integration which are formed within a context of unchanging military alliance patterns. In such a context, economic variables may take us a long way toward explaining puzzling aspects of integration.

By focusing on economic factors, I do not wish to imply that other variables are irrelevant or that economic variables are all that matter in understanding regional integration. Far from it. My study leaves some variation unexplained. Consider, for example, the finding regarding the timing of membership presented in chapter 4. It states that a country seeks to integrate its economy only when there is a significant positive cost of maintaining its present governance structure in terms of forgone growth as measured by a continuing performance gap between it and a more integrated rival governance structure. In the case of the European Community, a state tends to seek membership after growing for two and a half years, on average, at a rate significantly below EC average growth. The reaction time for all EC applicants appears to be normally distributed around that average. My analysis contents itself with this finding and could thus be labeled a macroanalysis; but it invites further research at the unit level to explain the varying reaction times. Differences in the domestic politico-institutional structures or in the sectoral composition of the economies of applicants may account for some of the variation in time lags.[12] A more general point is that by asking new questions and sketching possible answers my hope is not to provide complete and definitive solutions to puzzles regarding regional integration but, instead, to arouse curiosity for a fascinating research topic and invite refinements of the framework proposed in this book.

---

[12] A first systematic attempt to link domestic politics and international relations is offered in Helen Milner, *Interests, Institutions, and Information: Domestic Politics and International Relations* (Princeton: Princeton University Press, 1997). Milner's approach suggests several ways in which the present framework could be extended to provide a more fine-grained account of integration outcomes.

2 A review of theoretical approaches to integration

1 Introduction

Regional integration has been on the research agenda of social scientists at various times over the past fifty years (see table 2.1). Most political scientists studying integration have been primarily interested in understanding the institutional and policy dimensions of integration. They have sought to specify the political context in which integration occurs and have provided insightful accounts of the process of integration. One explanation of integration in political science is neofunctionalism. It refines the conceptual tools of its predecessor theory, functionalism, and embeds them in a rigorous utilitarian framework. It starts by assuming that supranationality is the only method available to states to secure maximum welfare and then offers a subtle account of how integration unfolds over time, using concepts such as functional spillover, updating of common interest, and subnational and supranational group dynamics. Intergovernmentalism is a contending analytical approach to integration. It is in most respects contrary to neofunctionalist premises. Integration is viewed as a sequence of interstate bargains triggered by a convergence of policy preferences among states. It serves to maximize states' wealth and power.

Economists have focused primarily on market relationships among goods and factors of production within a region and have assumed away the relevance of institutional and political forces. Economic explanations are positive theories of welfare gains and losses associated with regional integration, not explanations of the political choices that produce integrated areas. Most of these explanations are static: they do not address questions pertaining to the dynamics of integration such as changes in the rules and policies governing economic regions. The two main economic explanations are customs union theory and optimal currency area theory. Customs union theory seeks to understand the welfare implications of integration in terms of trade creation, trade diversion, and terms of trade. Optimal currency area theory specifies the

19

Table 2.1. *Theoretical approaches to regional integration*

		Main focus	Method	Timing of integration	Objective of integration	External effect of integration
Political-science approaches to integration	Function-alism	Supra-national institutions	Normative dynamic	Assumed (after war)	Peace through prosperity	n/a
	Neo-function-alism	Political actors at supra- and subnational levels	Positive dynamic	n/a	Welfare maximi-zation (assumed)	n/a
	Intergovern-mentalism	Heads of govern-ments	Positive (dynamic)	"Explained" (as convergence of member state preferences)	Welfare and power maximi-zation	n/a
Economic approaches to integration	Customs union theory	Markets (goods and services)	Positive static	n/a	Improve-ment of national income	Indirectly addressed
	Optimal currency area	Markets (goods and factors)	Positive static	n/a	Full employment and payments equilibrium	n/a
	Fiscal federalism (Casella approach)	Interaction of markets and excludable public goods	Positive dynamic	Explained	Improve-ment of market efficiency	n/a
Framework proposed in this book		Interaction of markets and political institutions	Positive dynamic	Explained	Improve-ment of economic growth and maintenance of political office	Addressed (central theme)

conditions under which integration in the monetary domain is economically efficient.

The fiscal federalism theory also speaks to issues of regional integration. Traditionally, the theory has focused on federal countries and has sought to identify the rules for the assignment of authority over different aspects of fiscal policy to different levels of government. The connection to integration is straightforward: as the removal of trade barriers increases the mobility of capital, labor, and consumers, regional differences in taxes and the supply of public goods can induce migration in any of these categories. This raises the potential for fiscal spillover across borders, creating incentives for redefining the assignment of fiscal policy tasks across different levels. Recent work in the fiscal federalism tradition also reflects more broadly on the relationship between the evolution of private markets and the provision of excludable public goods within integrated economic areas. It thus adds a dynamic dimension to the analysis of economic integration that is missing in customs union and optimal currency area theories.

2   Political-science approaches to integration

Functionalism

David Mitrany, the main proponent of functionalism, wrote in a 1943 essay entitled *A Working Peace System* that "the problem of our time is not how to keep nations peacefully apart but how to bring them actively together."[1] He proposed a solution which he called the pragmatic functional approach. It breaks away from the traditional link between authority and a definite territory by ascribing authority to activities based in areas of agreement. Peace "is more likely to grow through doing things together in workshops and marketplace than by signing pacts in chancelleries."[2] Coactivity rather than national coexistence defines the ideal of peace. Mitrany put his faith "not in a protected peace but in a *working peace.*"[3]

This functional method projects a gradual process towards peace and prosperity. Every function is left to generate others gradually; in every case the appropriate authority is left to grow and develop out of actual

---

[1] David Mitrany, *A Working Peace* (Chicago: Quadrangle Books, 1966), p. 28. On functionalism, see also James Patrick Sewell, *Functionalism and World Politics* (Princeton: Princeton University Press, 1966); Ernst Haas, *Beyond the Nation State* (Stanford: Stanford University Press, 1964), especially chapters 1–4; Inis Claude, *Swords into Plowshares* (New York: Random House, 4th edn,1971), especially chapter 17.

[2] Mitrany, *A Working Peace*, p. 25.   [3] *Ibid.*, p. 92.

performance.[4] A fundamental aspect of the functional method is that "sovereignty cannot ... be transferred effectively through a formula, only through a function. By entrusting an authority with a certain task, carrying with it command over the requisite powers and means, a slice of sovereignty is transferred from the old authority to the new; and the accumulation of such partial transfers in time brings about a translation of the true seat of authority."[5] This is the logic of "peace by pieces."[6] Functional cooperation does not start from the political but from the low-key economic and social planes such as the joint management of scarce resources, unemployment, commodity price fluctuations, labor standards, and public health. "Any political scheme would start a disputation; any working arrangement would raise a hope and make for confidence and patience."[7] Through gradual functional developments and through the provision of common services, the system may in time even build up solid foundations for closer political association.[8]

To summarize, the assumptions and propositions of functionalism are as follows: political divisions are a source of conflict among nations. These divisions can be transcended only gradually by seeking out areas of mutuality and establishing a "working" web of international functional institutions, managed by technical elites, in which and through which the interests of all nations are gradually integrated. Power and welfare, politics and economics are separable. Areas of functional cooperation are likely to be found in the "low-politics" area of economic and social life. Prosperity through global economic integration is the

---

[4] An elaboration of this theme is found on pp. 72 and 73. The passage merits being cited in full: "Here we discover a cardinal virtue of the functional method – what one might call the virtue of technical self-determination. The functional dimensions determine themselves. In a like manner the function determines its appropriate organs. It also reveals through practice the nature of the action required under the given conditions, and in that way the powers needed by the respective authority. The function, one might say, determines the executive instruments suitable for its proper activity, and by the same process provides a need for the reform of the instrument at every stage. This would allow the widest latitude for variation between functions, and also in the dimension or organization of the same function as needs and conditions change. Not only is there in all this no need for any fixed constitutional division of authority and power, prescribed in advance, but anything beyond the original formal definition of scope and purpose might embarrass this working of the practical arrangement."

[5] *Ibid.*, p. 31. Mitrany is cautious to add that "it would indeed be sounder and wiser to speak not of the surrender but of a *sharing* of sovereignty. When ten or twenty national authorites, each of whom had performed a certain task for itself, can be induced to perform that task jointly, they will to that end quite naturally *pool* their sovereign authority insofar as the good performance of the task demands it" (p. 31).

[6] The phrase is by Frederick Schuman, *The Community of Man* (London: Robert Hale, 1954), p. 314, cited in Claude, *Swords into Plowshares*, p. 381.

[7] Mitrany, *A Working Peace*, p. 99.   [8] *Ibid.*, p. 67.

guarantor of a stable and peaceful international system. Economic unification will ultimately lead to political unification.[9]

The weaknesses of functionalism are apparent. First, it is not properly speaking a theory of integration but rather a normative method. It describes a way that *should* be pursued to attain peaceful coexistence. However, it fails to specify fully the conditions under which such a scheme is feasible. For example, why should gradualism be as easily workable in "high politics" areas as it is in technical domains? Second, even a positive rendering of its main theme, that integration is in fact sought to secure peace, is not fully compelling. Why were not all European countries participating in the peace-building effort from the beginning? Did the United Kingdom, Denmark, and Ireland join the European Community in 1973 because of concerns about peace? Did Norway opt out because of opposition to the idea of peaceful coexistence? None of these suggestions is plausible.

Neofunctionalism

Neofunctionalism restates the assumptions of functionalism, refines its analytical tools, elaborates sketchy ideas and intuitions evoked in passing, and embeds earlier concepts into an analytical framework that proposes to study not international but regional integration. In a significant departure from functionalism, it shifts its analytical focus from the teleology, a working peace system, to the utilitarian dimension of the functional method. This enables it to shed the normative and utopian ballast of its predecessor, thus gaining analytical clarity and powerful implications.

The logic of integration was first systematically analyzed and elaborated by Ernst Haas, the chief exponent of neofunctionalism, in his pioneering study *The Uniting of Europe*.[10] This work and a collection of later contributions share a common neofunctional framework.[11] The

---

[9] Claude, *Swords into Plowshares*, pp. 378–391. For a later version of functionalism, see Karl Deutsch, *Political Community and the North Atlantic Area: International Organization in the Light of Historical Experience* (Princeton: Princeton University Press, 1957); and Karl Deutsch, *France, Germany, and the Western Alliance* (New York: Scribner and Sons, 1957). Deutsch held that increasing density of social exchange among individuals over prolonged periods of time would lead to the development of new communities (shared identity) and, ultimately, to the creation of a super-state with centralized institutions.

[10] Ernst Haas, *The Uniting of Europe* (Stanford: Stanford University Press, 1958).

[11] See in particular the following works by Ernst Haas: "International Integration: The European and the Universal Process," *International Organization* 15 (Summer 1961), 366–392; *Beyond the Nation-State* (Stanford: Stanford University Press, 1964); "Technocracy, Pluralism, and the New Europe," in Joseph Nye (ed.), *International Regionalism* (Boston: Little, Brown, and Co., 1968), pp. 149–179; "The Study of

approach is concerned with explaining "how and why nation-states cease to be wholly sovereign, how and why they voluntarily mingle, merge, and mix with their neighbors so as to lose the factual attributes of sovereignty while acquiring new techniques for resolving conflicts between themselves."[12] More precisely, neofunctionalism describes a process "whereby political actors in several distinct national settings are persuaded to shift their loyalties, expectations, and political activities towards a new and larger center, whose institutions possess or demand jurisdiction over the pre-existing states."[13]

Neofunctionalism's main analytical attributes are summarized below.

The actors

The primary players in the integration process are above and below the nation-state. Actors below the state include interest groups and political parties. Above the state are supranational regional institutions. These promote integration, foster the development of interest groups, cultivate close ties with them and with fellow-technocrats in the national civil services, and manipulate both if necessary.

The Commission of the European Union, for example, has the "power of initiative."[14] To have its proposals accepted by the Council of Ministers, the Commission forges behind-the-scene working alliances with pressure groups. As its policy-making role grows, interest groups coalesce across national boundaries in their pursuit of communitywide interests, thus adding to the integrative momentum. These groups need not be convinced "integrationist" groups. The very existence of the community alters their situation and forces them to adjust.[15]

What role is there for governments? According to neofunctionalism, government's role is "creatively responsive."[16] As holders of the ultimate political power, governments may accept, sidestep, ignore, or sabotage the decisions of federal authorities. Yet, given the heterogeneity of their interests in certain issue-areas, unilateral evasion or recalcitrance may

---

Regional Integration: Reflection on the Joy and Anguish of Pretheorizing," *International Organization* 24 (Autumn 1970), 607–646. See also Ernst Haas and Philippe Schmitter, "Economic and Differential Patterns of Political Integration: Projections about Unity in Latin America," *International Organization* 18 (Autumn 1964), 705–737. The summary of neofunctionalism presented in this section draws on Anne-Marie Burley and Walter Mattli, "Europe Before the Court: A Political Theory of Legal Integration," *International Organization* 47 (1993), 41–76.

[12] Haas, "The Study of Regional Integration," 610.

[13] Haas, "International Integration," 366. See also Haas, *The Uniting of Europe*, p. 12.

[14] Stuart Scheingold and Leon Lindberg, *Europe's Would-be Polity* (Englewood Cliffs, N.J.: Prentice-Hall 1970), p. 92.

[15] *Ibid.*, p. 92.

[16] The expression is borrowed from Reginald Harrison, *Europe in Question: Theories of Regional International Integration* (London: Allen & Unwin, 1974), p. 80.

prove unprofitable if it sets a precedent for other governments.[17] Thus governments may either choose to or feel constrained to yield to the pressures of converging supranational and subnational interests.

The motives

One of the important contributions of neofunctionalism is the introduction of an unambiguously utilitarian concept of interest politics that stands in sharp contrast to the notions of unselfishness or common good that pervade functionalist writing.[18] Assumptions of good will, harmony of interests, or dedication to the common good need not be postulated to account for integration. Ruthless egoism does the trick by itself.[19] As Haas puts it, "[t]he 'good Europeans' are not the main creators of the ... community; the process of community formation is dominated by nationally constituted groups with specific interests and aims, willing and able to adjust their aspirations by turning to supranational means *when this course appears profitable.*"[20] The supranational actors are likewise not immune to utilitarian thinking. They seek unremittingly to expand the mandate of their own institutions to have a more influential say in community affairs.

The process

Three related concepts lie at the core of the dynamics of integration: functional spillover, political spillover, and upgrading of common interests.

Functional spillover is based on the assumption that the different sectors of a modern industrial economy are highly interdependent and that any integrative action in one sector creates a situation in which the original goal can be assured only by taking further actions in related sectors, which in turn create a further condition and a need for more action, and so forth.[21] This process is described by Haas: "Sector

---

[17] Haas, *The Uniting of Europe*, p. xiv.
[18] Haas, *Beyond the Nation-State*, p. 34.
[19] This idea points to an affinity of neofunctionalism with rational choice theories. Self-interest need not be identical with selfishness. The happiness (or misery) of other people may be part of a rational maximizer's satisfaction.
[20] Haas, *The Uniting of Europe*, p. xiv, my italics.
[21] Leon Lindberg, *The Political Dynamics of the European Economic Integration* (Stanford, Calif.: Stanford University Press, 1963), p. 10. The text follows George's suggestion of strictly distinguishing those two types of spillover. See Stephen George, *Politics and Policy in the European Community* (Oxford: Clarendon Press, 1985), pp. 16–36. George also offers a compelling illustration of functional spillover. He argues that the removal of tariff barriers will not in itself create a common market. The fixing of exchange rates is also required in order to achieve that end. But the surrender of control over national exchange rates demands the establishment of some sort of monetary union, which, in turn, will not be workable without the adoption of central macroeconomic policy

integration ... begets its own impetus toward extension to the entire economy even in the absence of specific group demands."[22]

Political spillover describes the process of adaptive behavior, that is, the incremental shifting of expectations, the changing of values, and the coalescing at the supranational level of national interest groups and political parties in response to sectoral integration. Neofunctionalism does not postulate an automatically cumulative integrative process. Again, in Haas's words, "[t]he spillover process, though rooted in the structure and motives of the post-capitalist welfare state, is far from automatic,"[23] and "[f]unctional contexts tend to be autonomous; lessons learned in one organization are not generally and automatically applied in others, or even by the same group in a later phase of its life."[24] In other words, neofunctionalism identifies certain linkage mechanisms but makes no assumptions as to the inevitability of actor response to functional linkages.

Upgrading common interests is the third element in the neofunctionalist description of the dynamics of integration. It occurs when the member states experience significant difficulties in arriving at a common policy while acknowledging the necessity of reaching some common stand to safeguard other aspects of interdependence among them. One way of overcoming such deadlock is by swapping concessions in related fields. In practice, the upgrading of the parties' common interests relies on the services of an institutionalized autonomous mediator.[25] This institutionalized swapping mechanism induces participants to refrain from vetoing proposals and invites them to seek compromises, which in turn bolster the power base of the central institutions.

The context

The context in which successful integration operates is economic, social, and technical, that is, it is nominally apolitical. Here Haas seems to accept a key assumption of the predecessor to his theory, functionalism, which posits that functional cooperation must begin on the relatively low-key economic and social planes. However, economic and social problems are ultimately inseparable from political problems. Haas

coordination and which itself requires the development of a common regional policy, and so forth (pp. 21–22).

[22] Haas, *The Uniting of Europe*, p. 297.

[23] Haas, "Technocracy, Pluralism, and the New Europe," 165.

[24] Haas, *Beyond the Nation-State*, p. 48.

[25] "The European executives [are] able to construct patterns of mutual concessions from various policy contexts and in so doing usually manage to upgrade [their] own powers at the expense of the member governments." Haas, "Technocracy, Pluralism, and the New Europe," 152.

thus replaced the dichotomous relationship between economics and politics in functionalism by a continuous one: "The supranational style stresses the indirect penetration of the political by way of the economic because the 'purely' economic decisions always acquire political significance in the minds of the participants."[26] "Technical" or "controversial" areas of cooperation, however, might be so trivial as to remain outside the domain of human expectation and actions vital for integration.[27] The area must therefore be economically important and endowed with a high degree of "functional specificity."[28]

The advent of the first major EC crisis in 1965, initiated by de Gaulle's adamant refusal to proceed with certain aspects of integration he deemed contrary to French interests, triggered a crescendo of criticism against neofunctionalism. The theory, it was claimed, had exaggerated both the expansive effect of increments within the economic sphere and the "gradual politicization" effect of spillover.[29] Critics further castigated neofunctionalists for failing to appreciate the enduring importance of nationalism, the autonomy of the political sector, and the interaction between the international environment and the integrating region.[30]

Neofunctionalists accepted most of the criticism and engaged in an agonizing reassessment of their analytical framework.[31] Many thought their neofunctionalist approach wrong and thus rejected it. This move was unfortunate, for the growing inapplicability of the approach did not mean the framework was wrong. As noted by James Caporaso,

scholars (Haas included) did not adequately distinguish between the magnitude of values of the explanatory factors in the theory on the one hand (the independent variables) and the existence of the conditions required for the theory to work on the other. As the value of the explanatory variables become weak, we do not reject [a] theory; instead we should simply draw out the implications for variation in the phenomena to be explained – generally the smaller the values, the less the impact ... Thus, when integration slowed down ... integration theory was thought to be disconfirmed. But rather than being wrong, it was simply less relevant.[32]

[26] *Ibid.*   [27] Haas, "International Integration," 102.
[28] *Ibid.*, 372.
[29] Joseph Nye, "Patterns and Catalysts in Regional Integration," *International Organization* 19 (Autumn 1965), 870–884.
[30] See Stanley Hoffmann, "Obstinate or Obsolete? The Fate of the Nation-State and the Case of Western Europe," *Daedalus* 95 (Summer 1966), 862–915.
[31] See Ernst Haas, *The Obsolescence of Regional Integration Theory* (Berkeley: University of California Press, 1975).
[32] James Caporaso, "Regional Integration Theory: Understanding Our Past and Anticipating our Future," in Wayne Sandholtz and Alec Stone Sweet (eds.), *Supranational Governance: The Institutionalization of the European Union* (New York: Oxford University Press, forthcoming).

With the revival of European integration in the mid-1980s, neofunction-alism regained popularity in the international relations literature as a framework for explaining the process of integration, particularly in the legal domain.[33] Several of its analytical categories boast enduring relevance, notably the focus on subnational actors and its emphasis on the role played by supranational institutions in catalyzing the process of integration. Nevertheless, neofunctionalism has shortcomings. For example, it begins by stating that supranationality is the only method available to states to secure maximum welfare, but it fails to give a theoretical account of the link between welfare maximization and regional integration. It then focuses on institutional arrangements within a region in which economic transactions take place, but it leaves these transactions mostly unexamined. Further, the framework never fully specifies the conditions under which societal demands for inte-gration become accepted at the national level. The approach simply assumes that if there is a problem cutting across frontiers and there is a felt need, actors at the subnational and supranational levels will mobilize resources, and the problem will be solved.[34] This somewhat naive view is the result of inadequate attention to the preferences of governments and a lack of understanding of the nature of collective action problems that may impede progress towards integration. As a result, neofunction-alism leaves several important questions about integration unanswered, including: why is decision-making at the supranational level more efficient? Why have some integration schemes failed? Why does a country seek to join an already existing union and what explains the timing of such a request for membership? These are some of the questions that the framework developed in chapter 3 seeks to address.

Intergovernmentalism

Intergovernmentalism holds that integration can best be understood as a series of bargains between the heads of governments of the leading states in a region.[35] These political leaders, jealous of their national sovereignty, carefully circumscribe any sacrifice of sovereignty that may become necessary in order to attain common goals. Big states exercise a

---

[33] For a review of the literature, see Walter Mattli and Anne-Marie Slaughter, "Revisiting the European Court of Justice," *International Organization* 52 (Winter 1998), 177–209.

[34] Caporaso, "Regional Integration Theory."

[35] Andrew Moravcsik, "Negotiating the Single European Act: National Interests and Conventional Statecraft in the European Community," *International Organization* 45 (Winter 1991), 19–56. See also Paul Taylor, "Intergovernmentalism in the European Communities in the 1970s: Patterns and Perspectives," *International Organization* 36 (Autumn 1982), 741–766.

de facto veto over fundamental changes in the rules of integration. As a result, "bargaining tends to converge towards the lowest common denominator of large state interests."[36] Small states are often bought off with side-payments offered by the big ones.

The emphasis of intergovernmentalism on heads of states as central players is a key difference between it and neofunctionalism. There is ample evidence to suggest that governments do indeed play an important role in integration. But as a theory of integration, intergovernmentalism suffers from several shortcomings. By focusing only on episodes of interstate bargaining, the theory cuts into ongoing social processes and produces what Paul Pierson calls a "snapshot view of integration that is distorted in crucial respects."[37] Defining events that precede interstate bargains are overlooked, discounted, or treated in an *ad hoc* fashion, and events that follow instances of bargains appear to be irrelevant. Thus the theory implies, for example, that the implementation of interstate agreements is easy and automatic. This is hardly a plausible proposition considering that the majority of integration schemes have failed at the implementation stage.

Furthermore, a theory that focuses only on major interstate decisions or "celebrated intergovernmental bargains"[38] risks suffering from a particular type of selection bias: selection on the dependent variable. Such a theory offers no range of possible outcomes but only a constant event, "celebrated bargains"; it thus is difficult to test.[39] Intergovernmentalism argues that the "ups" of integration, that is, the big decisions, are the result of convergence of the preferences of the leading states. By implication, a slowdown or halt of the integration process must similarly reflect converging preferences. However, a theory that explains the meandering course of integration solely in terms of shifting preferences offers few ways of assessing its validity. A more challenging approach would be to seek to explain varying integration outcomes by examining how changes in external factors and constraints (parameters) affect integration, given fixed preferences of the member states. It is only when this approach fails that we can conclude with confidence that changes in outcomes are best explained by shifts in member-state preferences.

Aware of some of these weaknesses, intergovernmentalists have sought to expand their theoretical approach. Andrew Moravcsik, for

[36] Moravcsik, "Negotiating the Single European Act," 25–26.
[37] Paul Pierson, "The Path of European Integration: A Historical Institutionalist Analysis," *Comparative Political Studies* 29 (1995), 126.
[38] Andrew Moravcsik, "Preferences and Power in the European Community: A Liberal Intergovernmental Approach," *Journal of Common Market Studies* 31 (December 1993), 473.
[39] Caporaso, "Regional Integration Theory."

example, has minted a new theory that he calls "liberal intergovernmentalism." The theory posits a two-stage approach to account for major decisions in the history of the European Community. In the first stage, national preferences are primarily determined by the constraints and opportunities imposed by economic interdependence. In the second stage, the outcomes of interstate bargains are determined by the relative bargaining power of governments and the functional incentives for institutionalization created by high transaction costs and the desire to control domestic agendas.[40] This expanded approach is undoubtedly an improvement over the original version of intergovernmentalism, but the question arises as to why it is labelled "intergovernmentalist." Much that is "new" is strongly reminiscent of (neo)functionalism, notably the idea that domestic and transnational society starts the process of integration by expressing preferences which governments pursue in international bargains and through the creation of supranational organizations. In Caporaso's words: "Liberal intergovernmentalism muddies the waters in terms of a straight-up, comparative evaluation of neofunctionalism and itself. Much that is functionalist terrain is absorbed into [the expanded theory] . . . and some that is realist is dropped from the intergovernmental model . . . [T]he lines between classical realism and neofunctionalism have been blurred."[41]

Much of the remaining research on integration in the intergovernmental/realist tradition seeks not so much to build grand theories of integration but to address specific issues that relate to integration. Joseph Grieco, for example, seeks to explain variance in modern regional institutionalization by focusing on power-related variables. He argues that relative stability of power capabilities, which depends in part on the relative gains from regional cooperation and the expectation that such stability will persist, contributes to the establishment and deepening of formal regional institutions. In contrast, instability of power capabilities limits the likelihood that regional institutions will form; the reason is that weaker members may fear that liberalizing interstate economic relations will further undermine their political power relative to that of stronger members.[42]

The work by Edward Mansfield and Joanne Gowa examines the

---

[40] Moravcsik, "Preferences and Power in the European Community," 517.

[41] Caporaso, "Regional Integration Theory"; for a similar critique, see Alec Stone Sweet and Wayne Sandholtz, "European Integration and Supranational Governance," in Sandholtz and Sweet (eds.), *Supranational Governance*.

[42] See Joseph Grieco, "Systemic Sources of Variation in Regional Institutionalization in Western Europe, East Asia, and the Americas," in Edward Mansfield and Helen Milner (eds.), *The Political Economy of Regionalism* (New York: Columbia University Press, 1997), pp. 164–187.

effects of politico-military alliances and other factors, such as colonial relationships and wars, on bilateral trade. They find that trade is generally higher among countries that are allies and lower among countries that are actual or potential adversaries. The explanation is that alliances help to minimize the security risk associated with trade and thus promote commercial exchange among the members; this, in turn, generates wealth, thereby strengthening the alliance.[43]

This research establishes that the security dimension of integration is important, but it does not help to explain several of the questions posed in this book. For example: why did the United Kingdom, Norway, Denmark, and Ireland stay out of the European Community in the late 1950s and try to join it in the 1960s? Were these countries concerned about security externalities in the 1950s but not in the 1960s? This is hardly plausible. What explains the creation of several integration groups in Latin America in the 1960s? And why did all of these regional schemes fail? No shifts in alliances or power capabilities occurred in Latin America during this time. In short, the analysis must move beyond security consideration in order to be able to grasp many of the puzzling questions about integration.

3   Economic approaches to integration

Customs union theory

The focus of functionalism and neofunctionalism is on institutions and processes. Both theories analyze the dynamics of the distribution of policy tasks between the national and supranational levels. Customs union theory is neither dynamic nor concerned with institutions. It thoroughly discounts the importance of the political or common policy dimension of regional integration. It looks narrowly at markets of goods and considers the welfare implications of discriminating mergers of such markets.

The seminal contribution to the customs union theory is Viner's *The Customs Union Issue*.[44] According to Viner, the creation of a customs

---

[43] See Edward Mansfield, "Effects of International Politics on Regionalism in International Trade," in Kym Anderson and Richard Blackhurst (eds.), *Regional Integration and the Global Trading System* (London: Harvester Wheatsheaf, 1993), pp. 199–217; Joanne Gowa, *Allies, Adversaries, and International Trade* (Princeton; Princeton University Press, 1994); and Edward Mansfield and Rachel Bronson, "The Political Economy of Major-Power Trade Flows," in Mansfield and Milner (eds.), *The Political Economy of Regionalism*, pp. 188–208.

[44] Jacob Viner, *The Customs Union Issue* (New York: Carnegie Endowment for International Peace, 1950). See also Bela Balassa, *The Theory of Economic Integration* (Homewood, Ill.: Richard D. Irwin, 1961); "Trade Creation and Trade Diversion in

union involves the elimination of intra-area trade barriers and the equalization of tariffs on imports from non-member countries. Trade-creation effects arise if the output of inefficient industries is replaced, after the removal of tariffs, by cheaper imports from more efficient industries in a member state of the union. Trade creation makes a country better off because lower prices on newly imported goods increase the consumer's surplus and permit production gains. However, the union's common external tariff against third countries could have a trade diversion effect. The argument is as follows: let us assume that the third countries were the lowest-cost suppliers prior to the establishment of a customs union. The imposition of the common tariff puts these suppliers at a competitive disadvantage after the creation of the union. Thus the tariff may discourage imports from countries outside the union and encourage imports from less efficient sources of supply within the integrated area. The resulting trade diversion reduces a country's economic welfare. The net welfare effect of a customs union is an empirical question and will depend on the amount of trade created and diverted as well as on differences in unit costs.[45] The degree of trade diversion is likely to be small where the members of a union have extensive trade with each other and a low common tariff on imports from non-member countries.[46] The welfare effects of a customs union will also depend on transportation costs. *Ceteris paribus*, the lower the transportation costs among member countries, the greater the net gains from integration.[47]

the European Common Market," *Economic Journal* 77 (1967); "Monetary Integration in European Common Market," in Bela Balassa (ed.), *European Economic Integration* (Amsterdam: North-Holland, 1975), pp. 175–220; Melvyn Krauss, "Recent Developments in Customs Union Theory," *Journal of Economic Literature* 10 (1972), 413–436; Richard Lipsey and Kelvin Lancaster, "The General Theory of the Second Best," *Review of Economic Studies* 24 (1956–7), 11–32; James Meade, *Problems of Economic Union* (London: Allen & Unwin, 1953) and *The Theory of Customs Union* (Amsterdam: North-Holland, 1955); Tibor Scitovski, *Economic Theory and Western European Integration* (London: Allen & Unwin, 1958); Paul Wonnacott and Ronald Wonnacott, "Is Unilateral Tariff Reduction Preferable to a Customs Union? The Curious Case of the Missing Foreign Tariffs," *American Economic Review* 71 (1981), 704–714.

[45] Viner also discusses dynamic effects of integration such as enhanced competition among states with imperfectly complementary economies. These effects are likely to increase economic welfare.

[46] Richard Lipsey, "The Theory of Customs Unions: A General Survey," *Economic Journal* 70 (1960), 496–513.

[47] Bela Balassa, "Economic Integration," in *The New Palgrave Dictionary of Economics* (London: Macmillan, 1987), p. 44. The importance of taking transportation costs into consideration when deciding the welfare question is also highlighted in Paul Wonnacott and Mark Lutz, "Is There a Case for Free Trade Areas?," in Jeffrey Schott (ed.), *Free Trade Areas and US Trade Policy* (Washington: Institute for International Economics, 1989); Paul Krugman, "The Move Toward Free Trade Zones," in *Policy Implications of Trade and Currency Zones*, Proceedings of a Symposium by the Federal Reserve of

The concepts of trade creation and trade diversion remain important if the analysis is extended to take into consideration economies of scale on the plant level that may result from the merging of economic areas. Warner Corden examines this case, introducing two new concepts: the cost-reduction effect and the trade-suppression effect.[48] The first effect refers to reductions in average unit production costs as domestic output expands following the creation of an economic union. The trade suppression effect refers to the replacement of cheaper imports from non-member countries by domestic production under economies of scale. Corden concludes that a net benefit is likely to ensue because the cost-reduction effect tends to outweigh the trade suppression effect.

The customs union theory, however, is logically not impeccable. If countries establish customs unions to maximize national income, then only a union that encompasses all countries can meet that objective since only a global union will avoid *all* trade diversion.[49] This is a world of free trade. Similarly, Cooper and Massell, and Johnson have shown that participation in a customs union is inferior to unilateral tariff elimination, which leads to greater trade creation without giving rise to trade diversion.[50]

To rescue Viner's theory, economists have refined it by adding two further motives for the creation of customs unions. The first motive is strategic and considers the impact of integration on the terms of trade. The argument is as follows: if non-member countries are producers of competitive goods with high price-elasticities of demand, then the price of their exports is likely to fall after the imposition of a common external tariff. The resulting terms of trade gain to the union may offset the welfare loss due to trade diversion.[51] Empirical studies have found

Kansas City, Jackson Hole, Wyoming, 1991; and particularly Jeffrey Frankel, *Regional Trading Blocs in the World Economic System* (Washington: Institute for International Economics, 1997).

[48] Warner Corden, "Economies of Scale and Customs Union Theory," *Journal of Political Economy* 80 (1972), 465–475. For a more recent discussion of economies of scale in the context of regional integration, see Richard Baldwin and Anthony Venables, "Regional Economic Integration," in Gene Grossman and Kenneth Rogoff, *Handbook of International Economics* (Amsterdam: Elsevier, 1995), vol. III, pp. 1597–1644.

[49] Jan Tinbergen, 'Customs Unions: Influence of their Size on their Effect," *Zeitschrift der Gesamten Staatswissenschaft* 113 (1957), 404–414.

[50] See Charles Cooper and Benton Massell, "A New Look at Customs Union Theory," *Economic Journal* 75 (1965), 742–747; and Harry Johnson, "An Economic Theory of Protectionism, Tariff Bargaining, and the Formation of Customs Unions," *Journal of Political Economy* 73 (1965), 256–283.

[51] Robert Mundell, "Tariff Preferences and the Terms of Trade," *Manchester School of Economic and Social Studies* (January 1964), 1–13; Jaroslav Vanek, *General Equilibrium of International Discrimination. The Case of Customs Unions* (Cambridge, Mass.: Harvard University Press, 1965); Murray Kemp and Henry Wan, "An Elementary Proposition Concerning the Formation of Customs Unions," *Journal of International Economics* 6

support for the terms of trade argument. Howard Petith, for example, concluded in the mid-1970s that the terms of trade improvements were the major economic effect of European integration. He found that the Community's terms of trade effect on GNP is as high as 1 percent.[52]

The second motive refers to changed preferences. Some countries are assumed to have a preference for domestic industrial and agricultural production *per se*, rather than for straight maximization of national income. It is argued, for example, that countries at a comparative disadvantage opt for more domestic production to satisfy nationalist aspirations.[53] This raises, however, the question as to why such nationalist strategies are not implemented by means of taxes and export subsidies. A possible answer is that export subsidies outside agriculture do not conform with international trading agreements, whereas customs unions are compatible with frameworks such as the General Agreement on Tariffs and Trade (GATT). In short, constraints on the use of first-best domestic policies may help to explain the formation of customs unions.[54] While this argument is reasonably cogent, it still fails to explain customs unions in advanced societies with highly competitive industries. Furthermore, explanations based on *ad hoc* shifts in preferences are typically little more than thinly veiled acknowledgements of theoretical ignorance.

Optimal currency area theory

Customs union theory is concerned only with markets for goods. It considers the welfare implications of discriminating mergers of such markets. Optimal currency area theory has a slightly different focus. It seeks to understand the conditions under which it is economically efficient to create a currency union. The focus is on money, markets for goods, and markets for production factors.

The first contribution towards a theory of optimal currency areas was

---

(1976), 95–97; P. J. Lloyd, "The Theory of Customs Unions," *Journal of International Economics* 12 (1982), 41–63; Paul Collier, "The Welfare Effects of a Customs Union: An Anatomy," *Economic Journal* 83 (1979), 84–87.

[52] See Howard Petith, "European Integration and the Terms of Trade," *Economic Journal* 87 (1977), 262–272. The trade-creation gains are reported in Bela Balassa, "Trade Creation and Trade Diversion in the European Community."

[53] Charles Cooper and Benton Massell, "Towards a General Theory of Customs Unions for Developing Countries," *Journal of Political Economy* 73 (1965), 461–476. See also Johnson, "An Economic Theory of Protectionism, Tariff Bargaining, and the Formation of Customs Unions."

[54] A. Jones, "The Theory of European Integration," in Ali El-Agraa (ed.), *The Economics of the European Community* (Oxford: Philip Allan, 1985), pp. 71–92.

made by Mundell.[55] McKinnon, Kenen, and others extended the original model.[56]

A currency area is defined as an area in which exchange rates are immutably fixed or in which a common currency exists. Optimality is defined in terms of the ability of an area to achieve both internal balance (full employment and low inflation) and external balance (payments equilibrium) in the least costly way, that is, without interference from monetary and fiscal policies. The concept of optimal currency area was developed in the context of debates over the relative merits of fixed versus flexible exchange rate. Proponents of flexible exchange rates argued that a country afflicted with price and wage rigidities should adopt flexible exchange rates in order to maintain both internal and external balance.[57] Under fixed exchange rates with price and wage rigidities, any policy effort to correct international payments imbalances would produce unemployment or inflation, whereas under flexible exchange rates the induced changes in the terms of trade and real wages would eliminate payments imbalances without much of the burden of real adjustments.[58] Theorists of optimal currency areas, however, argued that fixed exchange rates (or a currency area) may reconcile internal and external balance more efficiently than flexible rates if a country is highly integrated within a region. More specifically, Mundell held that the creation of a currency area is efficient if a region exhibits high mobility of its factors of production. Such mobility assumes the role of exchange rate flexibility in the process of real adjustment to economic disturbances within the area.

McKinnon's criterion for establishing a currency union is the degree of external openness of a region as measured by the ratio of tradable to non-tradable goods. The higher the ratio the greater the benefit from

---

[55] Robert Mundell, "A Theory of Optimal Currency Areas," *American Economic Review* (September 1963), 657–665.

[56] Ronald McKinnon, "Optimum Currency Area," *American Economic Review* 53 (September 1963), 717–725; Peter Kenen, "The Theory of Optimum Currency Areas: An Eclectic View," in Alexander Swoboda and Robert Mundell (eds.), *Monetary Problems of the International Economy* (Chicago: University of Chicago Press, 1969), pp. 41–60. See also Herbert Grubel, "The Theory of Optimum Currency Areas," *Canadian Journal of Economics* 3 (May 1970), 318–324; and John Presley and Geoffrey Dennis, *Currency Areas* (London: Macmillan Press, 1976).

[57] See Milton Friedman, "The Case for Flexible Exchange Rates," in Milton Friedman, *Essays in Positive Economics* (Chicago: University of Chicago Press, 1953), pp. 157–203.

[58] Masahiro Kawai, "Optimum Currency Areas," in Peter Newman, Murray Milgate, and John Eatwell (eds.), *The New Palgrave Dictionary of Money and Finance* (London: Macmillan, 1992), p. 78. Note that if prices and real wages were assumed to be flexible, market clearance following disturbances would be instantaneous and real adjustments could be established without causing unemployment.

currency union. The reason, according to McKinnon, is that exchange-rate flexibility of an externally open region is not effective in rectifying payments imbalances because exchange rate variations would be offset by price changes without significant impact on the terms of trade and real wages. It follows that the optimal monetary arrangement of an internally open but externally relatively closed economy would be to peg its currency to the body of internally traded goods for price stability, and adopt externally flexible exchange rates for external balance.

Since the pioneering contributions by Mundell and McKinnon, work on optimal currency areas has examined the question as to whether particular countries should join with one another to form a currency area from a broader cost-benefit point of view than early studies.[59] The main cost of participation in a currency union is the loss of monetary independence. This cost varies, however. It is likely to be high for a country that has a low tolerance for unemployment and is subject to strong price and wage pressures from monopolistic industries and labor unions. A small and open economy, however, may be more willing to participate in a currency union because it does not have much freedom to choose its mix of inflation and unemployment in the first place. The main benefit that a currency area offers is greater usefulness of money. A single currency simplifies calculation and accounting, economizes on acquiring and using information for transactions, eliminates the risks of future exchange-rate fluctuations, and maximizes the gains from trade and specialization.[60]

Much of the recent theoretical work on optimal currency areas refines and extends the analysis of the calculus of participation in a currency union using game theory, paying particular attention to bargaining and cooperation issues that arise in strategic settings characterized by asymmetric information and unequal distribution of economic capabilities among possible members of a currency union.[61] Most of the recent

---

[59] See Yoshihide Ishiyama, "The Theory of Optimum Currency Areas: A Survey," *IMF Staff Papers* 22 (July 1975), 344–383; and Edward Tower and Thomas Willett, "The Theory of Optimum Currency Areas and Exchange-Rate Flexibility," *Special Studies in International Economics* 11 (Princeton: International Finance Section, Princeton University, 1976).

[60] Kawai, "Optimum Currency Areas," 80.

[61] See Willem Buiter and Richard Marston (eds.), *International Economic Policy Coordination* (Cambridge: Cambridge University Press, 1985); Matthew Canzoneri and Jo Anne Gray, "Monetary Policy Games and the Consequences of Non-Cooperative Behavior," *International Economic Review* 36 (1985), 547–564; Richard Cooper, *The International Monetary System* (Cambridge, Mass.: MIT Press, 1987); and Koichi Hamada, *The Political Economy of International Monetary Interdependence* (Cambridge, Mass.: MIT Press, 1985).

empirical work considers the question as to whether Europe satisfies the criteria for an optimal currency union.[62]

Neither customs union theory nor optimal currency area theory is concerned with explaining changes in the rules and policies that govern economic regions. In this sense, these two theories are static and fail to shed light on the process of deepening and enlarging communities. Their focus is on market relations among goods and factors of production; the importance of political and supranational institutions in the process of integration is assumed away. This is hardly a satisfactory state of affairs, for the implications of regional integration go beyond trade in goods, services, and factors. As recently acknowledged by three respected economists, regional economic arrangements, almost by definition, entail the imposition of some common rules of conduct for participating countries and a set of reciprocal commitments and obligations. "The importance of this political dimension of regional integration may well exceed that of the more direct implications having to do with trade flows."[63]

Robert Lawrence has similarly noted that

[m]ost theorizing about regionalism [in economics] considers these arrangements in the context of a traditional paradigm in which trade policy is characterized by changes to barriers at the border. Regional arrangements are modeled either as customs union ... or as free trade area ... But although the removal of internal border barriers is certainly an important feature, focusing only on these barriers overlooks much of what regional arrangements are about. The traditional perspective is at best incomplete and at worst misleading. In many cases these emerging arrangements are also meant to achieve deeper integration of international competition and investment. Once tariffs are removed, complex problems remain because of differing regulatory policies among nations.[64]

Thus, to understand regional integration, it is of critical importance to analyze how these complex problems are solved and to assess the political consequences of such solutions.

[62] See, for example, Peter Bofinger, "Is Europe an Optimal Currency Area?," *Centre for Economic Policy Research [CEPR] Working Paper* no. 915 (London, 1994); Paul De Grauwe and Wim Vanhaverbeke, "Is Europe an Optimal Currency Area? Evidence From Regional Data," *Centre for Economic Policy Research [CEPR] Working Paper* 555 (London, 1991); Barry Eichengreen, "Is Europe an Optimal Currency Area?" *National Bureau of Economic Research [NBER] Working Paper* no. 3579 (Cambridge, Mass.: NBER, 1991); and Jeffrey Frankel and Andrew Rose, "The Endogeneity of the Optimum Currency Area Criteria," NBER Working Paper no. 5700 (Cambridge, Mass.: NBER, 1996).

[63] Jaime de Melo, Arvind Panagariya, and Dani Rodrik, "The New Regionalism: A Country Perspective," in Jaime de Melo and Arvind Panagariya (eds.), *New Dimensions in Regional Integration* (Cambridge: Cambridge University Press, 1993), p. 176.

[64] Robert Lawrence, *Regionalism, Multilateralism, and Deeper Integration* (Washington: Brookings Institution, 1996), p. 7.

The general point is that an analysis of market integration that neglects to incorporate institutional elements risks being empty. Market integration takes place in a particular institutional setting. It also carries with it institutional implications which, in turn, affect the course of market integration. An account of integration that seeks to address the dynamic aspects of the phenomenon must consider the reciprocal relationship between economic and politico-institutional factors.

Fiscal federalism and economic integration

Fiscal federalism theory is an offshoot of public finance theory that analyzes the special fiscal problems which arise in federal countries, drawing on the literature on public goods, taxation and public debt incidence, and various parts of location theory. It examines the reasons for adopting a federal structure, identifies the rules for the assignment of authority over various parts of fiscal policy to different levels of government, and considers the efficiency implications of migration from one jurisdiction to another, as well as the role of intergovernmental revenue transfers and their most desirable forms in a federal structure.[65]

Many of the issues discussed in fiscal federalism are relevant to the study of regional institution-building, particularly in the European case where free trade and capital mobility, along with steps towards monetary union, have raised the question of the desirability of fiscal coordination among EU member states. Greater mobility of capital, labor, consumers, and taxpayers (individual or corporate) implies that regional differences in taxation and in supply of public goods can induce migration of each of these categories. This raises the potential for fiscal spillovers across borders creating incentives for fiscal policy coordination and thereby raising the problem of determining the appropriate levels for fiscal policy decision-making.[66] The forms of coordination which can be attained range from simple interstate agreements to mutually adopted centralized policies, depending on the scope of spillover, the cost of enforcement of an agreement, and the extent of economies of scale from centralization.[67]

---

[65] See Richard Musgrave, *The Theory of Public Finance* (New York: McGraw-Hill, 1959); Wallace Oates, *Fiscal Federalism* (New York: Harcourt Brace, 1972); and David King, *Fiscal Tiers – The Economics of Multi-Level Government* (London: Allen & Unwin, 1984).

[66] Willem Buiter and Kenneth Kletzer, "Fiscal Policy Coordination as Fiscal Federalism: Economic Integration, Public Goods and Efficiency in Growing Economies," *European Economic Review* 36 (1992), 647.

[67] See Robert Inman and Daniel Rubinfeld, "Fiscal Federalism in Europe: Lessons from the United States Experience," *European Economic Review* 36 (1992), 654–660; and Damien Neven, "Regulatory Reform in the European Community," *European Economic Review* 36 (1992), 98–103.

Allocative efficiency through coordination is not the only objective of policy-makers; another concern is the achievement of distributional goals. Mobility of taxpayers reduces the ability of local governments to use taxes and transfers to redistribute income locally. This raises a need for centralized redistributive policies.[68] Finally, economic integration is likely to raise questions as to how the winners will compensate the losers. The ensuing need for compensatory mechanisms is bound to widen the fiscal responsibility of the central authority in a region.

The contribution of the fiscal federalism literature to economic integration is not limited to the identification of the appropriate policy locus within a larger economic space. It has also triggered more general reflections on the link between the evolution of private markets and the creation of new institutions. The work of Alessandra Casella is particularly noteworthy in this context.[69]

Casella seeks to understand how the development of market integration is likely to shape the geometry of public-goods provision within a region. Her work links concepts and ideas developed in public finance with recent work on international trade and economic geography.[70] It thus connects well-established results on the determinants of optimal club size with characteristics of economic markets.

Casella uses institutions and jurisdiction interchangeably and defines them as "clubs whose members [jointly] decide [on], finance, and enjoy an excludable public good."[71] Markets, in turn, are defined as "sets of traders who exchange private goods."[72] Her argument can be summarized as follows: at first, the widening of markets requires centralized regional institutions to achieve coordination and reduce transaction

---

[68] See Dominique Bureau and Paul Champsaur, "Fiscal Federalism and European Economic Unification," *American Economic Review Papers and Proceedings* 82 (May 1992), 88–92.

[69] See Alessandra Casella, "Trade as an Engine of Political Change: A Parable," *Economica* (1994) 61, 267–284; Alessandra Casella and Jonathan Feinstein, "On the Formation of Markets and Political Jurisdictions," *NBER Working Paper* no. 3554 (Cambridge, Mass.: NBER, 1990); Alessandra Casella and Bruno Frey, "Federalism and Clubs: Towards an Economic Theory of Overlapping Political Jurisdictions," *European Economic Review* 36 (1992), 639–649; and Alessandra Casella and Barry Weingast, "Elements of a Theory of Jurisdictional Change," in Barry Eichengreen and Jeffry Frieden (eds.), *Politics and Institutions in an Integrated Europe* (Berlin: Springer, 1995).

[70] See Paul Krugman, *Geography and Trade* (Cambridge, Mass.: MIT Press, 1991).

[71] Alessandra Casella, "On Markets and Clubs: Economic and Political Integration of Regions with Unequal Productivity," *American Economic Review Papers and Proceedings* (May 1992), 115; see also Casella, "Trade as an Engine of Political Change," 268. Excludable public goods are goods whose consumption by one club member only marginally detracts from the consumption by other members of the good. Individuals outside the club have no access to the good.

[72] Casella, "On Markets and Clubs," 115.

costs. However, as integration deepens, the differences in economic roles and needs within the region become more marked, giving rise to demand for a broad range of public goods. "Jurisdictions must be redrawn to satisfy the requirements of unified, more competitive, more sophisticated markets."[73] What emerges is "functional federalism," that is, a regime where individuals and member states organize themselves into a pattern of overlapping jurisdictions, with each jurisdiction responsible for the provision of a specific class of public goods. These jurisdictions have variable membership depending on the scope of policy under consideration, and they represent a highly decentralized system of economic organization.[74]

Casella's analysis is congruent with and complementary to the framework developed in chapter 3 of this book. There are a few differences, however. Most of the institutional developments she describes presuppose the existence of a unified regional market. The framework of chapter 3 suggests that the achievement of such unification is far from automatic. Demand by market players alone does not typically generate a provision of functional goods. What Casella's analysis misses is an examination of the collective action problems involved in regional cooperation and the other supply-side conditions for successful integration, including the willingness of potential providers to supply common institutional arrangements. Another difference is that Casella does not consider the effects of regional institution-building on outsiders, an issue that is key to my framework. Finally, the theoretical departure point of her analysis varies somewhat from that which is presented in chapter 3. Her work is inspired by concepts developed in public finance, whereas chapter 3 builds, in part, on insights from property-rights theory, economic history, and new institutional economics. This difference is small, however, for we both agree on the key importance of market forces in driving the process of regional institution-building.

---

[73] Casella, "Trade as an Engine of Political Change," 267.
[74] Casella and Frey, "Federalism and Clubs," 640.

3   Explaining regional integration

1   Introduction

The general analytical framework for understanding regional integration begins with a discussion of the factors determining the outcome of regional integration schemes, which is followed by an examination of the consequences of integration for outsiders. Throughout the text integration is defined as the voluntary linking in the economic domain of two or more formerly independent states to the extent that authority over key areas of domestic regulation and policy is shifted to the supranational level. Unlike traditional political-science explanations, the account offered in this chapter stresses the importance of market factors in determining the outcome of integration schemes; but unlike purely economic theories it holds that market integration cannot be explained without reference to institutional factors.

This chapter seeks to address two related puzzles of regional integration, one implicating the insider countries in an integration process, the other the outsiders. The first puzzle can be stated as follows: why have so many attempts at integration failed while a few have been crowned with success? The second puzzle is: what explains when outsiders seek to become insiders? Outsiders can become insiders either by joining an existing economic union or by creating their own regional group.

The first puzzle, the variation in outcomes, is illustrated by the wide range of integration results. At one extreme, the highly successful European Union has managed over the past forty years to establish an array of institutions and policies, as well as a broad and clearly defined set of rules, which are hierarchically superior to domestic law and directly applicable in the member states of the Union. This novel European polity has boosted intraregional trade and investment, bringing unprecedented prosperity and stability to an area long known for internecine warfare and economic calamities. At the other extreme, projects such as the Latin American Free Trade Association, the Andean Pact, the Economic Community of West African States, and the

Middle German Commercial Union failed to make any significant progress towards integration. Their stated integration goals and subsequent achievements were far apart. Between these polar cases are a few integration projects with mixed results. Two such examples are the European Free Trade Association and the Central American Common Market. What explains the variation in these outcomes?

The analysis of the first puzzle takes the decision to adopt an integration treaty as a given, and is primarily concerned with identifying the conditions under which the process of integration is likely to succeed or to fail. Implementation of a promise by heads of states to tie the economies of their countries closer together entails a lengthy process of establishing common rules, regulations, and policies that are either based on specific treaty provisions or derived from the general principles and objectives written into integration treaties.

Two types of condition in particular need to be satisfied in order for integration to succeed. First, the potential for economic gains from market exchange within a region must be significant. If there is little potential for gain, perhaps because regional economies lack complementarity or because the small size of the regional market does not offer important economies of scale, the process of integration will quickly peter out. However, the potential for gain may grow with the diffusion of new technologies. Market players will then have an incentive to lobby for regional institutional arrangements that render the realization of these gains possible. The demand for regional rules, regulations, and policies by market players is a critical driving force of integration.

Second, there must also be a fulfillment of supply conditions. These are the conditions under which political leaders are willing and able to accommodate demands for regional institutions at each step of the integration process. Willingness depends on the payoff of integration to political leaders; they may be more willing to deepen integration if such a move is expected to improve their chances of retaining power, for example, by notably improving domestic economic conditions. But even willing political leaders may be unable to supply regional institutions because of collective action problems. One such problem, coordination, is particularly salient in integration. This leads to a key supply condition: the presence of a benevolent leading country within the region seeking integration. Such a country serves as a focal point in the coordination of rules, regulations, and policies; it may also help to ease tensions that arise from the inequitable distribution of gains from integration, for example, through side-payments. Contested institutional leadership or the absence of leadership makes coordination games very difficult to resolve.

The provision by an integration treaty for the establishment of "commitment institutions," such as centralized monitoring and third party enforcement, is a subsidiary (or weak) condition for successful integration. In its absence, cooperation may still be possible on the basis of repeat-play, issue-linkage, and reputation. Nevertheless, "commitment institutions" improve compliance with the rules of cooperation by acting as constraints in circumstances where self-help measures alone are insufficient to prevent reneging.

In sum, areas with strong market pressure for integration and undisputed leadership are most likely to experience successful integration; "commitment institutions" help to catalyze the process. Regional groups that do not satisfy either of the two strong conditions are least likely to succeed.

The second puzzle is the timing of the decision by outsider countries to seek integration either by joining an already existing economic union or by creating counter-unions. This puzzle is related to the first one, because the outcome of an integration project may have external effects on outsiders, for example, through diversion of trade, investment, and aid. These effects will trigger integrative responses if their negative impact on the economies of outsiders is felt. Affected outsiders will have an incentive to join an economic union, in the hope that accession will improve their economic performance and hence their governments' likelihood of staying in power. However, if the union has no interest in accepting new members because enlargement does not bring any economic or political advantages to the union, or if the price of membership in a union is prohibitive, countries in "relative deprivation" may decide instead to form their own regional group. Like any integration scheme, to succeed such a counter-union must satisfy both demand and supply conditions of integration. If these conditions are not met, counter-unions are likely to fail.

The chapter is organized as follows: section 2 summarizes the insights of several institutional schools of thought that offer fertile ground for thinking about the process of integration. Section 3 discusses some of these ideas in the context of regional integration and introduces the demand condition. Section 4 presents the supply conditions. Section 5 discusses the link between economic performance and regional institutional change. Section 6 complements the internal account of integration presented in sections 3 and 4 by considering the external dimension of integration, focusing on the effects of community building on outsiders. It sets the stage for an analysis of the timing puzzle. Section 7 links the theoretical analysis to the cases discussed in later chapters by identifying testable implications of the analysis and previewing the evidence presented in the remaining chapters.

2   Externalities, transaction costs, and demand for institutional change

Regional integration is the process of providing common rules, regulations, and policies for a region. What drives this process? Institutional theories, such as property-rights theory, economic history, new institutional economics, provide useful insights into this process. These theories are primarily concerned with explaining the evolution of domestic institutional arrangements, but their logic can be extended to shed light on the dynamics of regional institution-building. Their common definition of institutions is a set of formal and informal rules, regulations, and compliance procedures designed to constrain and shape human interaction and structure the incentives of actors involved in an exchange relationship in order to maximize the wealth or utility of these actors.[1]

Property-rights theory identifies key actors and motives driving institutional change. The theory holds that the impetus and demand for institutional change comes from the bottom, that is, from those actors incurring the greatest opportunity cost in the institutional *status quo*. For example, in a study of the evolution of property rights for mineral resources, Gary Libecap found that the law in the United States changed in response to changes in economic value: as the value of a resource increased, claimants of the resource had an incentive to demand more precision in the definition of property rights in order to capture more fully the potential rental stream from the resource.[2] Lance Davis and Douglass North have similarly argued that the possibility of profits that cannot be captured within an existing structure leads to the formation of new (or the mutation of old) institutional arrangements.[3] These views echo Harold Demsetz's argument that "property rights develop to internalize externalities when the gains of internalization become larger than the cost of internalization. Increased internalization, in the main, results from changes in economic values, changes which stem from the development of new technology and the

---

[1] Beth Yarbrough and Robert Yarbrough, *Cooperation and Governance in International Trade: The Strategic Organizational Approach* (Princeton: Princeton University Press, 1992), p. 11; and Douglass North, *Structure and Change in Economic History* (New York: Norton, 1981), p. 201.

[2] Gary Libecap, "Economic Variables and the Development of the Law: The Case of Western Mineral Rights," in Lee Alston, Thrainn Eggertsson, and Douglass North (eds.), *Empirical Studies in Institutional Change* (Cambridge: Cambridge University Press, 1996), pp. 34–58. See also Willard Hurst, *Law and Economic Growth* (Cambridge, Mass.: Harvard University Press, 1964).

[3] Lance Davis and Douglass North, *Institutional Change and American Economic Growth* (Cambridge: Cambridge University Press, 1971), p. 59.

opening of new markets, changes to which old property rights are poorly attuned."[4]

The economic history school refines the analysis of the impact of new technologies on markets and institutions by introducing the concept of transaction costs. Transaction costs are the costs of specifying, negotiating, monitoring, and enforcing contracts that underlie exchange. In other words, they are the costs of capturing the gains from market exchange.[5] North's account of the Industrial Revolution is a well-known example of this literature. His argument, in a nutshell, is that new technologies ease communications and shorten distances, thus increasing the size of markets. This had two effects. First, it created pressure to replace medieval and crown restrictions circumscribing entrepreneurs with better specified common law. Second, the growing size of the market caused a shift from vertically integrated (home and handicraft) production to specialized production. Specialization, however, increased the costs of measuring the inputs and outputs, thus catalyzing organizational innovation to reduce these transaction costs. In this account, technologies and transaction costs are inextricably intertwined: technological change led to increased specialization which induced organizational innovation; this in turn induced technical change, which required further organizational innovation in order to realize the potential of the new technology.[6]

Transaction costs also play a central role in the new institutional economics (NIE) literature, a rapidly growing field that has developed from the pioneering work of Oliver Williamson.[7] NIE theory takes as given the political rules of the game and the production technology. It seeks to explain industrial organization, from straightforward market exchange to vertically integrated exchange, based solely on differences in transaction costs. It postulates that "transaction costs are economized by assigning transactions (which differ in their attributes) to governance structures (the adaptive capacities and associated costs of which differ) in a discriminating way."[8] In particular, the higher the asset specificity

---

[4] Harold Demsetz, "Towards a Theory of Property Rights," *American Economic Review – Papers and Proceedings* 57 (May 1969), 350. Externalities arise when one person's actions affect others and the person is not penalized for the loss or damage caused (or rewarded for the benefits conferred).

[5] Douglass North, "Transaction Costs in History," *The Journal of European Economic History* 14 (Winter 1985), 558.

[6] North, *Structure and Change in Economic History.*

[7] See Oliver Williamson, *Markets and Hierarchies: Analysis and Antitrust Implications* (New York: Free Press, 1975); and Oliver Williamson, *The Economic Institutions of Capitalism* (New York: Free Press, 1985).

[8] Williamson, *The Economic Institutions of Capitalism*, p. 18.

(the degree to which durable investments are made to support particular transactions), the greater the institutional complexity required to promote efficient exchange.

Many of these ideas on institutional change can be extrapolated to an account of demand-side conditions for regional integration. Thus regional institution-building may be viewed as an attempt to internalize externalities that cross borders within a group of countries. The cost of these externalities increases as new technologies raise the potential for gain from market exchange, thus increasing the payoffs to regional rules, regulations, and policies.

3   Externalities, transaction costs, and demand for integration

The preceding section suggests a first building-block, for an account of regional integration. The argument can be stated as follows: as new technologies increase the scope of markets beyond the boundaries of a single state, actors who stand to gain from wider markets will seek to change an existing governance structure in order to realize these gains to the fullest extent.

What are the potential gains from wider markets? Theories of international trade and investment have identified several sources of gain from international exchange. Trade theorists argue, for example, that larger markets help firms achieve economies of scale in production; that is, an increase in production lowers the average cost of output per unit. The phenomenon of extensive intra-industry trade among industrialized countries attests to the importance of economies of scale in production. Another argument is that trade is beneficial because it permits countries to exploit their comparative advantage. A comparative advantage arises when the marginal opportunity costs of producing one good in terms of another good differ between countries. Thus a country gains from specializing in the production and export of those goods which it can produce at relatively low cost (i.e., goods in which it is relatively more efficient than other countries).

In addition to these gains from trade, there are specific gains to be had from investing abroad. Investment theorists view the sources of gain from international exchange as follows: firms operating in a given country may accumulate special production advantages over their counterparts in other countries such as cheaper sources of finance, special managerial and marketing skills, and patented or non-marketable technologies. These firm-specific intangible assets provide strong incentives for expanding production abroad, particularly if pulled by location-specific advantages in host countries. Location-specific advantag[e] include lower labor costs, skilled or non-unionized labor, lower material costs, access to extractive resources, market proximity, as well as invest- ment incentives such as cash grants, interest-free loans, fast-deprecia- tion schemes, tax credits, and training grants.[9]

Investment and trade are not necessarily separate activities. The existence of trade-related investment blurs the distinction. Trade- related investment is very common in international trade. One reason is that the process of specialization according to comparative advantage involves investment in increased productive capacity to service export markets. Trade-related investment can also involve vulnerable assets that are located abroad, such as transportation or storage facilities.[10] In short, investment generates trade, and trade attracts investment.

The costs of international trade and investment transactions, however, can be prohibitive, eroding many of the potential gains from exchange. The risks are numerous. First, there is uncertainty: civil unrest or economic mismanagement may render foreign assets or trade- related domestic investment worthless. Second, a wide range of *ex post facto* hazards due to either firm-level or government-level opportunism may severely curtail the profitability of international exchange.[11] Late deliveries, unexpected price hikes, poor-quality goods, tariff changes, new non-tariff barriers, differing rates of inflation, devaluations or foreign exchange restrictions to balance payment problems, all render reliance upon foreign markets precarious. In addition, a host country can revert to outright nationalization of foreign assets or implement measures of "creeping expropriation" through laws and regulations that deprive investors of the value of their contract. Such measures include local equity obligations, profit remittance controls, forced sales, export performance requirements, forced partnerships, local content require- ments, licensing restrictions, financing restrictions, restricted markets,

---

[9] For theories on foreign investment, see Richard Caves, *Multinational Enterprise and Economic Analysis* (Cambridge: Cambridge University Press, 1996); John Dunning, *Explaining International Production* (London: Unwin Hyman, 1989); Stephen Hymer, *The International Operation of National Firms: A Study of Direct Foreign Investment* (Cambridge, Mass.: MIT Press, 1976); Charles Kindleberger, *American Business Abroad: Six Lectures on Direct Investment* (New Haven: Yale University Press, 1969).

[10] For further examples and a discussion, see Yarbrough and Yarbrough, *Cooperation and Governance in International Trade*.

[11] I follow Oliver Williamson's definition of opportunism which is "self-interest seeking with guile." He adds: "This includes but is scarcely limited to more blatant forms, such as stealing and cheating ... More generally, opportunism refers to the incomplete or distorted disclosure of information, especially to calculated efforts to mislead, distort, disguise, obfuscate, or otherwise confuse." (See Williamson, *The Economic Institutions of Capitalism*, p. 47.)

tax discrimination, export quotas, supervision of transfer prices, and the prevention of local acquisition.[12]

Firms can seek to minimize transaction costs that arise from firm-level opportunism through private contractual arrangements (internal safeguards). Vertical integration, long-term licensing agreements, and multinationalism are organizational techniques that serve the purpose of internalizing externalities.[13] However, as Williamson has pointed out, internalized forms of production do not come without cost. Removing transactions from markets and organizing them internally may sacrifice economies of scale and scope. Internal organizations may also experience serious incentive and bureaucratic disabilities.[14]

These problems may raise the appeal of external safeguards in the form of an integrated governance structure, particularly as both efficiency costs of private contractual arrangements and efficiency gains of external safeguards increase with greater frequency of transactions. External safeguards can address not only firm-level problems but also government-level opportunism, thus enabling market players to economize optimally on trade and investment transaction costs.[15]

The institutional breadth and depth of external safeguards depend on the nature and intensity of functional demands which, in turn, reflect the density and extent of larger markets. Market density has been most pronounced in Europe and North America, as will be illustrated in the

[12] See Charles Lipson, *Standing Guard: Protecting Foreign Capital in the Nineteenth and Twentieth Centuries* (Berkeley: University of California Press, 1985), in particular pp. 7, 10, 22, 24–30, 97, 119, 162, 182; Michael Duerr, *The Problems Facing International Management* (New York: Conference Board, 1974), p. 5. See also Stephen Kobrin, "Foreign Enterprise and Forced Divestment in LDCs," *International Organization* 34 (1980), 65–88; "Expropriation as an Attempt to Control Foreign Firms in LDCs: Trends from 1960–1979," *International Studies Quarterly* 28 (1984), 329–348. Note that not all investment is equally vulnerable to government-level opportunism. For a discussion see Lipson, *Standing Guard.*

[13] Yarbrough and Yarbrough, *Cooperation and Governance in International Trade*, pp. 34 and 88; see also Farok Contractor and Peter Lorange (eds.), *Cooperative Strategies in International Business: Joint Ventures and Technology Partnerships between Firms* (Lexington, Mass.: Lexington Books, 1988).

[14] Williamson, *The Economic Institutions of Capitalism*, p. 163.

[15] The distinction between internal and external safeguards was first made by the Yarbroughs. They argue that preferential trade agreements are the "public sector equivalent of private non-standard contractual arrangements." My discussion in this section has been greatly inspired by their pioneering work. However, my overall argument is quite different from theirs and I am in disagreement with their analysis of European integration. For example, I argue that the Court of Justice has been the key enforcer of Community obligations; they argue instead that majority voting brought about enforcement. They also overlook the importance of coordination games in integration (Yarbrough and Yarbrough, *Cooperation and Governance in International Trade*). On the idea that international regimes serve to minimize transaction costs, see also Robert Keohane, *After Hegemony: Cooperation and Discord in the World Political Economy* (Princeton: Princeton University Press, 1984).

empirical chapters. It is thus not surprising that pressure for common rules and external safeguards has been strongest in these regions.

The successful provision of a new governance structure is likely to further market integration, hence putting the structure under pressure to adapt. Functional integration, that is, the provision of common rules, regulations, and policies embodied in an integrated governance structure, may begin with exchange rate coordination. As market integration accelerates it may expand to include common trade rules, common industrial standards, tax harmonization, macroeconomic policy coordination, common fiscal and monetary policies, as well as common social policies and institution of a regional transfer system to ease the burden of adjustment, to compensate losers, and to ensure the political viability of economic integration.

The critical role of market players in integration is amply illustrated in the empirical chapters. The "relaunching" of European integration in the mid-1980s, for example, is in great part attributable to pressure from the business community. European industrialists were the first to campaign for a single European market at a time of rapid technological change, even before the European Commission.[16] In 1983, they formed the Round Table of European Industrialists, a group comprising Europe's largest and most influential corporations, including Philips, Siemens, Olivetti, GEC, Daimler Benz, Volvo, Fiat, Bosch, ASEA, and Ciba-Geigy. Harping on the theme of economies of scale that would benefit business in a truly unified market, the European Round Table (ERT) became a powerful lobby *vis-à-vis* the national governments. Other business groups joined in the lobbying, notably the Union of Industrial and Employers' Confederations in Europe (UNICE), composed of over thirty industrial associations from throughout Europe.

As discussed in chapter 5, big business played a similarly important role in NAFTA. A wider market and a broader range of available labor skills would enable North American firms to rationalize production on a regional basis and thus compete more effectively against foreign producers both at home and in world markets. All of the major umbrella organizations, including the National Association of Manufacturers, the National Retail Federation, the Business Roundtable, and the United States Council for International Business, expressed support for deeper integration in North America.[17] Haggard notes that for big business

---

[16] The classic account is Wayne Sandholtz and John Zysman, "1992: Recasting the European Bargain," *World Politics* 42 (October 1989), 95–128.

[17] Stephan Haggard, *Developing Nations and the Politics of Global Integration* (Washington, D.C.: Brookings Institution, 1995), p. 90.

"the agreement offered new investment opportunities in Mexico and a chance to improve the overall climate of conducting business ... not only by lifting restrictions but [also] by *extending various guarantees,* for example, on the availability for foreign exchange, expropriation, and dispute settlement."[18]

A final illustration of the importance of business in promoting integration comes from the German Zollverein. In 1819, German business men, led by Friedrich List, founded the German Commercial and Industrial League (Deutscher Handels- und Gewerbeverein) which set as its aim the economic unification of Germany. In the same year, the League complained in a petition submitted to the German Diet that the numerous customs barriers "cripple trade and produce the same effect as ligatures which prevent the free circulation of the blood. The merchant trading between Hamburg and Austria, or Berlin and Switzerland must traverse ten states, must learn ten customs tariffs, must pay ten successive transit dues."[19] The League set up a network of correspondents all over Germany, printed pamphlets, memoranda, and their own periodical. List himself pleaded the League's cause with political leaders and wrote numerous articles, stressing the economic foundations of the project. Issues raised included the need for common weights and measures, a common coinage, and a single code of commercial law. Arnold Price notes: "It was undoubtedly due to [List's] influence that the governments were stirred out of their lethargy and began to discuss the problem seriously."[20]

In conclusion, the interests which are most important for spurring a drive for deeper integration are the same ones which economic theories of institutional change focus on. Clearly, however, demand for integration on the part of big business does not automatically translate into success. If demand is not met by supply, no change will occur. Some early institutional theories have been criticized and dubbed "naive" for overlooking the importance of supply conditions and assuming that demand alone would miraculously generate institutional change. The next section sheds light on necessary supply conditions.

4   The supply of integration

Supply conditions are the conditions under which political leaders are willing and able to accommodate demands for functional integration.

[18] *Ibid.,* p. 91, my italics.
[19] The petition is reprinted in W. von Eisenhart Rothe and A. Ritthaler, *Vorgeschichte und Begründung des Deutschen Zollvereins, 1915–1834,* vol. I (1934), pp. 320–324.
[20] Arnold Price, *The Evolution of the Zollverein* (Ann Arbor: University of Michigan Press, 1949), p. 37.

Willingness depends greatly on the payoff of integration to political leaders. If these leaders value political autonomy (absence of interference by supranational agents) and political power, they are unlikely to seek deep levels of integration as long as their economies are relatively prosperous. Why sacrifice national sovereignty and pay the price of membership in a regional group if the economy is growing relatively fast and voters are thus content? In other words, economically successful leaders are unlikely to pursue deeper integration because their expected marginal benefit from integration in terms of improved re-election chances (or simply in terms of retaining political power) is minimal and thus not worth the cost of integration. This argument is consistent with the insights from the rent-seeking literature which stipulates that political leaders value relative independence and "bribe-money" from small and effectively organized groups that stand to heavily lose from integration.[21] However, in times of economic difficulties, political leaders will be more concerned with securing their own survival and are thus likely to implement economic policies that enhance the overall efficiency of the economy; in other words, distributional considerations become of secondary importance, thus eliminating entrenched interest groups' resistance to integration.[22]

A cursory look at the data confirms the importance of economic difficulties as a background condition of integration. For example, the adoption of the Single European Act was a response to slow European growth in the early 1980s. Similarly, Canada and Mexico turned to the United States when their performance was in trouble, and Latin American economies liberalized in part through regional agreements in the face of the debt crisis.[23] Although Asian economies have adjusted since the 1960s by following selective liberalization strategies, they have not

---

[21] See Stephen Magee, William Brock, and Leslie Young, *Black Hole Tariffs and Endogenous Theory* (Cambridge: Cambridge University Press, 1989); Anne Krueger, "The Political Economy of the Rent-Seeking Society," *American Economic Review* 64 (June 1974), 291–303; Gordon Tullock, "The Welfare Costs of Tariffs, Monopolies, and Theft," *Western Economic Journal* 5 (June 1967), 224–232; Robert Tollison, "Rent Seeking: A Survey," *Kyklos* 35 (1982), 576–602; George Stigler, "The Theory of Economic Regulation," *Bell Journal of Economics and Management Science* (Spring 1971), 137–146; Sam Peltzman, "Towards a More General Theory of Regulation?," *Journal of Law and Economics* 19 (August 1976), 211–240; and Gary Becker, "A Theory of Competition among Pressure Groups for Political Influence," *Quarterly Journal of Economics* 98 (August 1983), 371–400.

[22] Dani Rodrik, "The Rush to Free Trade in the Developing World: Why So Late? Why Now? Will It Last?," in Stephan Haggard and Steven Webb, *Voting For Reform* (New York: Oxford University Press, 1994), pp. 61–88.

[23] Robert Lawrence, *Regionalism, Multilateralism, and Deeper Integration* (Washington: Brookings Institution, 1996), p. 86.

undergone institutional change through regional agreements to the same extent as less successful economies.[24]

Willingness brought about by economic difficulties, however, is no guarantee of successful integration. Willing leaders may still find it impossible to supply integration because of collective action problems. The work of Duncan Snidal and Arthur Stein provides useful insight into two types of collective-action dilemmas that are particularly relevant to the study of regional integration: Prisoners' Dilemma and coordination games.[25]

The Prisoners' Dilemma game has beneficially influenced the bulk of the international cooperation literature; but it has wrongly come to be viewed as the only, or the most important, collective-action problem.[26] Coordination problems are equally important in international cooperation and are of particular relevance for the study of regional integration. One reason is that regional integration schemes often go beyond the removal of border barriers (shallow integration) and include efforts to adopt common regulations and policies.[27] For example, one key element of the European Union's effort to create a common market is the promulgation of coordination equilibria, from common health and safety standards to the harmonization of excise taxes and the adoption of common macroeconomic policies.[28] The pressure for such coordination stems largely from the desire of big firms to establish regional production networks to reduce costs and maintain international competitiveness. The salience of coordination issues in integration will be illustrated in the following chapters.

[24] However, this may well change in the wake of the prolonged market turmoils of 1997 and 1998 in Asia.

[25] See Duncan Snidal, "Coordination Versus Prisoners' Dilemma: Implications for International Cooperation and Regimes," *American Political Science Review* 79 (December 1985), 923–942; and Arthur Stein, "Coordination and Collaboration: Regimes in an Anarchic World," in Stephen Krasner (ed.), *International Regimes* (Ithaca, N.Y.: Cornell University Press, 1983), pp. 115–140. See also Keohane, *After Hegemony*; Lisa Martin, "Interests, Power, and Multilateralism," *International Organization* 46 (Autumn 1992), 765–792; and Geoffrey Garrett and Barry Weingast, "Ideas, Interests, and Institutions," in Judith Goldstein and Robert Keohane (eds.), *Ideas and Foreign Policy: Beliefs, Institutions, and Political Change* (Ithaca: Cornell University Press, 1993), pp. 173–206. The PD and Coordination games provide a useful heuristic representation of two important strategic settings. However, the clean distinction between the two games breaks down under certain conditions. For good examples, see Barbara Koremenos, Charles Lipson, and Duncan Snidal (eds.), *Rational International Institutions* (forthcoming).

[26] Snidal, "Coordination Versus Prisoners' Dilemma," 923–924.

[27] Lawrence, *Regionalism, Multilateralism, and Deeper Integration*.

[28] The importance of Coordination games in international relations is stressed in Kenneth Abbott and Duncan Snidal, "Mesoinstitutions in International Politics," paper presented in the Program of International Politics, Economics, and Security, University of Chicago, April 1995, 31.

The normal (or strategic) forms of the Prisoners' Dilemma and coordination games are presented in figure 3.1. In both games, the policy options are x_1 and x_2 for state A, and y_1 and y_2 for state B. The entries in each cell represent ordinal payoffs for states A and B, respectively. (The ordinal payoffs are represented as ranging from 4 = "the most preferred outcome" to 1 = "the least preferred outcome.")

The Prisoners' Dilemma game

This game is the standard representation of externalities where in the pursuit of their own private gains actors impose costs on each other independently of each other's action.[29] State A will choose its dominant strategy x_2 and state B will pick its dominant strategy y_2. Both states end up being worse off than if both abstained from pursuing their narrow self-interest and cooperated (reaching payoff 3/3). The dilemma persists even if cooperation is achieved (x_1y_1 outcome), because both states will continue to have strong incentives to defect.

The extension of the two-actor Prisoners' Dilemma game to the n-actor situation tends to increase the difficulties of cooperation.[30] As the number of actors increases, information and communication problems become more severe and actors in cooperative arrangements may find it easier to cheat with impunity. However, the cooperation outlook brightens when the Prisoners' Dilemma game is played through time.[31] Repeated play makes cooperation more likely if the value of continued cooperation outweighs the benefits of defection at any one time.[32] Similarly, prospects of cooperation improve if Prisoners' Dilemma games are linked across space (issue linkage). Fear that noncooperation will spread into other areas provides an incentive for states not to succumb to immediate temptations to defect for short-run, issue-specific gains.[33]

Recent empirical studies, however, have shown that in a world of uncertainty and incomplete information, repeated play, issue-linkage, and reputation provide insufficient guarantees against violations of cooperation rules; more complex institutional arrangements may be

---

[29] Snidal, "Coordination Versus Prisoners' Dilemma," 926–927.

[30] Exceptions to this rule are discussed in Helen Milner, "International Theories of Cooperation among Nations," *World Politics* 44 (April 1992), 467–496; and Duncan Snidal, "The Politics of Scope: Endogenous Actors, Heterogeneity and Institutions," *Journal of Theoretical Politics* 4 (1994), 449–472.

[31] See Robert Axelrod, *The Evolution of Cooperation* (New York: Basic Books, 1984); and Russell Hardin, *Collective Action* (Baltimore: Johns Hopkins University Press, 1982).

[32] This result depends on the rate at which the players discount future gains; the higher the discount rate, the less likely is cooperation.

[33] Snidal, "Coordination Versus Prisoners' Dilemma," 939.

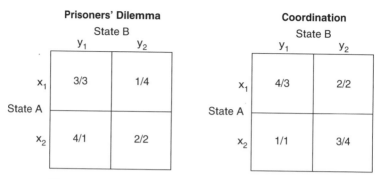

Figure 3.1 Collective action

needed to police violators.[34] Summarizing the evidence, Milgrom, North, and Weingast write:

> [A reciprocity] strategy requires that [an actor] know his current partner's previous history. When such information is difficult or costly to obtain, decentralized enforcement mechanisms break down. Institutions ... resolve the fundamental problems of restoring the information that underpins an effective reputation system while both economizing on information and overcoming a whole array of incentive problems that obstruct the gathering and dissemination of that information.[35]

This observation leads to a first (though weak) supply condition: in order to improve compliance with the rules of cooperation, a group of countries seeking integration must establish "commitment institutions," such as centralized monitoring and third party enforcement. A failure to satisfy this condition does not necessarily render integration impossible, but it makes success more elusive. Commitment institutions enhance the chances of sustained cooperation by acting as constraints in precisely those circumstances where self-help measures alone are insufficient to

[34] See Jeremy Bullow and Kenneth Rogoff, "A Constant Recontracting Model of Sovereign Debt," *Journal of Political Economy* 97 (February 1989), 155–178; John Veitch, "Repudiation and Confiscation by the Medieval State," *Journal of Economic History* 46 (March 1986); Elinor Ostrom, *Governing the Commons: The Evolution of Institutions for Collective Action* (Cambridge: Cambridge University Press, 1990); Avner Greif, Paul Milgrom, and Barry Weingast, "Coordination, Commitment, and Enforcement: The Case of the Merchant Guild," *Journal of Political Economy* 102 (1994), 745–776.

[35] Paul Milgrom, Douglass North, and Barry Weingast, "The Role of Institutions in the Revival of Trade: The Medieval Law Merchant, Private Judges, and the Champagne Fairs," *Economics and Politics* 2 (March 1990), 21. For a related argument, see Robert Axelrod and Robert Keohane, "Achieving Cooperation Under Anarchy," in Kenneth Oye (ed.), *Cooperation Under Anarchy* (Princeton: Princeton University Press, 1986), pp. 226–254.

prevent reneging.[36] Finally, commitment institutions are most effective if they offer direct access to those individuals with the greatest vested interest in seeing integration completed; examples here are the European Court of Justice and the Commission of the European Communities.

Coordination games

Coordination games are generally less well understood as examples of collective action. They raise different problems from Prisoners' Dilemma games. As Snidal puts it,

the problem in PD is that in pursuing its self-interest, each state imposes costs on the other independent of the other's policy, *whereas in the coordination game each imposes costs or benefits on the other contingent upon the other's policy.* The collective action problem is that neither state can choose its best policy without knowing what the other intends to do, but there is no obvious point at which to coordinate.[37]

In the coordination game in figure 3.1, state B prefers policy y_1 if state A chooses policy x_1 but prefers policy y_2 if A chooses x_2, and vice versa. Once a cooperative solution is achieved, it is self-enforcing. Neither state has an incentive to defect.[38] In other words, the problem in the coordination game is one of choice between multiple stable and efficient equilibria over which states have opposed interests; whereas in the Prisoners' Dilemma game the problem is how to get away from a single stable but inefficient equilibrium.[39]

Typically the collective action problem underlying an n-person co-ordination game is solved if there is one state (a regional leader) whose membership or cooperation in the group is perceived, by all or by a majority within the group, to be more important to the group than that of any other state. Adaptation to the policies of the leader makes not only political but also economic sense; that is, it is likely to be the least costly change within the group. For example, switching to German safety standards is, in the aggregate, less costly to the European Union than switching to Dutch standards, for example. Note, however, that even the "least costly" coordination arrangement involves typically immense organizational costs. Russell Hardin recently wrote that "the cost of re-coordination is the chief obstacle to moving to any supposedly

[36] Douglass North and Barry Weingast, "Constitutions and Commitment: The Evolution of Institutions Governing Public Choice in Seventeenth-Century England," in Alston, Eggertsson, and North, *Empirical Studies in Institutional Change*, pp. 134–165.

[37] Snidal, "Coordination Versus Prisoners' Dilemma," 931–932; see also Stein, "Coordination and Collaboration," pp. 125–127.

[38] The same result holds in an n-person coordination game.

[39] Snidal, "Coordination Versus Prisoners' Dilemma," 932.

superior order, even if it would be in virtually everyone's interest to be in the new order."[40]

Cost considerations aside, benevolent regional leaders can also help to ease distributional issues which arise as Coordination games are played over time. Repeated play makes coordination more difficult because it gives states incentives to be more concerned with the *distributional consequences* of coordination. If x_1y_1 (in figure 3.1) is the repeated outcome of an iterated coordination game, state A will be quite satisfied (it obtains 4 on each round), whereas state B only gets its second-best solution, namely 3. Small differences add up over time. Questions of fairness and equitable distribution of the gains from cooperation will need to be addressed to prevent discontent from derailing the integration process.[41] A dominant member state of a regional grouping may be able and willing to assume the role of regional paymaster, easing distributional tensions and thus smoothing the path of integration.[42]

These observations lead to a second (strong) supply condition: successful integration requires the presence of an undisputed leader among the group of countries seeking closer ties. Such a state serves as focal point in the coordination of rules, regulations, and policies; it also helps to ease distributional tensions through, for example, side-payments.

The following chapters illustrate that coordination problems are relatively easily solved in the presence of a regional leader, such as Germany in the European Union, Prussia in the Zollverein, or the United States in the North American Free Trade Area. However, they are likely to be insurmountable in the absence of an undisputed leader, such as, for example, in the case of the Middle German Commercial Union, ASEAN, or the Andean Pact. Likewise, coordination difficulties

---

[40] Russell Hardin, *Liberalism, Constitutionalism, Democracy* (forthcoming).

[41] Distributional issues have generally been neglected by students of International Political Economy, while scholars of the Realist school have exaggerated their importance. Realists argue that states refrain from cooperation because they fear the security implications of unbalanced distribution of the gains from cooperation (see Joseph Grieco, *Cooperation Among Nations* [Ithaca, N.Y.: Cornell University Press, 1990]; and Stephen Krasner, "Global Communications and National Power: Life on the Pareto Frontier," *World Politics* 43 (April 1991), 336–366). I argue that distributional issues matter – not primarily because of security reasons but because they can affect domestic politics or raise questions of fairness.

[42] Note that this account is different from hegemonic stability theory (see, for example, Keohane, *After Hegemony*). The latter is based on an analysis of public goods, a special case of the Prisoners' Dilemma, and deals with the implications of free-riding. The present account, however, refers to the Coordination game, where the issue is not free-riding but how to overcome distributional inequities.

will arise when two or more potential leaders belong to the same group. For example, within APEC, the United States and Japan are contending leaders. Their differing economic institutions and policy preferences in development, money, trade, and other domains make coordination very difficult.

Charles Kindleberger has put forth a similar idea by arguing that when countries are evenly matched in size and importance, agreement on international standards for output regulation, taxation, and the like is likely to be weakened by compromise. Thus he concluded in an essay written in the early 1980s: "In today's ... international economy with no one country any longer leading or dominant, there is risk of market failure in the sense of failure to adopt widely accepted standards in new goods, to keep old standards up to date as improvements become possible, and especially to achieve the international public good of world standards."[43]

5   Integration and economic performance

The implicit notion of a trade-off between economic growth and autonomy (i.e., absence of integration) is a very old theme. Dahl and Tufte, summarizing the views of influential Greeks from Pericles to Aristotle, note:

A democratic polity must be completely autonomous, because otherwise its citizens could not be fully self-governing: some of their decisions would be limited by the power or authority of individuals or groups outside the citizen body ... *To be sure, if a democratic polity was to be both small and completely autonomous, there was a price to be paid: the citizen body must be self-sufficient and life must be frugal.*[44]

Some 2,500 years after Aristotle, Britain's Prime Minister Callaghan echoed these themes while debating whether the United Kingdom should become a member of the European Monetary System (EMS):

When we joined NATO we removed some powers from ourselves but it was the general view of the House, continued for a quarter of a century, that in removing these powers we increased our security. That is surely the test that one needs to apply to this sort of proposal. *If it means less power in order to increase prosperity,*

---

[43] Charles Kindleberger, "Standards as Public, Collective and Private Goods," *Kyklos* 36 (1983), p. 393. He finds that the same logic applies at the domestic level and argues, for example, that in nineteenth-century England industrial standards failed to emerge in many areas because the country's industries typically were not dominated by a single large firm. By contrast, standardization in France and Germany was achieved because of the presence of dominant firms.

[44] Robert Dahl and Edward Tufte, *Size and Democracy* (Stanford: Stanford University Press, 1973), my italics.

the House would have to take a decision whether it wished to remain poor and independent or whether it was willing to sacrifice some powers and be more prosperous.[45]

In examining the relationship between integration and economic growth, my analysis draws on a literature that gives pride of place to institutions in accounting for growth.[46] Market transactions generate economic growth through exchange, specialization, and division of labor.[47] However, market players face disincentives to pursue exchange without the ability to engage in secure contracting. Institutions, that is, common rules, regulations, and policies, as well as compliance procedures, play a critical role in lowering contracting costs, thus promoting growth. The failure to insure transactions against the vagaries of foreign-market exposure can stifle growth in many ways. For example, technological change may involve new production techniques that make products cheaper to produce. Holding constant the product valuation by the marginal buyer and the delivery cost per unit distance, cheaper goods will cover larger markets. But an inadequately integrated governance structure will deter firms from expanding production to the full potential of the new production methods.[48] In other words, the new production technology will not be able to operate to capacity. This may even deter the adoption of new techniques and result in the deterioration of economic conditions as compared to integrated countries.[49]

The ensuing growth gap may widen for two reasons. First, firms in competitive industries will leave inhospitable jurisdictions and settle where the institutional environment is most conducive to profitable trade and investment. For such firms, exit is not just an option but is a question of survival. Exit of capital, entrepreneurship, and tax base will naturally depress economic growth. Second, foreign investors deciding

---

[45] Cited in Peter Ludlow, *The Making of the European Monetary System: A Case Study of the Politics of the European Community* (London: Butterworth Scientific, 1982), p. 144, my italics.

[46] See, for example, Alston, Eggertsson, and North (eds.), *Empirical Studies in Institutional Change*.

[47] For a good review of the theoretical and empirical literature on the growth effects of market integration, see Richard Baldwin and Anthony Venables, "Regional Economic Integration," in G. Grossman and K. Rogoff (eds.), *Handbook of International Economics* 3 (New York: Elsevier, 1995), pp. 1597–1644; see also Paolo Cecchini, *The European Challenge 1992 – The Benefits of a Single Market* (Aldershot, UK: Wildwood House, 1988); and Commission of the European Community, *The Impact and Effectiveness of the Single Market* (Luxemburg: Office for the Official Publications of the EC, 1996).

[48] See, for example, Joel Mokyr, *The Lever of Riches: Technological Creativity and Economic Progress* (New York: Oxford University Press, 1990), p. 245.

[49] For excellent discussions of the relationship between the size of country, new technologies, and economic growth, see essays by Simon Kuznets and Tibor Scitovski in E. A. G. Robinson (ed.), *Economic Consequences of the Size of Nations* (London: Macmillan, 1960).

whether to operate in the large and well-integrated market of a community or the functionally insufficiently integrated economy of a non-community country are likely to opt for the former, *ceteris paribus*. These capital inflows strengthen the competition-enhancing effects of market integration and thus help economic growth. Robust growth, in turn, may attract further capital investment, thereby accelerating growth.

Nevertheless, the nexus between integration and growth is neither necessarily immediate nor exclusive. First, the search for an integrated governance structure that is finely attuned to new market needs can involve considerable trial and error; furthermore, the effects of new institutional arrangements may take a long time to materialize. However, to the extent that a society gives weight to the achievement of efficiency, institutional competition is likely to weed out inefficient institutional arrangements in the long run. Secondly, this discussion does not imply that countries rejecting integration will automatically perform poorly. Some countries possess endowments, such as large oil fields, that may enable them to thrive economically even without integration. The argument is simply that the effect of institutional integration on growth is positive, controlling for all other factors that may influence growth.

6   The external effects of integration

A comprehensive explanation of regional integration requires that the discussion of the internal logic of integration be complemented by an account of the external logic, focusing on the effects of community building on outsiders. This is a topic that both political scientists and economists have mostly overlooked.[50]

Ironically, a successful regional process of internalization of externalities can create external effects (i.e., externalities) on countries that do not participate in the process. These effects differ from the symmetric (or diffuse) externalities that fuel the integration process within a group of countries discussed in the preceding sections. They are asymmetric (or spillover) externalities, that is, externalities that arise from the effort of creating an integrated governance structure and affect only outsiders.

What forms do external effects take? Historically, the most important is relative loss of market access. Countries outside an integrated group

---

[50] By their own admission, functionalists and neofunctionalists have neglected to study the impact of regional integration on countries outside a union. Economists have alluded to these effects indirectly by considering the effect of trade diversion on the economic welfare of members *within* a union. A recent exception in economics is Richard Baldwin, "A Domino Theory of Regionalism," Working Paper no. 4465 (Cambridge, Mass.: NBER, 1993).

may face temporary or lasting discriminatory trade policies. Even in the absence of a high common external tariff, discrimination may become lasting because rules of origin associated with free-trade areas can give protected firms a vested interest in maintaining protection, thus reducing the ability of the members of a free-trade area to engage in external trade liberalization.[51] However, there is a simple argument why the negative effects of discrimination may be temporary. If trade liberalization within a group has dynamic effects enhancing economic growth, or if scale economies stimulate the demand for imports from outside the region, income effects of liberalization may more than offset trade diversion, thus helping outsiders to raise their welfare.[52]

Another effect is investment diversion. Its importance has grown with the liberalization of capital markets. Rapid economic growth in a union may increase the share of international investment directed to union members at the expense of outsiders. Furthermore, improved competitiveness of the industries in a union could lead to increased production and lower prices, thus putting at a competitive disadvantage producers outside the union that do not experience comparable productivity gains and resulting in a reduction of external trade. Finally, to the extent that integration requires a dominant state to assume the role of paymaster dispensing funds to ease distributional frictions within a union, fewer funds may flow to needy outsider-states. In other words, integration could have the effect of aid diversion.

How will outsiders react to these externalities? The analysis assumes, as above, that leaders are utility maximizers who value both political power (authority, autonomy, etc.) and material resources (tax revenues, bribe-money, etc.). It also assumes that politicians' ability to hold on to political power depends on their relative success in managing the economy. Leaders who fail to maintain relatively high levels of economic growth will be ousted.[53]

---

[51] Anne Krueger, "NAFTA: Strengthening or Weakening the International Trading System?," in Jagdish Bhagwati and Anne Krueger (eds.), *The Dangerous Drift to Preferential Trade Agreements* (Washington: American Enterprise Institute for Public Policy Research, 1995), pp. 19–33.

[52] Lawrence, *Regionalism, Multilateralism, and Deeper Integration*, p. 26.

[53] For evidence on the link between economic performance and re-election chances, see Robert Erikson, "Economic Conditions and the Presidential Vote," *American Political Science Review* 83 (1989), 567–576 and "Economic Conditions and the Congressional Vote: A Review of the Macrolevel Evidence," *American Journal of Political Science* 34 (1990), 373–399; Helmut Norpoth, Michael Lewis-Beck, and Jean Dominique Lafay, *Economics and Politics: The Calculus of Support* (Ann Arbor, Mich.: University of Michigan Press, 1991); and Heinz Eulau and Michael Lewis-Beck, *Economic Conditions and Electoral Outcomes: The United States and Western Europe* (New York: Agathon Press, 1985).

These postulates suggest several answers to the question as to how outsiders may react to external effects. The answers are summarized as part of figure 3.2. If the impact of these effects is not noticeable, that is, if economic growth remains robust, the leaders in outsider countries will have no incentive to consider institutional change. Integration will not appear to be worth the candle, since the expected marginal benefit from integration in terms of improved re-election chances is minimal while a country is at high levels of economic growth, and the price of integration is substantial. The price is forgone control over important areas of the national economy and possibly even loss of bribe-money and support from powerful interest groups opposed to integration. Such political costs are not palatable to politicians. However, if the external effects are felt or are bound to be felt, elected officials, mindful of their re-election chances, are likely to change course and embrace pro-integration agendas. The reason is that the expected marginal value from integration in terms of the leaders' re-election chances (or, more broadly, the leaders' chances of retaining political power) is likely to increase as the economy declines. And as this value grows larger than the price of integration, rational outsiders will seek to become insiders.

Affected outsiders can pursue two integration strategies. First, they can seek to merge with the area generating the external effects. I call this "the first integrative response." Examples of this logic are the enlargement of the European Union and the German Zollverein, discussed in chapter 4.

Second, outsiders can respond by creating their own regional group. This I call "the second integrative response." There are many examples of this logic. As discussed in the following chapters, the creation of the customs union between Prussia and Hesse-Darmstadt triggered the Bavaria–Württemberg customs union, the Middle German Commercial Union, and the North German Tax Union. The establishment of the European Community triggered numerous integration projects, most notably the European Free Trade Association and the Latin American Free Trade Association. Likewise, efforts to deepen integration through the Single European Act raised fears of a "Fortress Europe," triggering a veritable tidal wave of integration projects throughout the world in the late 1980s. None of the projects of the second integrative response type is guaranteed automatic success. Like any integration scheme, the projects must satisfy the integration conditions discussed in this chapter.

At first sight, the first integrative response would seem less demanding than the second integrative response because by simply joining an existing union, an outsider country circumvents the strategic supply

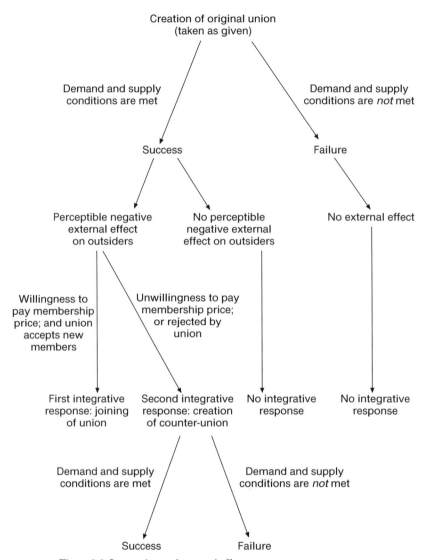

Figure 3.2 Integration and external effects

problems involved in designing common institutional arrangements. Joining simply requires a country to accept the clearly defined terms and conditions of "club" membership. Further, the incentive to join may increase as a regional group grows larger and more efficient. Richard Baldwin calls this the "domino effect" that is likely to spur the process of world-wide trade liberalization.[54] Nevertheless, there are two problems with the first integrative response. First, a union may simply have no interest in accepting new members. If an outsider is not a desirable candidate in the sense of being able to make a net positive contribution to the union (e.g., through net payments into the common budget, or by offering obvious commercial advantages), the union is unlikely to accept it, unless exclusion of such a candidate is costlier to the union than accepting it.[55] Second, the price of membership of a successful union is typically very high. For example, membership of the European Union requires that an applicant be willing and able to accept the so-called *acquis communautaire*, a body of rules that comprises not only union law as enshrined in the Treaty of Rome but also a very extensive body of secondary law as defined in the European Union's directives and regulations. Membership of the North American Free Trade group is similarly costly. A Latin American applicant must accept what John Williamson dubs the "Washington Consensus," which includes reducing fiscal deficits, shifting expenditure priorities, tax reform, interest-rate reform, exchange-rate adjustment, liberalization of rules governing foreign direct investment, privatization, deregulation, and protection of property rights.[56] Or consider a nineteenth-century example: Prussia required prospective members of the Zollverein to adopt Prussian customs law, tariffs, and auditing procedures. In some cases, Prussia even demanded that a newcomer agree to restrict its participation in future changes of the common legislation as well as in negotiations of commercial treaties between the Zollverein and neighboring states.

Historically, both rejection by a union and prohibitive membership price have led outsiders to experiment with their own regional schemes. Remarkably, the overwhelming majority of these schemes has failed. This result can be explained in all cases by the absence of the two strong integration conditions discussed in this chapter: undisputed leadership and strong market pressure for integration. The problems posed by the absence of leadership are discussed in detail in the empirical chapters, but several examples may be cited here. The Latin American Free Trade Association, for instance, was composed of three groups, the semi-industrial "giants" Brazil, Argentina, and Mexico, a middle group led by

---

[54] Baldwin, "A Domino Theory of Regionalism."

[55] As illustrated in chapter 5, a union may have an interest in accepting "undesirable" candidates when negative externalities originating in outsider countries threaten to disrupt the union's prosperity, stability, and security.

[56] See John Williamson (ed.), *Latin American Adjustment: How Much Has Happened?* (Washington: Institute for International Economics), p. 7; quoted in Stephan Haggard, *Developing Nations and the Politics of Global Integration* (Washington, D.C.: Brookings Institution, 1995), p. 79.

Chile, Colombia, and Venezuela, and the group of least-developed economies that included Bolivia, Ecuador, and Paraguay. The members of the third group complained almost from the beginning that integration was disproportionately benefitting Brazil, Argentina, and Mexico. None of these big countries was willing to address distributional issues, thus undermining the long-term prospects of integration. Absence of leadership also crippled the Andean Pact. A case in point is the failure to agree on a common external tariff. Peru favored an effective protection rate no higher than 40 percent, Colombia proposed a 60 percent tariff. Ecuador and Venezuela, however, insisted on a rate no lower than 80 percent. No country was willing to compromise or able to bribe the other into acquiescence. The Andean Pact's sectoral programs of industrial development failed similarly because governments were unable to agree on who was to produce what. The same coordination dilemma doomed industrial development projects within ASEAN.

Examples also abound of how an absence of market pressure for integration leads to failure. For instance, the members of ASEAN export the bulk of their primary commodities and manufactured goods to the same world markets. Most of their economies are not complementary. Excluding Singapore, intra-ASEAN exports have amounted to only 5 percent of total ASEAN trade since the late 1960s. Similarly, the members of the Andean Pact send most of their exports, consisting primarily of agricultural and mineral products, to the United States and Europe. The share of intra-regional trade in total trade of Andean countries amounted to only 1.2 percent in 1970 and to 2.5 percent in 1988. As shown in the following chapters, this situation is repeated in many cases.

In sum, when a region lacks an undisputed leader or when the potential for gains from integration is limited because regional economies lack complementarity or the small size of regional markets does not offer significant economies of scale, a counter-union – like any integration project – stands little chance of succeeding, in the sense of attaining stated integration goals.

7   Conclusion

Figure 3.3 summarizes the outcomes of several major integration schemes. As discussed above, if political leaders are willing to initiate an integration process, chances of sustained success are greatest if two strong integration conditions are satisfied: first, a regional group stands to reap important gains from integration; second, the group is led by a country able to serve as an institutional focal point and regional pay-master. A further (though weak) condition, the existence of monitoring and third-party enforcement, is likely to have a catalyzing effect on the integration process. The chances of success are weakest where none of these conditions is satisfied. The major success stories all satisfy the two strong conditions. They include the European Union and the Zoll-verein; their respective leaders are Germany and Prussia. NAFTA, led by the United States, stands a good chance of succeeding as well. No integration scheme that satisfies these two conditions has ever failed. At the polar end are very many integration projects, most of which are examples of the "second integrative response." Here again, no group failing to satisfy the two strong conditions of integration has ever succeeded.

Groups in cells with a success rate of 2 have mixed records. EFTA lost much of its momentum when the United Kingdom defected to the European Community in 1973. It was further weakened when three of its members, Finland, Sweden, and Austria, switched allegiance to the European Union in 1995. Progress within APEC has been stalled due to marked differences between the United States and Japan. The Central American Common Market (CACM) is a particularly fascinating case. Its place in a cell with a success rate of 2 appears anomalous. However, in CACM, unlike in the Latin American Free Trade Association, the United States came to play the role of the adopted regional leader, easing distributional problems and offering leadership in policy coordi-nation. As a quid pro quo, CACM countries had to accept the rules of integration defined by the United States, heavily favoring American multinational corporations. The outbreak of the "Soccer War" between El Salvador and Honduras in 1969 brought CACM's integration effort to an abrupt end. Finally, MERCOSUR emerged in the early 1990s from the failed Latin American Free Trade Association (LAFTA). The structure of the economies of its members has changed since the early 1960s. Industrialization has broadened the scope for mutually beneficial exchange of goods at the regional level. This has enabled MERCOSUR to raise the percentage of intraregional trade in total trade. Nevertheless, coordination and redistribution problems are no easier to solve today in Latin America than thirty years ago. They have, in fact, already derailed several integration goals of MERCOSUR, as discussed in chapter 5.

In chapter 4, the argument that the building of regional institutions serves to improve market efficiency is tested by analyzing foreign direct investment flows into Spain, Portugal, Greece, Denmark, Ireland, and the United Kingdom before and after these countries joined the European Union. If the efficiency view of integration is correct, it is

| | (Uncontested) regional leadership | |
	YES	NO
Relatively significant **(Potential) market gains from integration**	**3** European Union NAFTA Zollverein EFTA (until 1973)	**2** EFTA (after 1973) Asia Pacific Economic Cooperation Forum (APEC) MERCOSUR
Relatively insignificant	**2** Central American Common Market (until 1969)	**1** Bavaria–Württemberg Customs Union Middle German Commercial Union Central American Common Market (after 1969) ASEAN Economic Community of West African States LAFTA Andean Pact Caribbean Community Arab Common Market

Success rate: 3 = highest
1 = lowest

Figure 3.3 Outcomes of integration schemes

expected that the extension of the union's rules and enforcement mechanisms will mitigate the risks of investing in the periphery. And as these institutional safeguards lower the risks, the flow of transnational capital into the periphery should increase. The results, as will be seen, support this hypothesis. A country that joins the European Union experiences increased capital inflows, *ceteris paribus*.

The argument regarding the timing of enlargement of regional groups is also checked against data from the European Union and the Zollverein. One way of testing it is by examining whether the decision to join a union coincides with a sustained economic performance gap between insiders and outsiders (with insiders performing better than outsiders). Outsiders will have an incentive to join insiders when there is a performance gap; there will be no integration sought if there is no performance gap. Again, the empirical results strongly corroborate this proposition. Out of twenty applications for membership of the European Union by eleven countries, eighteen were submitted after one or, more typically, several years of growth rates substantially below the average growth rates of EU countries. The only countries that failed to seek EU membership in moments of relative economic decline were Europe's neutral countries during the Cold War. After the Cold War ended, they too sought membership. Similarly, in the nineteenth century the rulers of the many German kingdoms, electorates, and duchies clung to their sovereign rights and obstructed proposals for economic unification till empty treasuries forced them to seek membership of the Zollverein.

4   Integration in Europe

1   Introduction

This chapter seeks to illustrate and test the analytical framework elaborated in the previous chapter on integration schemes from nineteenth and twentieth-century Europe. It begins, in section 2, by examining one of the most successful examples of integration, the European Union. The section traces the EU's achievements to the existence of demand and supply conditions. First, demand conditions are examined through two examples chosen to illustrate the key role played by corporate actors in pressing for deeper integration: the constitutionalization of the Treaty of Rome and events leading up to the Single European Act. The section then turns to the enlargement issue and examines the conditions leading to acceptance or rejection of new potential members. Supply conditions are then considered. The section examines the role of two "commitment institutions," the Commission and the European Court of Justice, in fostering integration, and Germany's critical contribution as institutional leader and regional paymaster to the successful collective supply of integration. The section concludes with a statistical test of the relationship between integration and investment flows, adducing strong evidence of the efficiency view of integration. Section 3 provides a second test case of the analytical framework, namely the German Zollverein. Its structure is identical to that of section 2. The final section turns to failed European integration schemes and asks whether they can be explained in terms of absence of demand and supply conditions. The main empirical focus of the section is on an attempt at integration from a largely neglected period of European commercial history: the "United States of Europe" of the 1890s.

2   The European Union

The creation of the European Community is not easily captured by any simple theoretical argument. It appears as a phenomenon *sui generis*.

The beginning of European integration is taken as given. The focus in this chapter is on the conditions that made the process of European integration a success, and on the external effects of community-building in Europe.

It is commonly thought that the Community's main function is to preserve peace and security in Europe. After the Second World War, there was deep-seated opposition to restoring full sovereignty to West Germany – a country blamed for aggression in 1870, 1914, and 1939. The policy-makers in the West, however, faced a quandary in the 1950s as the Cold War intensified. The Soviet Union had just acquired the atomic bomb, Euro-communism was on the rise, and in 1950 the Korean War broke out. A strong Germany was essential for the security of the West. But would a revitalized Germany not pose a renewed political and military threat to its neighbors? To preempt this possibility, a new European institution needed to be created which could cement the economies of its member countries into an interdependent maze out of which independent aggressive action by a single country would be impossible.

The Schuman Plan of 1950 constituted the first step in this direction. It proposed to place the entire French and German coal-and-steel industry under a common High Authority and to abolish all tariffs restricting free exchange of coal-and-steel products. The treaty establishing the European Coal and Steel Community (ECSC) for fifty years was signed in 1951 by France, Germany, Italy, Belgium, Holland, and Luxemburg. Its preamble stresses the concern for peace as the driving force of European integration. It reads:

[The six governments] considering that *world peace* may be safeguarded only by creative efforts equal to the dangers which menace it; convinced that the contribution which an organized and vital Europe can bring to civilization is indispensable to the maintenance of *peaceful relations*; ... desirous of assisting through the expansion of their basic production in raising the standard of living and in furthering the works of *peace*; resolved to substitute for historic rivalries a fusion of their essential interests [and] to establish, by creating an economic community, the foundation of a broad and independent community among *peoples long divided by bloody conflicts* ... have decided to create a European Coal and Steel Community.[1]

Past plans designed to bring peace to Europe, however, have been many. These include the Abbé de St. Pierre's *Project of Perpetual Peace*, Immanuel Kant's *Perpetual Peace*, Count Richard Coudenhove-Kalergi's *Paneuropa*, and Aristide Briand's projects in the 1920s and 1930s for a

---

[1] *Treaties Establishing the European Communities* (Brussels: Office for Official Publications of the European Communities, 1987), my italics.

lasting European peace. None came to fruition. The peace motive was insufficient to assure success for these plans. It may explain the establishment of the ECSC and has certainly helped European integration in the way suggested by Robert Jervis when he wrote that "expectations of peaceful relations were a necessary condition for the formation of the European Common Market ... Had the Europeans thought there was a significant chance that they would come to blows, they would not have permitted their economies to grow so interdependent."[2]

Other motives were also important in accounting for the creation of European integration. Consider for example external developments. Europe, once the world's focus, found itself in danger of being eclipsed to the point of insignificance after the Second World War in a universe controlled by two superpowers. The Suez Crisis provided a particularly sobering demonstration of how limited the freedom of action of European states had become. "It was felt that if Europe were to become something more than a footnote to history, the individual nations would have to combine their power and speak with a unified voice."[3] The Spaak Report of 1956, which served as blueprint for the Treaty of Rome establishing the European Communities, contains the following nostalgic note in its foreword: "Europe, which once had the monopoly of manufacturing industries and obtained important resources from its overseas possessions, today sees its external position weakened, its influence declining and its capacity to progress lost in its divisions."[4] Even more revealing is the following statement by Walter Hallstein, first President of the European Commission: "It may be said in all frankness that an essential factor in the establishment of the European Economic Community has been egoism, European insistence on self-assertion ... The old world has waked up; it is shaking off its feeling of second-rateness and is ready to play the game of world economics according to the rules of its traditional liberalism."[5] To restore its influence in the world, Europe had to unite and create a "third force" between the two superpowers.[6]

[2] Robert Jervis, "The Future of World Politics: Will It Resemble the Past?," *International Security* 15, no. 3 (Winter 1990/1991), 51.

[3] Laurence Krause (ed.), *The Common Market: Progress and Controversy* (Englewood Cliffs, N.J.: Prentice Hall, 1964), p. 4.

[4] Comité Intergouvernemental Crée par la Conférence de Messine, *Rapport des Chefs de Délégation aux Ministres des Affaires Etrangères* (Brussels, Secrétariat, April 21, 1956), p. 9.

[5] Foreword by Walter Hallstein in Elizabeth Marting (ed.), *The European Common Market: New Frontier for American Business* (New York: American Management Association, 1958), pp. 12–13.

[6] This thinking was particularly prevalent in the writings of Jean Monnet, the pro-American "founding father" of the European Community. See Sophie Meunier, "The Paradox of Unity: European Integration and US-EC Trade Negotiations, 1958–1993," dissertation in progress (MIT, Department of Political Science).

   This reasoning applied not only to the political realm but particularly to trade relations. A united Europe was bound to be in a stronger bargaining position in trade negotiations. Pierre Uri, a longtime collaborator of Jean Monnet and presumed author[7] of the economic sections of both the Schuman plan and the Spaak Report, acknowledged:

We could not conceal the fact that one reason for setting up the Common Market was to enhance the bargaining power in tariff negotiations of all member countries taken together. It was all to the good that bargaining power of "the Six" would match the power of the United States in tariff negotiations and would make more likely the lowering of the US tariff which would be trade-creating. We should think, not in static terms, or of effects on paper, but of reality.[8]

   The US role as security guarantor was a crucial factor in the beginning of European integration. The US presence in Europe contained Germany, giving the French sufficient confidence in their security to build a bilateral relationship with Germany, and allowed West European governments to avoid questions of West European foreign policy and defense by letting them be absorbed into the Atlantic Alliance under American leadership.[9]

   Why, then, did the US support plans for European integration? There are three main reasons. First, it was thought that only a strong ally is a good ally. Economic integration would strengthen the United States' European partners and thereby improve the overall military position of the West *vis-à-vis* the Soviet bloc. Second, Americans assumed that integration would produce economic growth in Europe and thus increase the demand for American products and investments. Third, the United States hoped that a prosperous and united Western Europe would accept a larger share of the common defense spending, increase its aid to developing countries, and take a more active role in solving international currency and commodity problems. "As the members merge their economies and develop their capacity for acting as a unit, they will for the first time be able to play the role of an equal partner . . .

---

[7] See Richard Mayne, *The Community of Europe* (London: Victor Gollancz, 1962), p. 90 and p. 117.

[8] Pierre Uri made this statement during a conference of economists held in Lisbon in 1958. The proceedings of the conference are collected in E. A. G. Robinson (ed.), *Economic Consequences of the Size of Nations* (London: Macmillan, 1960), p. 430. For an excellent account of the effectiveness of the united European bargaining front during the Kennedy Round negotiations, see Thomas Zeiler, *American Trade and Power in the 1960s* (New York: Columbia University Press, 1992).

[9] William Wallace, *Regional Integration: The West European Experience* (Washington: Brookings Institution, 1994), p. 9.

sharing equitably in the responsibilities and burdens which have hitherto rested mainly upon [the United States]."[10]

What emerged from this unique confluence of security, political, and economic motives was an ambitious blueprint for merging individual European economies into an "ever closer union."[11] The Treaty of Rome establishing the European Communities came into force on January 1, 1958. It committed the EC-Six (Germany, France, Italy, the Netherlands, Belgium, and Luxemburg) to a far-reaching exercise in economic integration which envisaged free movement of goods, services, capital, and labor, aided by common policies in agriculture, transport, regional development, external commerce, economic cohesion, and other domains. By the end of the transition period in 1969, the basic ingredients of the customs union – elimination of internal tariffs and quotas and erection of a common external tariff – were established. The member states agreed to deepen integration on two further occasions: in the mid-1980s by signing the Single European Act, and in the early 1990s by agreeing to the Maastricht Treaty on European Union.

This chapter provides an illustration of the importance of the demand-side and supply-side factors of chapter 3 in explaining the process of European integration. The following sections consider, first, the role of corporate actors in pushing legal integration through the constitutionalization of the Treaty of Rome and in bringing about the Single European Act; second, they examine supply conditions, particularly the role of Germany as the region's institutional leader.

The demand for integration

William Wallace, a perceptive student of European integration, has made a helpful distinction between formal and informal integration.[12] Formal integration refers to the institutional framework established by the various treaties of European integration (Treaty of Rome, the Single European Act, and the Maastricht Treaty). It is by definition a discontinuous process, proceeding treaty by treaty. Informal integration, on the other hand, refers to the patterns of interactions and exchange triggered by the formal framework and amplified by technological

---

[10] Robert Bowie and Theodore Geiger, *The European Economic Community and the United States*, Report of the Subcommittee on Foreign Economic Policy of the Joint Economic Committee, Congress of the United States (Washington, D.C.: US Government Printing Office, 1961), p. 12.

[11] Objective as stated in the preamble of the Treaty of Rome of 1957. See European Communities, *Treaties Establishing the European Communities* (Brussels: Office for Official Publications of the European Communities, 1978), p. 213.

[12] Wallace, *Regional Integration*.

advance and market dynamics. Wallace argues that informal integration, in turn, "creates pressures for further deepening of the formal structures of rules and institutions in order to manage their impact."[13] This idea is akin to the "logic of demand" elaborated in the previous chapter

Corporate actors and pressure for legal integration

A first illustration of the demand logic is provided by the critical role played by private firms in bringing about legal integration in Europe, that is, in constitutionalizing the Treaty of Rome.[14] This was the process by which the Treaty evolved from a set of legal arrangements binding upon sovereign states, into a vertically integrated legal regime conferring judicially enforceable rights and obligations on all legal persons and entities, public and private, within the European Union. This section focuses primarily on corporate actors, but it must not be overlooked that these actors were assisted by key "commitment institutions" on the supply side, notably the European Court of Justice (ECJ). Thus the section also illustrates the catalyzing effect on integration that may result when demand forces meet "commitment institutions." These institutions will be more fully discussed in a later section.[15]

A quick perusal of the Treaty of Rome articles suggests that the founders intended the Court and its staff to interact primarily with other community organs and the member states. Articles 169 and 170 provide for claims of noncompliance with community obligations to be brought against member states by either the Commission or other member states. Article 173 gives the Court additional jurisdiction over a variety of actions brought against either the Commission or the Council by a member state, by the Commission, by the Council, or by specific individuals who have been subject to a Council or Commission decision directly addressed to them. Almost as an afterthought, Article 177 authorizes the Court to issue "preliminary rulings" on any question involving the intepretation of Community law arising in the national courts. Lower national courts can refer such questions to the ECJ at their discretion.

In practice, the Article 177 procedure served as a channel of corporate pressure and demands for deeper integration. It established the framework for the constitutionalization of the Treaty by providing links

---

[13] *Ibid.*, p. 5.
[14] The section draws on Anne-Marie Burley and Walter Mattli, "Europe Before the Court: A Political Theory of Legal Integration," *International Organization* 47 (1993), 41–76; and Walter Mattli and Anne-Marie Slaughter, "Law and Politics in the European Union," *International Organization* 49 (1995), 183–190.
[15] See pp. 99–101 below.

between the Court and subnational actors – private litigants, their lawyers, and lower national courts. Referrals to the ECJ under Article 177 rely on the initiatives of private actors who deem governmental regulation incompatible either with existing Community rule or with the spirit of the Treaty of Rome. Without individual litigants, there would be no cases presented to national courts and thus no basis for legal integration. The various identities, motivations, and strategies of litigants have inevitably influenced the nature and pace of integration.

An early example of this influence is provided by the famous *Van Gend & Loos* case of 1963. Through an Article 177 reference, a private Dutch importer raised the question whether he was entitled to invoke directly the common market provision of the Treaty of Rome against the Dutch government's attempt to impose customs duties on some of his imports from Germany.[16] Over the explicit objections of the member states, the Court proclaimed that

the Community constitutes a new legal order ... for the benefit of which the states have limited their sovereign rights, albeit within limited fields, and the subjects of which comprise not only member states but also *their nationals* ... Community law therefore not only imposes obligations on individuals but it also intended to *confer upon them rights* which became part of their legal heritage.[17]

The effect of this case was that firms and private individuals who stood to gain from European integration could now push their governments, through the Article 177 procedure, to live up to paper commitments by pointing to Treaty provisions that supported an activity they wished to undertake; a national court would then certify the question of how Community law should be applied to the European Court of Justice, and if the Court's interpretation of a Treaty obligation implied a conflict between national law and Community law, national courts would have to set aside domestic rule.

Another example of the importance of business in pushing legal integration is given by the role played by big French firms in forcing the Conseil d'Etat, the politically influential supreme administrative court in France, to accept the judge-made doctrines of direct effect and supremacy of Community law.[18] Until the beginning of the 1980s, the French Conseil d'Etat felt little pressure to endorse direct effect and

---

[16] Case 26/62, *N.V. Algemene Transport & Expeditie Onderneming Van Gend & Loos v. Nederlandse Administratie der Belastingen*, ECR, 1963, p. 1.

[17] *Ibid.*, p.12, my italics.

[18] This section draws on Walter Mattli and Anne-Marie Slaughter, "Revisiting the European Court of Justice," *International Organization* 52 (1998), 177–209. "Direct effect" means that EU law can confer on individuals legal rights that public authorities must respect and national courts protect. The supremacy doctrine states that in any conflict between community law and national law the former must be given primacy.

supremacy. Two of its major partners, Germany and Italy, had supreme courts that refused to comply fully with the ECJ's jurisprudence. In 1984, however, the Italian Constitutional Court authorized lower national judges to declare national law incompatible with treaty obligations without having to refer the case to the Constitutional Court.[19] The German Federal Constitutional Court announced in 1986, in the *Solange II* case, that it would no longer control the constitutionality of Community legal acts. The legal context in which corporate interests in France now found themselves put them increasingly at a competitive disadvantage relative to firms operating in member states where supremacy and direct effect doctrines were fully accepted. According to Jens Plötner, "solid economic reasons [existed rendering] ... full integration of Community law into French law paramount. How could the Project of 1992 become effective if the almost three hundred directives intended to transform it into legal reality were not to be directly enforced by the Conseil d'Etat?" He adds: "[T]he impossibility of referring to certain community regulations was bound to represent a serious economic disadvantage [to French firms] in comparison to their European competition. In the long run, this could have led to a movement of forum shopping, combined with some delocalization of head offices."[20]

To remedy this situation, major import-oriented and export-oriented companies in France launched systematic attacks on government decisions that they felt were contrary to Community law. Their aim was to provoke a chain of verdicts by the ECJ condemning France for breach of Community law. This increased the pressure on the French government and the Conseil d'Etat to comply with Community rule. It is no coincidence that the decision by the Conseil d'Etat confirming the direct effect of Community directives in France was initiated by Philip Morris and Rothmans, firms with sufficient resources to engage in repeat litigation strategies.[21]

Richard Rawlings provides another account of the litigation strategy of corporate actors in the European context in his study on the Sunday

---

[19] Italian Constitutional Court decision 170/84, Granital, [1984] CMLRev 756.

[20] Jens Plötner, *The European Court and National Courts – Doctrine and Jurisprudence: Legal Change in Its Social Context – Report on France*, Working Paper, RSC No. 95/28 (Florence: European University Institute, 1996), pp. 29 and 24.

[21] *Ibid.*, 27. Reporting on the Netherlands, Claes and de Witte note similar pressures by Dutch business companies seeking to enforce in the early years of the Community the competition rules of the Treaty of Rome before national courts. See Monica Claes and Bruno de Witte, *The European Court and National Courts – Doctrine and Jurisprudence: Legal Change in Its Social Context – Report on the Netherlands*, Working Paper, RSC No. 95/26 (Florence: European University Institute, 1995), p. 7.

trading saga, appropriately entitled *The Eurolaw Game.*[22] At issue was the British Shops Act of 1950 that places statutory restrictions on Sunday trading. Large retailers used an Article 177 reference to the ECJ with the practical effect of freezing the enforcement of the national law. The economic incentive for such action is clear. For large retailers Sunday trading represents up to 23 percent of their turnover.[23] The "European Defense" put forth by the retailers stated that the Shops Act contravenes Article 30 of the EEC Treaty which prohibits "quantitative restrictions on imports and all measures having equivalent effect." If a shop is prohibited from trading on a Sunday, they argued, its overall sales will be reduced; if sales are reduced, imports from the European Community will be reduced (by about 15 percent). Ergo the Shops Act amounts to a measure having equivalent effect to a quantitative restriction on imports within the meaning of Article 30.[24]

The Sunday trading saga – too long and convoluted to be narrated here in full – demonstrates the potential for the use of "Euro-litigation" strategies to achieve gains by powerful corporate interests. It contains a subplot that Rawlings calls "the Multi-national Game." In this game, large British retailers were part of a coordinated Europe-wide litigation strategy by corporate interests in other member states that used Article 177 references almost simultaneously to intensify the pressure for abolition of restrictions on Sunday trading in their respective countries. Rawlings characterizes the Eurolaw game played in the Sunday trading saga in terms of outflanking or "trumping" the domestic system.[25]

The importance of Article 177 as a channel of corporate pressure and demands for deeper integration has been confirmed in a recent study by Alec Stone and James Caporaso. The study examines whether the pressure by private litigants for supranational rule increases as the number of cross-national transactions rises.[26] The data set comprises 2,978 Article 177 references by national courts to the European Court of Justice. Strikingly, the authors find that the relationship between references and intra-EU trade is nearly linear, with litigants in countries

[22] Richard Rawlings, "The Eurolaw Game: Some Deductions Form a Saga," *Journal of Law and Society* 20 (1993), 309–340. The term "saga" has been used in the legal literature to denote the situation where a single policy attracts litigation over a period of time through a series of attacks.

[23] Paul Diamond, "Dishonorable Defences: The Use of Injunctions and the EEC treaty – Case Study of the Shops Act 1950," *The Modern Law Review* 54 (1991), 72–87.

[24] *Ibid.*, 79.   [25] *Ibid.*

[26] Alec Stone and James Caporaso, *From Free Trade to Supranational Polity: The European Court and Integration*, Working Paper No. 2.45 (Berkeley: Center for German and European Studies, University of California, 1996); see also Alec Stone and Thomas Brunell, "Constructing a Supranational Constitution: Dispute Resolution and Governance in the European Community," *American Political Science Review*, (forthcoming).

that trade more with other EU countries generating higher levels of references.

Second, Stone and Caporaso examine whether there is any relationship between these references and Community legislation (regulations and directives). They find that the relationship is positive and significant, suggesting that references lead to legislation.[27] They conclude their study by noting, based on their evidence, that governments do not control the integration process in any determinative sense. Governments behave reactively rather than proactively. They act to ratify transfers of governing authority from the national to the supranational level that have already begun or to slow down the pace at which these transfers are made. In other words, this behavior can be seen as a response to subnational level demand for integration.

Corporate pressure and the Single European Act

The introduction of computers, microelectronics, fibre optics, satellites, cable television, digital switches, lasers, electronic reproduction, and many other innovations deeply transformed the economy of Europe and the developed world in the 1970s and 1980s. The consequence of these advances has been, in a sense, to "shrink" distances and put pressure on governments to adjust the scale of political and economic organization to the level implied by the new technologies.

Major manufacturers who began in those years to produce and market on a European rather than a nation-by-nation basis were confronted with burdensome obstacles: different national tax regimes that necessitated detailed paperwork and checks on fuel and goods at each frontier, resulting in lengthy border delays for trucks moving parts from plant to plant, and different regulations on axle weights, truck safety, vehicle exhaust emissions, and hours permitted behind the wheel.[28]

These impediments to free trade gave European big business, struggling to compete with their American and Japanese rivals, reason to think of ways to reduce the costs of producing and transacting in Europe. One solution promoted by big business was the completion of a truly single European market.[29] To increase its clout in European economic affairs, a group of the largest and most influential corporations, including Philips, Siemens, Olivetti, GEC, Daimler Benz, Volvo, Fiat, Bosch, ASEA, and Ciba-Geigy, formed the Round Table of European Industrialists in

---

[27] More refined tests remain to be done. As the authors note, a further implication of their main proposition is that levels of integration are expected to vary across economic sectors, depending on the differential rates of transnational exchange.

[28] Wallace, *Regional Integration* p. 22. See also Jacques Pelkmans, Alan Winters, and Helen Wallace, *Europe's Domestic Market* (London: Routledge, 1988), p. 22.

[29] Sandholtz and Zysman, "1992: Recasting the European Bargain," 116–120.

1983.[30] In one of their first meetings, the members of ERT concluded that "in reality, despite ambitions to liberalize trade, and the measures taken by the EEC, Europe remains a group of separate national markets with separated national policies and separated industrial structures. This prevents many firms from reaching the scale necessary to resist pressure from non-European competitors."[31]

The ERT urged political leaders to take the following policy steps:[32] (1) revamp public policies to improve the risk/return relationship for European private investment – for example, by allowing tax allowances for incremental research and development expenditures; (2) harmonize economic and monetary policies; (3) end subsidies to obsolete industries; (4) integrate the European market by allowing for the development of common standards; (5) promote the free flow of people, information, and ideas; (6) facilitate the emergence of transnational industrial structures by eliminating fiscal impediments to mergers and restructuring and simplifying the transactions between parent companies and their subsidiaries; and (7) redefine EC regional and social policies.

These demands were given voice through an effective lobbying campaign orchestrated by big business. Many ERT members had privileged access to key decision-makers in the member states. A member of the Delors cabinet declared: "These men are very powerful and dynamic ... when necessary they can ring up their own prime ministers and make their case."[33] For example, the Chief Executive Officers (CEOs) of Fiat and Philips, both leading investors in France, met several times with French President Mitterand to discuss the idea of a single European market and suggest specific policies to improve the health of the European economy. Some of these proposals eventually found entry into Mitterand's European industrial initiative. Cowles concludes that "in many respects, the French President's agenda ... had been set for him by the ERT."[34] ERT members also lobbied the Commission.[35]

---

[30] For an excellent study on the European Round Table, see Maria Green Cowles, "The Politics of Big Business in the European Community: Setting the Agenda for a New Europe," PhD dissertation (Washington: The American University, Department of Political Science, 1994). See also Rob Van Tulder and Gerd Junne, *European Multinationals in Core Technologies* (New York: John Wiley & Sons, 1988), pp. 214–216.

[31] Quoted in Maria Green Cowles, "Setting the Agenda for a New Europe: The ERT and EC 1992," *Journal of Common Market Studies* 33 (December 1995), 506.

[32] Cowles, "The Politics of Big Business," 219.

[33] Quoted in Van Tulder and Junne, *European Multinationals in Core Technologies*, p. 215.

[34] Cowles, "Setting the Agenda for a New Europe," 513.

[35] See Axel Krause, "Many Groups Lobby on Implementation of Market Plan," *Europe* (July/August 1988), 24–25; Sonia Mazey and Jeremy Richardson (eds.), *Lobbying in the European Community* (Oxford University Press, 1993); R. Pedler and M. Van Schendelen (eds.), *Lobbying the European Union: Companies, Trade Associations, and*

Ludlow notes: "Business advocacy was ... a central factor in propelling [the Single Market project] to the top of the Community's agenda, and in clarifying the range of measures involved and the need for a comprehensive, time-tabled strategy."[36] Lobbying at the Community level was relatively easy since the Commission had nothing to lose and much to gain from endorsing demands by business groups. In fact, senior Community officials regularly attended ERT business discussions. Delors himself explained: "We count on business leaders for support."[37] Besides ERT, many other business groups lobbied the Commission. One was the Union of Industrial and Employer's Confederation in Europe (UNICE), which included over thirty industrial associations from throughout Europe.[38] Its Secretary-General described the Union's lobbying as follows: "Nine-tenths of our work comprises the regular, invisible interchange of ideas between our experts and the EC Commission's civil servants."[39]

By all accounts, the lobbying effort of big business was effective. Businesses' success was helped by bad economic conditions. The European economies had suffered through more than ten years of industrial unrest and stagflation, and the economic recovery beginning in 1982–1983 was frail and slow.[40] As argued in chapter 3, in times of economic difficulties, the marginal value of integration in terms of the leaders' re-election chances is likely to be relatively high. Concerns about forgoing national sovereignty become of secondary importance to leaders intent on surviving politically. This allows leaders' dependence on big business to grow since this group's investment is of vital importance to economic recovery.

Thus, the bargaining position of European big business was exceptionally strong in the first half of the 1980s. Business could effectively threaten to move capital out of Europe if political action were not

Issue Groups (Brookfield: Dartmouth Publishing Co., 1994); and Andrew McLaughlin, Grant Jordan, and William Maloney, "Corporate Lobbying in the European Community," *Journal of Common Market Studies* 31 (June 1993), 191–211.

[36] Peter Ludlow, *Beyond 1992: Europe and Its Western Partners* (Brussels: Centre for European Policy Studies, 1989), p. 29.

[37] Quoted in Krause, "Many Groups Lobby on Implementation of Market Plan," 24.

[38] Sandholtz and Zysman, "1992: Recasting the European Bargain," 117.

[39] Quoted in Krause, "Many Groups Lobby on Implementation of Market Plan," 24; see also Sandholtz and Zysman, "1992: Recasting the European Bargain," 117.

[40] Japan and the United States performed in the same period considerably better than Europe. See Geoffrey Garrett, "International Cooperation and Institutional Choice: The European Community's Internal Market," *International Organization* 46 (Spring 1992), 539. From 1974–1984, EC economic growth averaged 1.8% compared to 2.7% in the United States and 4.4% in Japan. See Organization for Economic Cooperation and Development (OECD), *Economic Outlook: Historical Statistics. 1960–1985* (Paris: OECD, 1987).

forthcoming. The following example serves as an illustration of this power: Wisse Dekker, the CEO of the Dutch multinational Philips, said in a speech that received front-page coverage in the *Financial Times* that if European political leaders failed to establish a single market "there were not so many reasons why ... Philips should stay in the Netherlands ... I am European enough to wait until the last possible moment ... [but] if Europe is neither able nor willing to develop its economic structure, then the consequences ... must be drawn."[41] A few months later, just before the EC Council was to take the final vote on the Single European Act, the CEOs of over thirty European firms sent the following remarkable telex to the Council members:

As leading industrialists based in the European Communities ... we urge you to exercise your full influence so that the forthcoming top meeting ... will produce concrete results. STOP. Not only is the credibility of European political leaders at stake but European industry badly needs a clear signal that the major objectives of the Treaty of Rome will be realised within the next 5 years. STOP. Even a clear statement that this would not be the case, would – although not hoped for – be helpful as this would end the prolonged period of uncertainty with which industry has to cope under the present situation and which forms a significant obstacle on the way to expanding our activities and intensifying our efforts to build a strong and competitive European position.[42]

Even though it is impossible to assess *ex post facto* the exact historical importance of the telex, it is not farfetched to conclude that it served as a powerful reminder to political leaders of the dire financial and economic consequences that a failure to accommodate the demands of big business for deeper integration might produce. The member states duly signed the Single European Act in February 1986.

The enlargement issue

Chapter 3 has argued that states which fail to adapt their governance structure adequately to the exigencies of new technologies will suffer economic damage for one or several of the following reasons. First, cost-saving new production techniques requiring large markets are unlikely to be implemented in imperfectly integrated markets where they could only be operated below capacity. Second, firms in competitive industries will leave the jurisdiction of such states and settle where the institutional environment is most conducive to profitable trade and investment. Third, foreign investors deciding whether to operate in the large and well-integrated market of a community country or the functionally

---

[41] Jonathan Carr, "Multinationals May Leave, If Europe Does Not Unite," *Financial Times* (25 April 1985), 1; quoted in Cowles, "The Politics of Big Business", 243.

[42] Quoted in Cowles, "Setting the Agenda for a New Europe," 517.

insufficiently integrated economy of a non-community country are likely to opt for the former, *ceteris paribus*. Finally, by remaining outside a union, states may also suffer the damage of trade diversion.

If these external effects are strongly felt and the economies of outsiders decline markedly, elected officials, mindful of their re-election chances, are likely to change course and embrace pro-integration agendas. The reason is that the expected marginal value from integration in terms of the leaders' re-election chances (or, more broadly, the leaders' chances of retaining political power) is likely to increase as the economy declines. And as this value grows larger than the price of integration, rational outsiders will seek to become insiders. The following sections examine this proposition in detail.

One immediately testable hypothesis deriving from this analytical framework suggests that a country seeks to integrate its economy only when there is a significant positive cost of maintaining its present governance structure in terms of forgone growth (as measured by a continuing performance gap between it and a more integrated rival governance structure). This proposition is broadly supported by the data.

Table 4.1 compares the timing of applications for membership in the EC with the evolution of growth rates for countries inside and outside the EC. The results show that out of twenty applications for membership by eleven countries, eighteen were submitted after one or – more typically – several years of growth rates mostly substantially below the average growth rates of EC countries.[43]

The empirical analysis shows more generally that there is no integration sought when there is no performance gap, and that a sustained

---

[43] The average growth rate is based on the six founding countries of the European Community (EC-Six). For the second, third, and fourth enlargements, an average growth rate based on all present members yields essentially identical results. Data is from the *IMF Yearbook* (Washington, D.C.: 1984) for GDP data at constant prices for years 1957–1960; *IMF Yearbook* (Washington, D.C.: 1991) for GDP data at constant prices for years 1961–1990; Commission of the European Communities, Directorate General for Economic and Financial Affairs, *European Economy: Annual Economic Report 1991–92* (Brussels: December 1991) for GDP data at constant prices for European Community countries during the years 1990–1991; and Organization for Economic Cooperation and Development, *OECD Economic Outlook* 51 (Paris: June 1992) for all other data for 1990–1992. The same calculations were done on economic growth data reported in the *National Accounts* by the OECD and in the Penn World Tables by Heston and Summers. (The Penn World Table [Mark 5.5] of 1993 is an updated [to 1990] and revised version of the original Table that was prepared for the article "The Penn World Table (Mark 5): An Explained Set of International Comparisons: 1950–1988" by Alan Heston and Robert Summers, in the *Quarterly Journal of Economics*, May 1991.) The results based on the OECD and Penn World Table data are essentially identical to the findings in Table 4.1 and thus are not reported here.

Table 4.1. *The timing of application for membership the European Community (based on IMF data)*

Country	Application number	Year of application	Growth-rate differential with EC (year prior to application with amount)	Number of years of below EC-6 growth rates (prior to application)	Growth-rate differential of country with EC-6 a year after membership
United Kingdom	First	1961	**Below** (6.1%)	3	
	Second	1967	**Below** (1.5%)	3	**Above** EC
	"Third"	1970	**Below** (7.1%)	6	
Ireland	First	1961	**Below** (5.5%)	3	
	Second	1967	**Below** (2.5%)	3	**Above** EC
	"Third"	1970	**Below** (2.3%)	1	
Denmark	First	1961	**Below** (4.3%)	1	
	Second	1967	**Below** (1.3%)	1	*Below* EC
	"Third"	1970	**Below** (1.9%)	2	
Norway	First	1961	**Below** (5.5%)	3	
	Second	1967	*Above* (0.3%)	0	
	"Third"	1970	**Below** (3.9%)	2	n/a
	Fourth	1992	**Below** (0.2%)	5	
Sweden	First	1991	**Below** (2.7%)	3	**Above** EC
Switzerland	First	1992	**Below** (2.5%)	5	n/a
Finland	First	1992	**Below** (8.1%)	2	**Above** EC
Austria	First	1989	**Below** (0.2%)	3	[Same as EC]
Spain	First	1977	**Below** (1.9%)	1	*Below* EC
Portugal	First	1977	*Above* (2.0%)	0	**Above** EC
Greece	First	1975	**Below** (7.3%)	1	[Same as EC]

performance gap always eventually triggers demands for integration.[44] Countries that fail to experience such a gap see no reason to pay the price of integration and thus stay out. However, as discussed below in detail, there is one interesting exception to the rule that countries seek membership if there is a performance gap: Europe's neutral countries failed to seek full EC membership in moments of relative economic decline *during the Cold War*. After the Cold War ended, they too opted to pursue full integration. Finally, another regularity is that growth-rate differentials tend to be mostly above the EC average during the first year of membership. Growth rates for advanced newcomers then tend to

---

[44] For extensive statistical evidence, see Walter Mattli, "The Logic of Regional Integration," PhD thesis, University of Chicago (1994).

fluctuate around the Community average, while they typically remain higher for poorer countries during the first few years. As suggested in the concluding section, such trends are linked to beneficial investment inflows following membership.

The countries of the first enlargement of the EU

The Treaty of Rome establishing the European Communities came into force on January 1, 1958. As briefly outlined above, it committed the EC-Six (Germany, France, Italy, the Netherlands, Belgium, and Luxemburg) to a far-reaching exercise in economic integration which envisages free movement of goods, services, capital, and labor, aided by common policies in agriculture, transport, regional development, external commerce, research and development, economic cohesion, education, environment, and other domains. Most other Western European countries which were not part of the EEC – the United Kingdom, Sweden, Norway, Denmark, Austria, Switzerland, and Portugal – at first reacted to the formation of the European Community by establishing the European Free Trade Association (EFTA) on January 4, 1960. Finland signed an association agreement with EFTA in 1961. This rival organization with a minimalist integrative program committed its members to establishing free trade in industrial goods only.

To foreign investors, the European Community was more attractive than EFTA. The percentage of the value of US direct investment in Western Europe which was apportioned to Community countries rose from 40.5 percent in 1957 to 44.7 percent in 1964. Yannopoulous relates this increase to a diversion of the flow of US investment from the non-EC countries of Western Europe, particularly the United Kingdom, to members of the Community.[45] Numerous other studies have likewise concluded that the EC attracted significantly more of the growth in total US foreign direct investment than EFTA countries (see table 4.2.).[46]

This investment diversion undoubtedly contributed to the UK's

---

[45] George Yannopoulos, "Foreign Direct Investment and European Integration: The Evidence from the Formative Years of the European Community," *Journal of Common Market Studies* 28 (March 1990), 236.

[46] Andrew Schmitz, "The Impact of Trade Blocs on Foreign Direct Investment," *Economic Journal* 80 (1970), 724–731; Andrew Schmitz and Jurg Bieri, "EEC Tariffs and US Direct Investment," *European Economic Review* 3 (1972), 259–270; John Lunn, "Determinants of US Direct Investment in the EEC: Further Evidence," *European Economic Review* 13 (January 1980), 93–101 and "Determinants of US Direct Investment in the EEC: Revisited Again," *European Economic Review* 21 (January 1983), 391–393; Anthony Scaperlanda and Robert Balough, "Determinants of US Direct Investment in the EEC: Revisited," *European Economic Review* 21 (May 1983), 381–390. For a useful review of the empirical studies, see Yannopoulos, "Foreign Direct Investment and European Integration," especially 238–247.

Table 4.2. *Flows of US direct investment to Western Europe (%)*

	1950	1957	1964
Western Europe	100	100	100
European Community (EC) countries	45.6	36.5	50.5
European Free Trade Association (EFTA) countries	48.9	59.7	44.1

Source: Yannopoulos, "Foreign Direct Investment and European Integration," 237.

worsening economic condition. The UK grew in the late 1950s and early 1960s well below the Community average. To stem economic losses, the United Kingdom formally announced in 1961 that it had decided to apply for full membership in the EC. It was soon followed by Ireland, Denmark, and Norway. Subsequently, Austria, Sweden, and Switzerland made separate applications for association. Negotiations regarding the British application dragged on until January 13, 1963, when General de Gaulle declared at a Paris press conference that Britain was not ripe for membership. Two weeks later, all negotiations were adjourned indefinitely. At that time, talks with Norway and Denmark were advanced. Formal negotiations on the Irish application had hardly begun. In the case of the three applicants for association – Austria, Sweden, and Switzerland – a first round of talks had taken place between the EC Commission and a delegation from the countries concerned, to ascertain the problems to be addressed. But no formal negotiations had been opened.[47]

Continuing poor economic performance relative to that of the EC-Six led the British Prime Minister, Harold Wilson, to announce in May 1967 that the United Kingdom had decided to submit its second application.[48] Ireland, Denmark, and Norway followed suit. Negotiations were immediately initiated, but only a few months later de Gaulle, in one of his famous press conferences, declared that full membership for Britain would lead to the destruction of the Community. This closed the door to entry yet again. Events in May 1968 led to the resignation of de Gaulle, and under President Pompidou France no longer objected in

[47] Dennis Swann, *The Economics of the Common Market* (London: Penguin Group, 6th edn, 1988), p. 24.
[48] For a lucid study on the economic performance gap between the EC-Six and the EFTA countries, see Fritz Breuss, *Integration in Europa and gesamtwirtschaftliche Entwicklung: EG- und EFTA-Staaten im Vergleich* (Vienna: Oesterreichisches Institut für Wirtschaftsforschung, 1990).

principle to British membership. The United Kingdom, along with the three other applicants, was invited back to the negotiating table.[49] The United Kingdom, Ireland, and Denmark continued to grow at rates substantially below the Community average after the resumption of talks. This trend narrowed or reverted only as the three acceded to membership in 1973.

Norway's planned membership in the Community was vetoed by a national referendum held in October 1972. Why? Norway was the only country of four applicants where the performance gap of the years 1968–1970 had completely disappeared in 1971–1972, thus possibly giving Norwegians the impression that membership was no longer worth the candle. This is not a farfetched conclusion considering that membership not only entails a relative loss of sovereignty but also usually net contributions to the Community's budget by wealthy members.[50] The reversal of Norway's economic fortune can be attributed to a stroke of good luck. In 1969, the first commercially important discovery of petroleum on Norway's continental shelf was made at the Ekofisk field, just as foreign oil companies were about to give up after four years of exploratory drilling. Later major finds have included the Frigg field, one of the largest offshore natural gas deposits, and the huge Statfjord field. The estimated reserves below the 62nd parallel alone ensured an annual production for twenty years that is several times Norway's domestic consumption of petroleum products.[51]

In the mid-1980s, times changed for the worse in Norway. World crude-oil prices fell to $8 a barrel in 1985–1986, delivering a severe blow to Norway's economy from which it took a long time to recover. The reduction in petroleum revenue slashed Norway's spendable real income by 9 percent. By the late 1980s registered unemployment climbed to nearly 6 percent, the highest suffered in Norway for over sixty years.[52] Consistent with the framework of chapter 3, Norway announced in November 1992 its intention to seek membership of the EC. At the last minute, however, Norway opted to stay out, as it had done in 1972, when a majority of Norwegians voted against EU membership in

---

[49] Table 4.1 records this as application "Third." Formally, however, no new applications were submitted. For an overview of this enlargement process, see Christopher Preston, *Enlargement and Integration* (London: Routledge, 1997), pp. 23–45.

[50] Christopher Anderson and Shawn Reichert write: "[P]ublics in ... member states ... that are considering membership ... will be more reluctant to support integration if they will be net payers." See C. Anderson and S. Reichert, "Economic Benefits and Support for Membership in the EU: A Cross-National Analysis," *Journal of Public Policy* 15 (1995), 246.

[51] See country report on Norway in the *Encylopaedia Britannica (Macropaedia)* (1992), pp. 1082–1096.

[52] See survey on Norway in *Financial Times*, June 2, 1992, Section IV.

November 1994. Most analysts have explained Norway's latest rejection in terms of successful coalescing of rural interests, nationalists, leftists, and environmentalists. This, however, does not explain why this coalition succeeded in 1994 while only a few years earlier, during the height of the recession, its views had been marginal. The conventional explanation would benefit from a reference to the development of differential growth rates between the EU and Norway, as suggested in this analysis. By the early 1990s oil prices had recovered from their mid-1980s' slump and they quickly propelled the Norwegian economy out of the recession. In 1994, the year of the referendum, Norway's real GDP growth was a remarkable 5.7 percent, a rate well above the EU average. Oil revenues were largely responsible for Norway's relative economic strength.[53] Predictions were that the North Sea petroleum bounty would continue to buoy the economy for a number of years.[54] For Norway, membership of the EU had once again lost its urgency. Moses and Jenssen conclude that "oil incomes have become a determinative factor in influencing Norwegian attitudes on membership . . . Norwegians apparently feel that they can afford to remain outside the Union."[55]

Europe's neutral countries and enlargement

Prima facie, the data on Europe's neutral countries seem to contradict our explanation, at least partially. Austria, Sweden, Finland, and Switzerland submitted or announced the intention to submit applications only between 1989 and 1992, after several years of growth rates continually below the Community average.

Why did they fail to apply during earlier periods of widening performance gaps? There are two parts to the answer. First, while it is true that these four EFTA countries did not seek application until the late 1980s and early 1990s, they nevertheless repeatedly sought closer ties with the Community. For example, when the United Kingdom and Denmark decided to leave EFTA in 1972, the remaining members negotiated free-trade agreements (FTAs) in industrial goods with the EC. The FTAs with Austria, Portugal, Sweden, and Switzerland came into force on January 1, 1973, with Iceland in April 1973, and with Norway in July 1973.[56] A joint EC–EFTA ministerial meeting in

---

[53] Jonathon Moses and Anders Todal Jenssen, "Nordic Accession: An Analysis of the EU Referendums," in Barry Eichengreen and Jeffry Frieden (eds.), *Forging an Integrated Europe* (Ann Arbor: University of Michigan Press, 1998), pp. 211–246.

[54] See special report on Norway in *Financial Times* (November 20, 1995), 1–4.

[55] Moses and Jenssen, "Nordic Accession: An Analysis of the EU Referendums," 222.

[56] See Finn Laursen, "The Community's Policy Towards EFTA: Regime Formation in the European Economic Space (EES)," *Journal of Common Market Studies* 28 (1990), 311.

Luxemburg on April 9, 1984, produced a declaration which sought to continue, deepen and extend cooperation between the EC and the EFTA with the aim of creating a dynamic European Economic Area (EEA).[57] The dialogue on the EEA intensified and in 1992 a treaty signed by the two organizations established a European free-trade zone in goods, services, labor, and capital. The EEA came into force on January 1, 1994.[58] While not, therefore, officially applying for EC membership, the EFTA countries clearly demonstrated a recognition of the benefits of association with the dynamic regional grouping.

Another policy to narrow the institutional gap between insiders and outsiders, short of membership, is *policy mimicry*. Europe's neutral countries have repeatedly adopted norms and policies forged outside their jurisdiction to avoid economic marginalization. For instance, in 1988 the Swiss government introduced the so-called "Europe Clause" requiring all proposed legislation or amendments to be examined for compatibility with Community rule.[59] In 1993 the Swiss government announced plans to press ahead on harmonizing of its laws and regulations with those of the Community, even though it did not consider membership.[60] In the same year, Switzerland introduced a value-added tax as a further step to align its fiscal and economic policies with those of the European countries. In Norway, steps were taken as early as 1987 to create a new Secretariat in the Foreign Ministry, together with a Committee of Permanent Secretaries, in order to ensure better coordination of European policies. These agencies scrutinize all new Community directives and seek to involve a wider range of bodies in European affairs. Legislative adaptation proceeded on a wide scale in various ministries, in close consultation with export industries, labor and employers' organizations, and other interest groups.[61]

In Sweden, an extraordinary decree was adopted by the government in June 1988 that required every expert inquiry or Royal Commission proposing a policy in fields related to the internal market or European integration to evaluate the policy's compatibility with corresponding EC legislation and EC Commission proposals. The burden of proof of compatibility rested on the proposer and every proposal that diverged

[57] See Philippe Nell, "EFTA in the 1990s: The Search for a New Identity," *Journal of Common Market Studies* 28 (June 1990), 327–358.
[58] In a referendum held in December 1992, Switzerland rejected the EEA by a narrow majority.
[59] Richard Senti, "Switzerland," in Helen Wallace (ed.), *The Wider Western Europe: Reshaping the EC/EFTA Relationship* (London: Pinter Publishers, 1991), p. 220.
[60] *Bericht über die Aussenpolitik der Schweiz in den 1990er Jahren* (Bern: Bundesrat, November 1993).
[61] Martin Saeter and Olav Knudsen, "Norway," in Wallace (ed.), *The Wider Western Europe*, 189.

from Community legislation had to be justified. EC compatibility also needed to be considered in the judicial review of government bills.[62] Furthermore, a secretariat for integration questions was established, which was responsible for internal adjustments and the implementation of domestic integration policy.[63] Sweden unilaterally adopted and implemented more than twenty directives by the end of 1989. At the same time, it enlarged its value-added tax base in line with that of the Community, changed its somewhat restrictive banking and currency laws, and undertook some deregulation.[64]

In the monetary domain, acts of mimicry are also quite common. For example, in the 1980s and early 1990s Austria, Switzerland, and Sweden were not members of the European Monetary System (EMS), yet their respective central banks pegged their currencies to the Deutschmark, the EMS's anchor currency.[65]

In short, even before seeking formal membership Europe's neutral countries went a long way down the road of unilateral adaptation to EC law and policies to avoid being effectively left out. Their national sovereignty remained intact *de jure*, but *de facto* it had lost much of its value.[66]

A second reason why these countries have been more reluctant than other West European states to seek full membership of the EU is that neutrality during the Cold War may well have served them better than membership. This is perhaps most apparent in the Finnish case. For Finland, which shares a 780-mile border with Russia, neutrality was not

---

[62] Carl-Einar Stalvant and Carl Hamilton, "Sweden," in Wallace (ed.), *The Wider Western Europe*, p. 203.

[63] *Ibid.*, p. 202.

[64] Finland also followed the beat of legislative calibration to Community norms. See Esko Antola, "Finland," in Wallace (ed.), *The Wider Western Europe*, pp. 146–158.

[65] A Swedish diplomat was quoted in the *Washington Post* as saying: "How long can anyone remain 'independent' *vis-à-vis* a decision by the *Bundesbank* to change the interest rate or the value of the German Mark? About 20 minutes?" Quoted in an article by Jim Hoagland, "A Bogeyman Theory of Government," *Washington Post* (June 2, 1992).

[66] Philippe Nell, "EFTA in the 1990s," 352. An interesting example of the logic of policy mimicry in a different historical era can be found in Hendrik Spruyt, "Institutional Selection in International Relations: State Anarchy as Order," *International Organization* 48 (Autumn 1994), 527–557. Spruyt writes that "sovereign states proved better at mobilizing their societies and enhancing their domestic economies [than the cities of the Hanseatic league]. Territorial units gradually encroached on the independence of the cities ... The German princes thus started to *mimic the administrative processes and legal framework of territorial states* ... When political elites recognized the consequences of localism and the lack of economic integration in their city-states, they turned to the territorial rules of Frederick and Catherine the Great as models worthy of emulation ... [I]ndividuals had reasons to mimic those successful institutions ... [They] emulated what they perceived to be successful arrangements in order to reduce uncertainty and gain legitimacy" (*ibid.*, 546 and 550, my italics).

only a political imperative but also above all an economic advantage, permitting it to maintain steady and profitable trade relations with Moscow. The loss of economic benefits due to the collapse of the Soviet Union contributed to Finland's deepest recession since the 1930s.[67] As a result, Finland no longer felt any compunction about betraying its principle of neutrality. Its application to the EC contained no reference to preserving neutrality as a precondition to membership.

While Europe's neutral countries failed to seek *full* EC membership in moments of relative economic decline during the Cold War, they too sought membership after the Cold War ended. Despite rapid progress towards a European Economic Area and despite sweeping policy mimicry, the neutral countries were unable to reverse relative economic decline in the late 1980s and early 1990s. Corporate pressure on governments to move towards full membership grew intense in those years. Big firms became increasingly discontented with the uncertainty and lack of transparency of many of the measures taken by their governments to bridge the institutional gap with the EU. They argued that such measures did not provide conditions favorable enough to compete successfully with the big firms within the common market. In particular, they felt that their governments could not commit themselves to implement EC policies as credibly as EC governments.[68] This created lingering doubts about the comprehensiveness and thorough- ness of policy mimicry and also made outsiders vulnerable to discrimi- natory treatment by the EC in several domains, such as research and development and public procurement. As a result, multinationals in outsider countries began to invest more and more of their resources away from home, within the EC. This enabled them to lower production costs and get a stronger foothold in the European market.[69] In Sweden, for example, the result of this process was a striking gap between outward investment and inward investment in the late 1980s (see figure 4.1).

Disinvestment of such magnitude came at a particularly inopportune

[67] Real output declined by 10 percent over 1991 and 1992 and was flat in 1993. Unemployment reached 20 percent. The banking sector lurched into losses so severe that the state had to spend some 60 billion markkas to bail it out. The budget deficit ballooned to around 10 percent of gross domestic product and foreign debt doubled to almost 50 percent of GDP. Finally, the value of the Finnish markka fell by 50 percent between 1991 and the end of 1992. See *Financial Times*, special survey on Finland (October 11, 1993), 2.

[68] Carl-Einar Stalvant and Carl Hamilton, "Sweden," in Wallace (ed.), *The Wider Western Europe*, p. 208.

[69] Karl-Orfeo Fioretos, "The Anatomy of Autonomy: Interdependence, Domestic Balances of Power, and European Integration," *Review of International Studies* 23 (1997), 312.

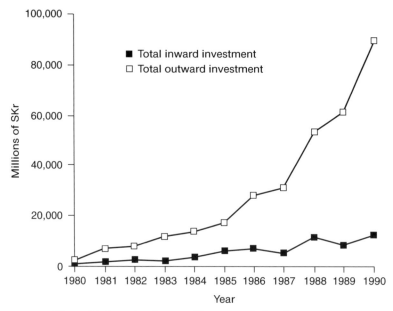

Figure 4.1 Inward and outward investment in Sweden.
Source: Karl-Orfeo Fioretos, "The Anatomy of Autonomy: Interdependence,
Domestic Balances of Power and European Integration," *Review of International
Studies*, 23 (1997), 312.

time. Sweden was grappling with its most severe recession since the
1920s.[70] The recovery package that the government had designed was
to a large extent dependent on retaining Swedish companies. In dire
need of improving the investment climate, the Swedish government was
left with no option but to apply for full EC membership. Even after the
application was filed in 1991, Swedish firms kept pressing government
officials for rapid membership negotiations, repeatedly issuing explicit
threats of exit.[71] Fioretos concludes unequivocally: "The engine of
Sweden's integration … has been its large multinational corporations
… The Swedish government had little option but to secure access for
Swedish firms to the Union if it was to retain domestic investment,

[70] Sweden's economy declined by 1.2 percent in 1991 and 1 percent in 1992.

[71] Moses and Jenssen, "Nordic Accession: An Analysis of the EU Referendums," 217.
The two authors also note that in public-opinion polls conducted in the run-up to the
referendum, a majority of Swedes thought that EU membership would improve
domestic economic fortunes. In contrast, only 28 percent of Norwegians felt that
membership would be an advantage to Norway's economy.

promote growth and employment, as well as make Sweden an attractive site for foreign investment in the future."[72]

The Austrian case is similar to the Swedish one, and thus fits well the general logic of the first integrative response elaborated in the previous chapter. In a recent case study, Tim Büthe summarizes the key motives of Austrian membership application as follows: "Austria – first some of its firms, eventually its government on behalf of Austria's economic growth perspective – had sought EC membership to ensure access to the EC market for Austrian exports and ... to ensure competitiveness."[73] The membership issue was first brought up in Austria by export-oriented firms in the mid-1980s, during the period of negotiations for the Single European Act. The textile industry of Vorarlberg in western Austria felt increasing discrimination from the EC, despite free-trade agreements.[74] The Federation of Austrian Industrialists was the first important interest group to endorse the demands for EC membership made by the textile industry. In 1987 it issued an "urgent appeal to the Federal Government to do everything so that full membership in the EC can be accomplished at the earliest possible moment."[75] The idea of membership was also endorsed by the Federal Chamber of Commerce and quickly enjoyed widespread popularity. Such positive public response is best understood against the backdrop of an Austrian economy in distress. Paul Luif notes:

In November 1985, Austria's large state-owned industry was on the brink of bankruptcy and the federal government had to come to the rescue, but the already high budget set limits for such intervention. The nationalized industry had to abandon one of its most cherished policies and to dismiss workers and employees on what was, for Austria, a massive scale. These problems were only one indication of the precarious state of the Austrian economy, which in the mid-1980s was growing more slowly than ... the EC economies taken as a whole.[76]

---

[72] Fioretos, "The Anatomy of Autonomy," 313.

[73] Tim Büthe, *European Union and National Electorates: The Austrian Public Debate and Referendum on Joining the European Union in June 1994*, Working Paper 5.8 (Cambridge, Mass.: Harvard University, Center for European Studies, July 1995), p. 22.

[74] Paul Luif, "Austria," in Wallace (ed.), *The Wider Western Europe*, p. 135.

[75] Vereinigung Oesterreichischer Industrieller, "Europa – unsere Zukunft. Eine Stellungnahme der Vereinigung Oesterreichischer Industrieller zur Europäischen Integration" (Vienna, May 1987), 46; quoted in Luif, "Austria," p. 129. Note that most of Austria's trade has always been with Community members. In 1985, for example, the EC countries received a 56.1 percent share of Austrian total exports whereas the EFTA countries got only 10.5 percent. At the same time, Austria imported 62.1 percent of goods from the EC and only 7.6 percent from EFTA countries. See International Monetary Fund, *Directions of Trade* (Washington D.C.: IMF), various issues.

[76] Luif, "Austria," p. 135.

On July 17, 1989, Austria submitted its EC application to the Commission – an application that had been authorized by a 95 percent majority of the lower chamber of the Austrian Parliament.[77]

Like big firms in Sweden, firms in Austria strongly preferred full EC membership to membership of the EEA.[78] They felt that EEA membership alone would neither provide sufficient guarantee against EC discrimination nor create the right investment climate. Büthe notes, for example, that investments in Austria which were financed on international capital markets in 1994 still cost a premium over investments in the EU, despite Austrian membership in the EEA.[79] Only EC membership seemed to offer big Austrian business the necessary safeguards and advantages to compete effectively with EC firms.

The more general expected gains from full membership on Austria were illustrated in a series of influential studies published in the early 1990s by the Austrian Institute of Economic Research. The studies predicted that GDP would be 2.8 percent higher by the year 2000 if Austria were a full EU member instead of simply belonging to the EEA.[80] Persuaded by such arguments, two-thirds of Austria's voters endorsed EU membership in a 1994 referendum. The strong vote in favor of membership was possibly influenced by renewed economic difficulties in the early 1990s. Austria's recession peaked in 1993 when GDP declined by about 0.25 percent. Along with Sweden and Finland, Austria joined the European Union on January 1, 1995.

Finally, the Swiss case is, in parts, consistent with the first integrative response logic of chapter 3. Swiss economic growth fell significantly below average Community growth in the late 1980s. In late 1990, Switzerland entered into a recession that lasted for around three years.[81] At the same time, internationalized sectors of the Swiss economy, most notably the engineering and chemical industries, began to lobby for EU membership. In 1988, engineering exports represented 28.3 percent of total Swiss exports to the EC market. Products by the chemical industry accounted for 21.4 percent of total Swiss exports to the EC.[82] These

---

[77] Büthe, *European Union and National Electorates*, p. 7.
[78] See Paulette Kurzer, *Business and Banking: Political Change and Economic Integration in Western Europe* (Ithaca: Cornell University Press, 1993).
[79] Büthe, *European Union and National Electorates*, p. 23.
[80] Sven Arndt, "Alpine Contrasts: Swiss and Austrian Responses to the EU," in Eichengreen and Frieden (eds.), *Forging an Integrated Europe*, pp. 260–261.
[81] The Swiss economy started to move back into growth in the last quarter of 1993. The jobless rate rose during the recession to over 5 percent
[82] Kristina Plavsak, "Why Do Small States Want to Join European Integration? Responses of Austria, Norway, and Switzerland to the EC Challenge," unpublished paper (New York: Columbia University, Department of Political Science, May 1996), 32.

industries were expressing concern about negative externalities from the deepening process of European integration, particularly in the form of discrimination in the areas of technical harmonization, public procurement, and research and development. In light of growing economic unrest, the Swiss government declared its intention to seek EU membership in October 1991. It sent a formal application to the Community on May 18, 1992. How did it justify such a move, considering the "sacredness" of Swiss neutrality? In a 1993 foreign policy report, the Swiss government explained that neutrality had never been an end in itself but merely a means of preserving Swiss independence. In the post-Cold War world, Swiss independence was threatened more by not having a say in EU matters than by any hostile military power. Prosperity through integration became the declared objective of Swiss foreign policy.[83]

Considering all of these factors (economically troubled times, corporate pressure for EU membership, willingness by political leaders to accommodate these demands), the political-economy approach of chapter 3 would predict in the Swiss case a smooth move towards membership. Instead, in December 1992, 50.3 percent of Swiss voters opposed EEA membership as against 49.7 percent in favours, thus in effect barring any further talks on EU membership. The economic cost of the "no" vote was estimated to be high. Several studies suggested that by not joining the EEA, investments in Switzerland would grow at only 0.5 percent instead of 3.5 percent. As a result, GNP would rise by less than 1 percent compared to 2.3 percent, and unemployment would double.[84] Considering the continuing economic difficulties of the Swiss economy in the wake of the "no" vote, many of these estimates seem to have been validated.[85]

Why this negative vote? The approach of chapter 3 cannot explain it. This need not imply that the approach is wrong. First, many of the dynamics leading up to the referendum were well captured by the approach; further, the outcome of the referendum was extremely tight, thus hardly an outcome that convincingly "falsifies" the approach. Nevertheless, it does suggest that, at least in the Swiss case, the political-economy approach is *analytically* incomplete. But the approach remains

[83] *Bericht über die Aussenpolitik der Schweiz in den 1990er Jahren* (Berne: Bundesrat, November 1993).
[84] Rene Schwok, "Switzerland: The European Union's Self-appointed Pariah," in John Redmond (ed.), *Prospective Europeans: New Members for the European Union* (New York: Harvester Wheatsheaf, 1994), p. 34.
[85] See William Hall, "Switzerland: Isolation Is Now Being Questioned," *Financial Times*, survey (March 1997), 27.

useful because it provides a benchmark by which to assess the extent and impact of non-economic motivations in deciding for or against integration. It thus suggests that a more fine-grained analysis is needed in the Swiss case, that takes into consideration factors such as the country's socio-political characteristics, or elements that capture the peculiarity of Swiss political decision-making.[86]

The remaining countries

Spain was virtually a closed economy under Franco's dictatorship, and up to 1970 it established trading links neither with EFTA nor with the EC. In 1970 it began a trade agreement with the EC which reduced tariffs, with some exceptions for sensitive products and with a slower pace for dismantling tariffs on the Spanish side. In July of 1977, the Suarez government submitted its application to the EC. Spain became a full member on January 1, 1986. Portugal began to consider membership in the EC upon restoration of full democracy after the departure of Caetano in 1974. An application was filed in March of 1977 and the country joined simultaneously with Spain.[87] The relationship between Greece and the Community goes back to the 1960s. A Treaty of Association came into operation in 1962 and provided for the eventual formation of a customs union between Greece and the Six. Following the *coup d'état* in 1967, the Greek association agreement was frozen, but it was reactivated in 1974 with the restoration of democracy. In June 1975 the Karamanlis government submitted an application to the EC. Greece became a full member on January 1, 1981.[88]

The data on economic growth for Spain, Portugal, and Greece show some correlation between economic slowdown and the timing of their application for membership. The evidence of a link between economic performance and timing, however, is considerably weaker for these three countries than for most other countries in the sample. This is not surprising. As noted in chapter 3, a test of the timing hypothesis is only meaningful for countries that are generally viewed by a union as desirable prospective members. These are typically countries within the region that are at a comparable level of socio-economic development. Countries that are significantly poorer than even the least wealthy

---

[86] See, for example, Pascal Sciarini and Ola Listhaug, "Single Case or a Unique Pair? The Swiss and Norwegian 'No' to Europe," *Journal of Common Market Studies* 35 (September 1997), 407–437.

[87] For an overview of the EC's third enlargement, see Preston, *Enlargement and Integration in the European Union*, pp. 62–86.

[88] For further reading, see G. N. Yannopoulos (ed.), *Greece and the EEC* (Basingstoke: Macmillan, 1986); and Preston, *Enlargement and Integration in the European Union*, pp. 46–61.

members of the EU have an interest in improving their rate of economic growth if it has fallen but also have a continuing interest in reducing the glaring per capita income gap between themselves and the Union. They stand to gain handsomely from the EU's Regional Development and Structural Readjustment Funds and are likely to attract foreign private capital as members of the EU. The timing of applications for EU membership, for example, by formerly communist countries, such as Poland, Hungary, Romania, and others, is therefore primarily determined by the willingness of the EU to accept them as new members.

As argued in chapter 3, a union will have an interest in accepting poor peripheral economies typically only when the net cost of excluding them is bigger than the cost of accepting them. More precisely, the argument is that an incentive for accepting these poor countries exists when negative externalities originating in these outsider countries threaten to disrupt the union's stability, security, and prosperity. The sources of these externalities may reside in economic mismanagement, political instability, or social unrest. A particularly common form of negative externality is illegal immigration. Economic inclusion through integration rather than exclusion, goods rather than people, trade instead of migration may become an expedient integrative formula for defusing the threat of social disruption caused by such illegal immigration – especially when a union's labor market is saturated.[89] Trade and investment may raise living standards and increase employment opportunities, thus easing the pressure to migrate.[90]

Events in Eastern Europe in the early 1990s suggest that the scope of negative externalities originating in the periphery of the Community did indeed shape the attitude of EC members regarding enlargement to the

[89] The "push" factor of migration, namely marked differences in the marginal productivities of labor and capital from one economy to another, will disappear, according to the factor-price equalization theorem, when free trade and investment are allowed. See Wolfgang Stolper and Paul Samuelson, "Protection and Real Wages," *Review of Economic Studies* 9 (1941), 58–73; Paul Samuelson, "International Trade and the Equalization of Factor Prices," *Economic Journal* 58 (June 1948), 163–184. Perfect factor-price equalization, however, is not a necessary condition for migration to cease, for migration is costly. It involves separation from family and friends, acclimatization to a new cultural and linguistic environment, and sometimes even payment to smugglers. Rational expectations about improved domestic opportunities may thus suffice to dampen emigration pressures.

[90] See James Hollifield, "Migration and International Relations: Cooperation and Control in the European Community," *International Migration Review* 26 (Summer 1992), 568–595. See also James Hollifield, *Immigration, Markets and States: The Political Economy of Postwar Europe* (Cambridge, Mass.: Harvard University Press, 1992); Ulrich Hiemenz and Klaus Werner Schatz, *Trade in Place of Migration* (Geneva: International Labor Office, 1979).

East. The European Union's eastern periphery was moving from an era of communism and rigid command economies towards a goal of democratic pluralistic regimes with market economies. This transformation represented a gargantuan social experiment of uncertain outcome. Its failure threatened to play havoc with West European projects for monetary and political union and seriously risked undoing most of the European Union's progress up to that point in economic integration. Above all, Western Europe feared massive migratory movements if the process of political transition and economic restructuring in the East went awry. Economic "push" factors, such as rising unemployment, food shortages, and a decline in the already precarious standard of living, combined with ethnic tensions and mounting criminality, had already motivated hundreds of thousands to move west. In the early 1990s the United Nations High Commissioner for Refugees predicted as many as 25 million refugees from all over Eastern Europe if political instability and unfavorable socio-economic conditions continued.[91]

The threat of such massive migration caught Western Europe at a particularly unwelcome time. In 1991, there were 15 million unemployed workers in Western Europe, of which 12 million resided in the EU. This amounted to some 6 percent of the population of Western Europe. The unemployment rate among those aged under 25 averaged 35 percent. With the onset of the recession in the early 1990s these numbers stood to rise significantly. Immigration was rapidly becoming a core issue of electoral campaigns in many European countries. The growing number of foreigners who were competing with indigenous workers for a dwindling number of jobs fomented xenophobia and exacerbated social tensions.

Clearly the problem of migration had to be tackled at the source rather than through a policy of containment. The West responded to the plight in the East initially by offering technical assistance and advice in areas such as food distribution, privatization, banking, civil service reform, education, environment and energy through the PHARE and

---

[91] Baudoin Bollaert, "L'Occident face à la misère de l'autre Europe," *Le Figaro* (November 22, 1990), 4. See also Norbert Kostede, "Igor Ante Portas," *Die Zeit* (December 14, 1990), 13; Kuno Kruse and Brigit Schwarz, "Neue Freiheit, Neue Grenzen," *Die Zeit*, Dossier (February 15, 1991), 13–15; J. Dempsey, "Seven Million May Leave the Soviet Union," *Financial Times* (January 26, 1991); "Poor Men at the Gate," *The Economist* (March 16, 1991), 11–12; Lilia Shevtsova, "Post-Soviet Emigration Today and Tomorrow," *International Migration Review* 26 (Summer 1992), 241–257. The crisis proportion of such an influx becomes clear, when this predicted number of refugees is compared with past averages. The yearly average net migration into the twelve EC countries was 161,400 for 1980 to 1984; and 533,000 for 1985 to 1989. See David Coleman, "Does Europe Need Immigrants? Population and Work Force Projections," *International Migration Review* 26 (Summer 1992), 449.

the TACIS programs.[92] Economic loans were provided by the European Investment Bank (EIB). The European Bank for Reconstruction and Development (EBRD) concentrated its lending to the nascent private sector. Such traditional aid, however, proved insufficient. The attempted Soviet coup of August, 1991, signalled to the West that more effort was needed to avert chaos.[93] Only integration of Eastern and Western Europe seemed to offer a way of stimulating economic growth and producing sufficient political stability to mitigate the pressure for large-scale migration. Jackie Gower notes that "[u]ntil the summer of 1991 the prevailing view in Brussels was that none of the former Comecon states could realistically be regarded as candidate members of the Community until well into the next century. Indeed, it is arguable that the EU's overriding objective at this time was to avoid the question of membership." Gower concludes that the shock of the attempted Moscow coup changed the EU's attitude towards enlargement.[94] Avoidance was simply no longer a sensible policy option.

Instead, the Community initiated negotiations on gradual integration with Czechoslovakia, Hungary, and Poland. On December 16, 1991, far-reaching association agreements (also called "Europe Agreements") were signed, under which the EU promised to remove its barriers to industrial imports from the three countries within five years. Each of these states in turn committed themselves to take concrete steps towards a market economy and pluralist democracy. They agreed, notably, to model their competition laws on those of the Community and also to bring their laws regarding intellectual and commercial property, public procurement, banking, financial services, company accounts and taxes, indirect taxation, technical rules and standards, consumer protection, health and safety, transport, and the environment into line with EU practice.[95]

[92] PHARE is the acronym for "Pologne, Hongrie: Activité pour la Restructuration Economique." (The word *phare* also means lighthouse in French.) The PHARE program now includes ten countries in Eastern Europe. It is funded by the EU budget and the money is given by way of grants. The total sum allocated to PHARE was raised to 1 billion Ecu in 1992. (See Heinz Kramer, "The European Community's Response to the New Eastern Europe," *Journal of Common Market Studies*, 213–244, especially 221–226.) TACIS stands for Technical Assistance to the Commonwealth of Independent States. Its budget amounted to 450 million Ecu in 1992.

[93] Edward Mortimer, *European Security after the Cold War*, Adelphi paper no. 271 (London: International Institute for Strategic Studies, 1992), p. 21.

[94] See Jackie Gower, "EC Relations with Central and Eastern Europe," in Juliet Lodge, *The European Community and the Challenge of the Future* (New York: St. Martin's Press, 1993, 2nd edn), pp. 289–290.

[95] Commission of the EC, *Association Agreements with the Countries of Central and Eastern Europe: A General Outline*, COM (90) 398 (Brussels 1990); Commission of the EC, *Association Agreements with Poland, Czechoslovakia and Hungary, Background Briefs* (Brussels, 1992). After the dissolution of Czechoslovakia, separate negotiations were conducted between the EU and the Czech and Slovak Republics.

Romania and Bulgaria signed similar association agreements with the EU in 1993.[96]

During the Copenhagen Summit in June 1993, the EU offered more formal political ties and greater market access. New vehicles for cooperation – so-called "association councils" composed of foreign ministers of the Twelve and their counterparts in the "associate" states – were set up. Foreign ministers also agreed to an Anglo-Italian plan for formal cooperation at international conferences and joint foreign-policy actions with the associate states. A year later, German Foreign Minister Klaus Kinkel announced a comprehensive program for a European Union *Ostpolitik* and pledged to promote it during Germany's presidency of the Union which started on July 1, 1994. Kinkel stressed in particular the need to bring the Ukraine rapidly within the European cooperation system and to defuse tensions between Kiev and Moscow. Kinkel justified such a policy by saying that "the economic crisis [in the Ukraine] and the tensions with Russia affect us directly ... They could have far-reaching consequences."[97] After two years of negotiations, Russia signed an agreement with the Community during the EU Summit on Corfu in June 1994. The agreement removed quotas on most Russian exports except some textiles and steel products, and set forth an intention to undertake negotiations on a free-trade agreement in 1998. Similar cooperation agreements are being negotiated with the Ukraine, Byelorussia, and Kazakhstan.[98]

Further EU concessions to Eastern Europe included promises to phase out gradually limits on imports of so-called "sensitive" goods (iron, steel, farm products, chemicals, textiles, clothing, and footwear) from the East and the adoption in May 1995 of a so-called "white paper" on Eastern Europe. The 300-page paper was addressed to Poland, Hungary, the Czech Republic, Slovakia, Bulgaria, and Romania and constituted a specific road-map for these countries to align their

---

[96] The association agreements sought to establish not only gradual market integration but also wide-ranging cooperation that included industrial collaboration aimed at structural change, promotion of scientific research and technological development, support of vocational training and higher education, cooperation in the energy, environmental, and telecommunications sectors, regional development, and cooperation in the fight against money laundering and drug trafficking. See Heinz Kramer, "The European Community's Response to the New Eastern Europe," 229–230.

[97] Quoted in Quentin Peel, "Bonn and Paris plan EU Ostpolitik," *Financial Times* (March 25, 1994), 2.

[98] Germany's sensitivity to the migration issue can be explained by its proximity to Eastern Europe. There is little doubt that Germany would bear the main cost of massive emigration from the East. See Klaus Manfrass, "Europe: South–North or East–West Migration?," *International Migration Review* 26 (Summer 1992), 389.

economies to the internal market as a step towards full membership of the European Union.

This remarkable flurry of initiatives notwithstanding, the political will in the EU to carry out plans for further integration cooled markedly in 1995. There are two simple reasons, both of which are consistent with the logic of the externality argument. First, the early market concessions of the EU were successful in warding off the threat of mass migration. The Union's share of former Comecon countries' exports and imports rose from 20 percent in 1988 to almost 50 percent in 1992 and has grown continuously ever since.[99] Increased trade, in turn, led to brisk export-led economic growth that helped to re-establish a semblance of order and stability in the East. Second, in view of this success it was not clear why the EU would have had an incentive to deepen integration with the East. The price of continuing the process of enlargement no longer appeared worth the marginal benefit. The European Commission calculated that it would cost the enormous sum of Ecu 38 billion ($47 billion) in aid to extend regional and social policies of the EU to the countries of Eastern and Central Europe.[100] This meant that Greece, Ireland, Spain, and Portugal risked losing generous payments from Brussels, and that taxpayers, particularly in Germany, would be asked to foot the additional bill of enlargement. The cost promised to increase significantly if the Common Agricultural Policy (CAP) were extended, because subsidies would have to be paid to Eastern farmers. Alternatively, the EU would have to reform the CAP, reducing farmers' reliance on price support before proceeding with enlargement. However such a move was likely to be foiled by powerful farmer lobbies in the West. Enlargement would also necessitate institutional reforms including the widening of majority voting, a change that was vehemently opposed by Britain. None of these steps were politically palatable. Unsurprisingly, a senior Commission official noted in the mid-1990s that "the [current] level of seriousness about enlargement is not minimal, it simply does not exist."[101]

Supply of integration

Chapter 3 argued that integration is most likely to succeed when two supply conditions are satisfied in addition to the demand condition. There are two primary supply conditions: first, "commitment

---

[99] See Eurostat, *Balance of Payments, Monthly Statistics*, various issues.
[100] Lionel Barber, "Brussels Keeps Shut the Gates to the East," *Financial Times* (November 16, 1995), 17.
[101] Quoted in *ibid.*, 17.

institutions" such as centralized monitoring and third-party enforcement enhance the chances of sustained cooperation by acting as constraints on member states in circumstances where self-help measures alone are insufficient to prevent reneging of contractual obligations. Second, the presence of an undisputed leader state among the group of countries seeking closer ties serves as focal point in the coordination of rules, regulations, and policies; it also helps to ease distributional tensions by assuming the role of regional paymaster.

The European Union satisfies both of these conditions. It possesses the most far-reaching commitment institutions of any recent regional integration scheme and it benefits from the presence of Germany, which, in the process of deepening, has provided critical institutional leadership and has been willing to ease distributional tensions through generous side-payments.

Two EU institutions, in particular, are responsible for monitoring and enforcing Community obligations: the Commission and the European Court of Justice. An important task of the Commission is to see that individuals, companies, and member states do not act in ways which run counter to the treaties or EU secondary law.[102] For example, if firms enter into an agreement that restricts competition, the Commission may seek a voluntary termination of such an agreement or issue a formal decision prohibiting it and inflicting fines on the parties to the agreement. It can also take member states to task by demanding termination of an infringement, or by taking the matter to the Court of Justice for a final decision.[103]

The Court also plays a key monitoring and enforcing role in integration. Most notably, it has improved the effectiveness of the EU enforcement mechanism through two judge-made doctrines: supremacy and direct effect.[104] The supremacy doctrine holds that EU law has primacy over national legislation; and the direct-effect doctrine (discussed above) provides that EU law is directly applicable to the citizens

---

[102] Treaty and secondary law has been considerably broadened in scope over the years. It was originally confined to issues dealing with trade in a narrow sense. Today it regulates a wide range of areas, including competition, intellectual and commercial property, public procurement, state aid, telecommunications, banking, financial services, company accounts and taxes, indirect taxation, technical rules and standards, consumer protection, health and safety, transport, environment, research and development, social welfare, education, and even political participation.

[103] Swann, *The Economics of the Common Market*, p. 50. Besides the Commission, member states also have the right to bring cases to the Court. In practice, however, legal proceedings initiated directly by member states against each other are relatively rare. See Ulrich Everling, "The Member States of the European Community Before their Court of Justice," *European Law Review* 9 (1984), 215–241.

[104] See Burley and Mattli, "Europe Before the Court: A Political Theory of Legal Integration."

of the member states without prior intervention by their governments. Direct effect authorizes private parties (firms and individuals) to seek enforcement of treaty obligations against member governments ("vertical" enforcement) and also against private parties ("horizontal" enforcement).[105] Individuals have even been empowered recently to pursue legal actions against member governments that fail to implement community directives (i.e., secondary legislation) correctly or in a timely fashion.[106] This direct participation of private parties in the enforcement of the Treaty of Rome, a treaty of international law, is without precedent. It has greatly improved the Court's role as central monitoring agent. By the same token, it has increased the Court's caseload. In response, the EU added a new institution, the Court of First Instance, to its enforcement system in 1988. This new Court was established to hear and give judgement on a number of specific types of legal action, particularly on complaints or disputes arising from the EU's competition policy.[107] Finally, in a notable step to further the Court's effectiveness, the EU empowered the ECJ to impose heavy penalties upon member states that fail to comply with Court rulings.

The second supply condition refers to institutional leadership. Here Germany has played a key role, particularly since the mid-1970s. By then Germany had begun moving into a league of world economic powers of which the only other members were the United States and Japan.[108] Germany had weathered the economic crisis triggered by the oil-shocks considerably better than any other European economy. "The picture that emerge[d was one with] Germany firmly at the top ... rather than [one of] an association of more or less equal states progressing harmoniously and happily towards Union."[109]

Germany's economy exhibited greater productivity than the other European economies in the sectors most threatened by international competition (steels, textiles, clothing, etc.); it was home to a higher proportion of the most dynamic industries (equipment goods, chemicals, and agrifood industries) and it showed continuing capacity to

---

[105] See case 36/74, *B.N.O. Walrave and L. J. N. Koch* v. *Association Union Cycliste Internationale, European Court Reports, (ECR)* (1974), 1405; and case 149/77, *Gabrielle Defrenne* v. *Société Anonyme Belge de Navigation Aérienne Sabena, ECR* (1978), 1365.

[106] See case 152/84, *Marshall* v. *Southampton and South West Hampshire Area Health Authority (Teaching), Common Market Law Review* 1 (1986), p. 688; and case 152/84, *ECR* (1986), 737.

[107] Clive Archer and Fiona Butler, *The European Community Structure and Process* (New York: St. Martin's Press 1992), p. 37.

[108] Peter Ludlow, *The Making of the European Monetary System* (London: Butterworth, 1982), p. 8.

[109] *Ibid.*

specialize and concentrate on products with a high technology input.[110]
The strength of the German economy was reflected by the value of the
Deutsche Mark (DM) which rose over 30 percent against the currencies
of Germany's twenty-three major trading partners between 1972 and
1977.[111]

The German economy has remained the strongest in terms of gross
domestic product (GDP); its represents almost one-quarter of the
Community's GDP and contributes about one-quarter to the EU's
external and internal trade. Germany is the main trading partner of
thirteen EU member states, as well as Switzerland, Turkey, and the
former Yugoslavia; and it is the second most important economic
partner after Russia for most East European states. Germany's centrality
to Europe is of course not a new fact; John Maynard Keynes wrote
before the First World War: "Round Germany as a central support the
rest of the European economy system group[s] itself, and on the
prosperity and enterprise of Germany the prosperity of the rest of the
Continent mainly depend[s]."[112]

German economic preeminence is bound to translate into political
influence within the Union. Germany has indeed been the key policy
initiator and institutional agenda setter in a wide range of issue areas.
For example, it is credited with launching the European Monetary
System, "arguably the first major act of German leadership in the
history of the European Community."[113] It played central roles in the
initial outline of the budget compromise at the Stuttgart Council
summit in June 1983; in relaunching the EMU at the Hanover summit
in June 1988; and in calling for an inter-governmental conference (IGC)
on political union paralleling the proposed EMU.[114] Germany's contribution to the institutional architecture of the Union further includes
the strengthening of common macroeconomic, social, and environmental policies, as well as the introduction of concepts such as

---

[110] See Commission of the European Communities, Directorate-General for Economic
and Financial Affairs, *Changes in Industrial Structure in the European Economies since the
Oil Crisis, 1973–78* (Luxemburg: Office for Official Publications of the EC, 1979).

[111] Ludlow, *The Making of the European Monetary System*, p. 8.

[112] Quoted in Simon Bulmer, "Germany and European Integration: Toward Economic
and Political Dominance?," in Carl Lankowski (ed.), *Germany and the European
Community* (New York: St. Martin's Press, 1993), p. 88. See also William Wallace,
"Germany's Unavoidable Central Role: Beyond Myths and Traumas," in Wolfgang
Wessels and E. Regelsberger (eds.), *The Federal Republic of Germany and Beyond*
(Bonn: Europa Union Verlag, 1988), pp. 276–285.

[113] Ludlow, *The Making of the European Monetary System*, p. 290.

[114] Peter Katzenstein, "United Germany in an Integrating Europe," in Peter Katzenstein
(ed.), *Tamed Power: Germany in Europe* (Ithaca: Cornell University Press, forthcoming).

subsidiarity[115] and multitiered governance.[116] Another illustration of Germany's influence is the widespread acceptance of the Bundesbank as the model of statute for the European Central Bank, and the adoption by the Union of the "Rhineland model of capitalism," a form of economic liberalism with strong provisions for social policy cushioning.[117] German influence is also felt in the field of technical standards. The German national standards-setting organization Deutsches Institut für Normen (DIN) has long set the tone in a wide range of European industries. DIN's influence is also felt indirectly through its active participation in European standards-setting organizations such as CEN and CENELEC.[118] A measure of this indirect influence is DIN's control of the largest number of secretariats for technical committees within CEN and CENELEC.[119] For example, in March 1989, DIN held 75 out of 212 CEN/CENELEC secretariats for technical committees, that is, 35.4 percent. The British Standards Institution (BSI) held 18.4 percent and the Association Française de Normalisation (AFNOR) 17.9 per cent.

This shaping of EU institutional arrangements by Germany may favor German interests more directly than those of other member states, thus possibly giving rise to distributional concerns. Simon Bulmer notes:

The adoption of German institutional rules (e.g. on EMU) and norms (e.g. subsidiarity) mobilizes a procedural bias that should facilitate the articulation of German interests. There is, of course, a time-lag in how this institutional power comes into play. Shaping the EU's constitutive politics in one time period will only mobilize bias enabling Germany to advance its interests in the regulative politics of the EU in a subsequent time period.[120]

For example, German insistence on fiscal rectitude in the Maastricht

---

[115] Subsidiarity means that the Community should take action only if the objective of a proposed action cannot be sufficiently achieved by the member states at the domestic level.

[116] See Simon Bulmer and William Paterson, "Germany in the European Union: Gentle Giant or Emergent Leader?," *International Affairs* 72 (1996), 9–32. On the broader influence of Germany's pragmatic version of monetary policy, see Kathleen McNamara, *A Currency of Ideas: Monetary Politics in the European Union* (Ithaca: Cornell University Press, 1998).

[117] Simon Bulmer and William Paterson, *The Federal Republic of Germany and the European Community* (London: Allen & Unwin, 1987), p. 12; and Michael Hodges and Stephen Woolcock, "Atlantic Capitalism versus Rhine Capitalism in the EC," *West European Politics* 16 (July 1993), 329–344.

[118] European Standards Committee and European Electrical Standards Committee; both are known by their French acronyms.

[119] Stephen Woolcock, Michael Hodges, and Kristin Schreiber, *Britain, Germany and 1992* (London: Pinter, 1991), pp. 48–49.

[120] Simon Bulmer, "Shaping the Rules? The Constitutive Politics of the European Union and German Power," in Katzenstein (ed.), *Tamed Power*.

convergence criteria will come into play in the run-up to the decision on who proceeds to stage three of EMU beginning in 1999.[121]

Nevertheless, German leadership has largely been gentle rather than imposing.[122] Germany strongly prefers to build consensus from within the Union and, if necessary, offers concessions to preserve that consensus. To avoid the risk of political isolation in Brussels, Germany has been careful to launch nearly all its initiatives in tandem with other major EU partners.[123] The EMS was presented as a Franco-German project, as were proposals for an intergovernmental treaty on foreign policy coordination, tabled at the 1985 Milan Council summit. The German initiative for reviving the integration project, originally put forth by Foreign Minister Hans-Dietrich Genscher in 1981, became the Genscher–Colombo initiative, once Italian support was canvassed.[124] Similarly, Chancellor Helmut Kohl's letter of April 1990 to the Irish presidency, calling for an IGC on political union, was co-signed by the French President Mitterand.

Leadership is also expressed by Germany's willingness to ease distributional tensions and act as regional paymaster. Germany is by far the largest net contributor to the EU budget (measured both in absolute and per capita terms) which redistributes substantial resources, notably through the European Regional Development Fund, the European Social Fund, and more recently the Cohesion Fund. The primary beneficiaries of these funds are the poorer EU members. The existence of the funds depends much on continuing German prosperity and generosity. Germany's net contribution to the budget has increased from DM 10.5 billion in 1987 to DM 22 billion in 1992. It is estimated to exceed DM 30 billion by the end of this decade. In 1996, Germany's financial contribution to the EU amounted to about two-thirds of the net income of the Union, double the relative size of the German GDP in the EU.[125]

In conclusion, it is worth pondering why Germany has assumed the role of institutional leader and regional paymaster. In part, the answer is that Germany acts out of economic self-interest. Germany depends

---

[121] *Ibid.*

[122] "Gentle giant" is how Simon Bulmer characterizes Germany in his writings. See p. 103, note 116.

[123] Jeffrey Anderson, "Hard Interests and Soft Power, and Germany's Changing Role in Europe," in Katzenstein (ed.), *Tamed Power.*

[124] Bulmer, "Germany and European Integration: Toward Economic and Political Dominance?"

[125] Katzenstein, "United Germany in an Integrating Europe," p. 32. See also Michael Shackleton, "The Budget of the European Community," in Juliet Lodge (ed.), *The European Community and the Challenge of the Future* (London: Pinter, 1989), pp. 129–147.

economically on its European partners as much as they depend on Germany, and thus any measure that improves stability and security in trade and investment in Europe is likely to suit Germany. For example, in the late 1970s German industrialists expressed serious concern over the continuing appreciation of the Deutsche Mark against other European currencies. Such a trend posed serious risks to German exports. A return to a fixed exchange rate regime, as proposed in the EMS, seemed in Germany's obvious interest. The EMS also promised to rid the European economies of monetary disturbances that tend to give rise to protectionist pressures, hurting German export interests.[126] More generally, unobstructed access to a single and prosperous European market is of obvious interest to Europe's most powerful and efficient economy. It enables German firms to expand through increased exports, mergers and acquisition. Regional production networks, in turn, reduce production costs and raise the international competitiveness of German firms.

However, not all interests are purely economic. In the early years, German elites embraced European integration to gain international rehabilitation and establish an equality of sovereign right between Germany and its neighbors. Later, participation in the deepening process of integration reinforced commitment to values such as support for basic human rights, democracy, social justice, and the rule of law.[127] Interestingly, Germany has been promoting these same values vigorously of late at the supranational level, pressing for greater transparency and accountability, insisting that human and social rights be respected, and pushing for greater empowerment of the European Parliament.

Integration and efficiency: a concluding note

A main argument of this chapter has been that integration serves to economize on trade and investment transaction costs. If this efficiency view of integration is correct, it is expected that the completion of the Single European Market program will, for example, provide an important stimulus to inward investment flows. Recent studies have confirmed such a prediction. The EU absorbed 44 percent of global foreign investment flows in the early 1990s, compared to 28 percent in the mid-1980s.[128]

---

[126] Ludlow, *The Making of the European Monetary System*, pp. 35–47 and 73.

[127] Rudolf Hrbek and Wolfgang Wessels, "National-Interessen der Bundesrepublik Deutschland und der Integrationsprozess," in R. Hrbek and W. Wessels (eds.), *EG-Mitgliedschaft: Ein Vitales Interesse der Bundesrepublik Deutschland?* (Bonn: Europa Union Verlag, 1984), pp. 29–69.

[128] See Commission of the European Communities, *The Impact and Effectiveness of the Single Market* (Luxemburg: Office for Official Publications of the EC, 1996), p. 4.

The efficiency view of integration also holds that the extension of the Union's rules and enforcement mechanisms through EU membership will mitigate the risks of investing in the periphery. And as these institutional safeguards lower the risks, the flow of transnational capital into the periphery should increase. What is the evidence? Is EU membership positively related to growth in capital inflows holding other factors constant?

I test this using a balanced panel. The spatial temporal domain includes sixteen European states for the years 1970 to 1994.[129] During the chosen time period, six of the sixteen states entered the union (the UK, Ireland, and Denmark in 1973; Greece in 1981; Spain and Portugal in 1986). Of the other ten states, six were members throughout the time period covered (Germany, France, Italy, and the Benelux), and four were non-members for the entire time period (Finland, Norway, Sweden, and Austria).

The dependent variable is the percentage change in foreign direct investment in constant dollars. The primary independent variable represents the first five years of membership of the European Union. This is a dummy variable coded as one in the year a state joins the European Union and the following four years. All other cases are coded as zero. Two control variables were added: real interest rates (calculated as discount rate minus inflation rate) and economic growth.[130]

Combining cross-sectional and time-series observations in a single analysis poses a number of potential estimation problems. Most importantly, this type of analysis requires simultaneous correction for temporal autocorrelation and heteroskedasticity across cases. In order to accomplish this, I use a technique developed by Kmenta which he calls a "cross-sectionally heteroskedastic and timewise autocorrelated model."[131] In my use of the Kmenta technique, however, I assume that the serial correlation of the errors follows the same process across cases. The assumption in pooled series analysis is that similar patterns exist across cases. This should be true not only of the relationships among variables, but also of the process underlying serial correlation.[132] Thus,

---

[129] The analysis begins with the year 1970 because data for the 1960s are sketchy and incomplete.

[130] Data on foreign direct investment, discount rates, inflation rates, and economic growth were obtained from the International Monetary Fund's *International Financial Statistics*, various issues.

[131] Jan Kmenta, *Elements of Econometrics* (New York: Macmillan, 1986), pp. 618–622.

[132] Nathaniel Beck and Jonathan Katz. "What To Do (And Not To Do) With Time-Series Cross-Section Data," *American Political Science Review* 89 (1995), 634–647; and N. Beck and J. Katz, "Nuisance Versus Substance: Specifying and Estimating Time-Series Cross-Section Models," *Political Analysis* (1996).

Table 4.3. *Effects of new membership in the European Union and economic factors on growth in foreign direct investment*

(Dependent variable: growth in foreign direct investment)

Economic growth (prior year)	Real interest rates	New membership in EU	Constant	R-square	N
3.873[a]	1.111[a]	13.013[b]	0.028	0.24	330
(0.637)	(0.277)	(5.245)			

Notes: each cell contains the estimated coefficient on the first line and its corresponding standard error below.
[a] indicates statistical significance at the 0.001 level
[b] indicates statistical significance at the 0.01 level

I calculate a single value of "rho" to be used for each cross-section. The results are reported in table 4.3.

As expected, economic growth and real interest rates are positively related to increased rates of foreign investment. The coefficients are positive and the relationships are statistically significant at the 0.001 level. Most importantly, the first five years of membership in the European Union are positively related to an increase in foreign investment inflows independent of economic factors. The coefficient for new membership in the EU is positive and statistically significant at the 0.01 level.[133]

The statistical evidence presented here can be plausibly attributed to membership only if factors not yet considered can be ruled out as having had an impact on investment flows. One counterfactual hypothesis is that government intervention in the form of enticing depreciation allowances, investment grants, and favorable performance requirements may have attracted sudden large inflows of capital. However, there is little reason to believe that this consideration was important. The general evidence clearly suggests that incentives written into liberal investment legislation do not induce large foreign direct investment (FDI) inflows by themselves.[134] In the European context, Portugal, for

[133] It would be desirable to run the analysis differentiating intra-EU investment (i.e., investment originating within the EU) from extra-EU investment (i.e., investment originating outside the EU). However, reliable data are available only from the 1980s, which renders a test for the entire period impossible.
[134] See United Nations Conference on Trade and Development (Programme on Transnational Corporations), *World Investment Report 1993: Transnational Corporations and Integrated International Production* (New York: United Nations Publications, 1993), p. 216.

example, introduced a far-reaching foreign investment promotion program in 1980 which provided a variety of fiscal and financial incentives in the form of tax holidays, interest rates subsidies, and grants.[135] Its effect on foreign investment was very small compared to the big jump in FDI which occurred subsequent to membership. Another example is the Spanish case. Two royal decrees were introduced in Spain in 1981 to liberalize foreign direct investment. They did not significantly increase Spain's capital base. Output remained stagnant, with employment declining, inflation rampant and the current account heavily in the red.[136] The turning point came only in 1986 after its accession to the Treaty of Rome. FDI soared from $2 billion in 1985 to $3.4 billion during Spain's first year of membership and $4.7 billion in 1987.[137]

3   The Zollverein

In the early years of the nineteenth century, Germany was fragmented into over three hundred independent kingdoms, electorates, duchies, imperial cities, ecclesiastical territories, and estates of imperial kings.[138] These territories had enjoyed increasing independence ever since the close of the Middle Ages, but were enabled to claim full sovereignty only with the abolition of the Holy Roman Empire in 1806.[139] After the defeat of Napoleon in 1815, Germany's political entities were consolidated into 38 states, which grouped themselves into the German Confederation (Deutscher Bund).[140] This union of sovereign states

135 Peter Buckley and Patrick Artisien, "Policy Issues of Intra-EC Direct Investment: British, French and German Multinationals in Greece, Portugal and Spain, with special reference to Employment Effects," *Journal of Common Market Studies* 26 (December 1987), 222.

136 J. B. Donges and K. E. Schatz, "The Iberian Countries Facing EC Membership: Starting Conditions for their Industries," *Weltwirtschaftliches Archiv* 121 (1985), 756–778.

137 See Tom Burns, "The Open-Door Policy Continues," *Financial Times* (October 21, 1992), p. 6 of *Times* special Survey on European business locations. See also Buckley and Artisien, "Policy Issues of Intra-EC Direct Investment," and P. Buckley and P. Artisien, *North–South Direct Investment in the European Communities* (London: Macmillan, 1987).

138 William Otto Henderson, *The Zollverein* (Chicago: Quadrangle Books, 1958, 2nd edn), p. 1.

139 Arnold Price, *The Evolution of the Zollverein*, pp. 12–19.

140 See Hermann Oncken and F. E. M. Saemisch (eds.), *Vorgeschichte und Begründung des Deutschen Zollvereins 1815–1834. Akten der Staaten des Deutschen Bundes und der Europäischen Mächte* (Berlin: Reimar Hobbing, 1934), vols. I–III; especially vol. I, section 2, entitled, "Die Verhandlungen am Bundestag, die Wiener Konferenzen und die süddeutschen Einigungsbestrebungen," pp. 297–548. For a carefully detailed study of the Vienna Final Conferences, see Karl Ludwig Aegidi, *Aus der Vorzeit des Zollvereins. Beitrag zur Deutschen Geschichte* (Hamburg: Noyes & Geister, 1865).

(*Staatenbund* as opposed to *Bundesstaat*), where unanimity was required for joint action, proved utterly inadequate to provide for either economic or political unity. Political jealousies and the desire for independence blocked any attempt at economic unification. In a period where income taxes were non-existent, and customs and excise duties were the main sources of state revenues, the submission to a common customs system with an independent customs administration would have amounted to giving away a vital part of sovereignty.[141] Not surprisingly, the many conferences of the postwar period which were convened to discuss the rationalization of the German economy came to nought.

> It is ... almost unbelievable that negotiations were kept up for so many years, and it is easily understood why they failed in their purpose ... [E]verybody was thinking first of his own state and hardly anybody ever considered the interests of the union they were going to establish, took broad views, or pursued a farsighted policy ... [A]ll of them refused to give up an iota of their own sovereignty.[142]

The first step towards an improvement of Germany's antiquated economic structure was taken by Prussia when it announced a customs reform in 1818 that abolished internal duties, established one single customs line along the boundaries of the monarchy, and replaced the chaotic system of over sixty different rates of customs and excises by a standardized tariff.[143] In addition, transit dues were introduced in the eastern and western parts of Prussia, which lay on important European trade routes.[144] This new customs law put Prussian state finances back on a sound basis, aided Prussian industry and commerce and thus consolidated Prussian monarchy.[145]

In 1828, Prussia formed a customs union with Hesse-Darmstadt, thus forming the nucleus of the German Zollverein. Between 1828 and

---

[141] Price, *The Evolution of the Zollverein*, p. 97.

[142] *Ibid.*, p. 90.

[143] J. A. R. Marriott and C. G. Robertson, *The Evolution of Prussia* (Oxford: Clarendon Press, 1915), p. 290.

[144] Prussia's Eastern possessions stretched from the Memel at the mouth of the Vistula to Mühlhausen in the south of the Harz mountains. They comprised East Prussia, Posen, Pomerania, Brandenburg, Saxony, and Silesia. The Western possessions included Westphalia and the Rhineland Province (from 1824). Prussia was divided by Hesse-Cassel, Brunswick, and the southern portion of Hanover.

[145] Hans-Werner Hahn, *Geschichte des Deutschen Zollvereins* (Göttingen: Vandenhoeck & Ruprecht, 1984), pp. 20–27. Emmanuel Roussakis, *Friedrich List, the Zollverein, and the Uniting of Europe* (Bruges: College of Europe, 1968), pp. 46–60. A good measure of the relative efficiency of the new law is reflected by the fact that it reduced administrative costs in Prussia to only 14 to 15 per cent of total receipts (see Price, *The Evolution of the Zollverein*, p. 121). This contrasts with rates well over 50 percent for most other states. See also August Sartorius von Waltershausen, *Deutsche Wirtschafts-geschichte 1815–1915* (Jena: Gustav Fischer, 1923, 2nd edn) esp. pp. 1–69.

Figure 4.2 Central Europe in 1815. Reprinted by permission from
The Zollverein by W. O. Henderson published by Frank Cass & Company,
900 Eastern Avenue, Ilford, Essex, England. Copyright Frank Cass & Co. Ltd.

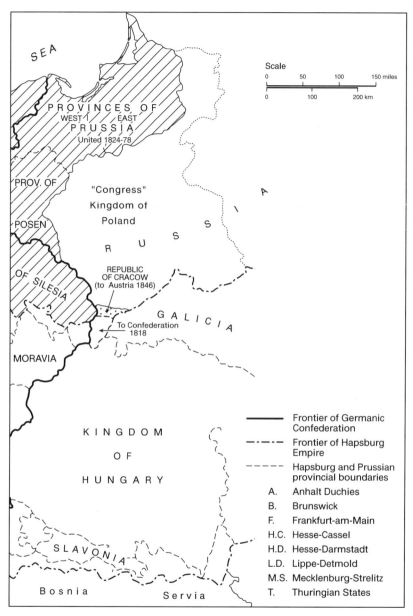

SEA

PROVINCES OF
WEST | EAST
PRUSSIA
United 1824-78

PROV. OF

POSEN

"Congress"
Kingdom of
Poland

R   U   S   S   I   A

REPUBLIC
OF CRACOW
(to Austria 1846)

OF SILESIA

GALICIA

To Confederation
1818

MORAVIA

KINGDOM

OF

HUNGARY

SLAVONIA

Bosnia   Servia

Scale

| 0 | 50 | 100 | 150 miles |
| 0 | 100 | 200 km | |

——————— Frontier of Germanic
           Confederation

—·—·—·— Frontier of Hapsburg
           Empire

— — — — Hapsburg and Prussian
           provincial boundaries

A.   Anhalt Duchies
B.   Brunswick
F.   Frankfurt-am-Main
H.C.   Hesse-Cassel
H.D.   Hesse-Darmstadt
L.D.   Lippe-Detmold
M.S.   Mecklenburg-Strelitz
T.   Thuringian States

the Seven Weeks' War of 1866, when the old Zollverein came to an end, over sixteen major states joined the German Customs Union.

The account of the process of German integration must begin with an examination of the demand-side factors of integration. The following section illustrates the key role played by German business groups in fostering economic integration. It also highlights how a new generation of transportation and production techniques catalyzed the process of integration. The study then turns to an analysis of the conditions under which political leaders acceded to the demands for integration. It concludes with an examination of the supply factors, particularly Prussian leadership, in securing the success of the process of integration.

The demand for integration

Germany's interstate commerce of the early nineteenth century was thwarted by poor communications and a multitude of antiquated trade restrictions. German roads were notoriously poor. In 1816, a traveler took no less than five hours to go by coach from Weimar to Erfurt, a distance of about twelve miles,[146] and about a week to complete the 336 miles between Berlin and Königsberg.[147]

Duties were levied not at the frontiers but on roads and rivers, at town gates and at markets. Some eighteen hundred customs frontiers existed in Germany in those years. "The Germans trade like prisoners behind prison bars," declared a Frenchman.[148] And Clive Day noted:

It was impossible to travel far on any German river without reaching a staple, where the boatsman was subject to delay, inconvenience, and considerable expense. On the Rhine, for instance, there were thirty-two stations of this character where dues were still levied in 1800. As far as regarded the effect on commerce the flow of the rivers might as well have been interrupted by cataracts.[149]

In a petition drafted in 1819 on behalf of the German Commercial and Industrial League (Deutscher Handels- und Gewerbeverein) and submitted to the German Diet, Friedrich List complained:

Thirty-eight customs boundaries cripple inland trade, and produce much the same effect as ligatures which prevent the free circulation of the blood. To make a commercial shipment from Hamburg to Austria and from Berlin to Switzerland, one must cross ten states, study ten sets of customs regulations, pay six different transit duties. He who has the misfortune to reside at a frontier where

---

[146] Sartorius von Waltershausen, *Deutsche Wirtschaftsgeschichte 1815–1915*, pp. 23–24.
[147] Roussakis, *Friedrich List*, pp. 30–31.
[148] Quoted in Henderson, *The Zollverein*, p. 21.
[149] Clive Day, *A History of Commerce* (New York: Longmans, 1914), p. 347.

three or four states touch each other, passes his entire life bickering with customs officials; he has not got a fatherland.[150]

Comparing conditions in Germany with those of France, List went on to comment that German businessmen "cast envious glances across the Rhine where, from the Channel to the Mediterranean, from the Rhine to the Pyrenees, from the Dutch to the Italian borders, a great nation carries on its trade over free rivers and free roads without ever meeting a custom-house official."[151]

Similar views were expressed in a petition dated July 1819 and signed by some 5,000 German workers, factory-owners, and merchants. In the same year, Rhineland merchants petitioned the King of Prussia to encourage a revival of German industry by removing all customs barriers within Germany and by simply levying duties on land frontiers and at ports.[152] The Commercial and Industrial League set up a network of liaisons all over Germany, printed pamphlets and memoranda on economic unification and published a periodical – the *Organ of the German Commercial and Industrial Union* (*Organ für den deutschen Handels- und Fabrikantenstand*).[153] List himself pleaded the League's cause with political leaders and wrote numerous articles, stressing the economic foundations of the project.[154] In several instances, business exerted pressure on political leaders by threatening to emigrate or by exporting capital and setting up subsidiaries in the large Prussian market.[155]

German business kept pressing for deeper integration even after political leaders had signed the treaty establishing a German customs union. Countervailing duties, state monopolies, differences in internal excises, lack of a uniform system of weights, measures, and coinage, and the absence of a single code of commercial law still hampered commerce in Germany. The insistence of demands for deeper integration grew especially as new technologies increased the opportunity cost of transacting in the unfinished German market. Higher opportunity cost translated into greater pressure on political leaders to adjust the scale of

---

[150] The petition is reprinted in Oncken and Saemisch (eds.), *Vorgeschichte und Begründung des Deutschen Zollvereins, 1815–1834*, vol. I, pp. 320–324. A translation of the petition can be found in Margaret Hirst, *Life of Friedrich List and Selections from his Writings* (London: Smith, Elder & Co., 1909), pp. 137–144.

[151] Hirst, *Life of Friedrich List and Selections from his Writings*, p. 140.

[152] Henderson, *The Zollverein*, p. 27.

[153] Price, *The Evolution of the Zollverein*, p. 37.

[154] See Friedrich List, *Schriften, Reden, Briefe*, edited by the Friedrich List Gesellschaft (Berlin: Reiman Hobbing, 1927–1936).

[155] See, for example, Pierre Benaerts, *Les Origines de la Grande Industrie Allemande* (Paris: F. H. Turot, 1933), p. 53.

political and economic organization to the level implied by the new techniques.

Two areas of innovation affecting the costs of transacting in the German market deserve special mention: improvements in river transport and the introduction of the railway. The invention of the steamboat revolutionized river traffic well before it affected overseas trade. As early as 1816, a steamboat made its way from Rotterdam to Cologne.[156] By the middle of the nineteenth century, steamships were six times as numerous as sailing vessels on Germany's main rivers. Paddle-driven steamboats, introduced in the 1830s, were soon replaced by much faster screw-driven boats. The efficiency of steamboats was later further enhanced by the compound expansion engine and the Parson turbine. And as river traffic grew, river channels were cleared and deepened.[157] Traffic on water was further eased in the first half of the nineteenth century by an ambitious canal-building program that created a comprehensive network of waterways.

Important as river steam-navigation was in lowering transport costs and in extending the home market, it was soon overshadowed by the development of the railway.[158] The railways brought what Pollard called "the single most substantial alteration of the earth's surface undertaken by man up to that time."[159] Their advantages over the traditional means of transportation lay in speed, low cost, and regularity of service. German railway construction began in 1835 with the opening of a four-mile-long suburban line from Nürnberg to Fürth, in Bavaria. It was followed by the Berlin–Potsdam railway. Both lines were built and run by private companies.[160] Fifteen years later, the aggregate mileage of the German railway system amounted to 3,747 miles of railway. Roussakis notes: "Railway lines crossed the country from north to south and east to west, providing links between regional centers of growing importance. Raw materials could now be carried more quickly and cheaply to factories; this stimulated the growth of concentrated, large-scale production. New markets for industrial and agricultural products were opened up, and old markets became more accessible."[161]

The railway served not only to reduce transaction costs and widen markets, but also provided the single most powerful stimulus to Germany's industrial development and growth. It created an unprecedented demand for iron as well as other materials used in the manufac-

---

[156] Henderson, *The Zollverein*, p. 148.
[157] Roussakis, *Friedrich List, The Zollverein, and the Uniting of Europe*, p. 81.
[158] *Ibid.*
[159] Pollard, *European Economic Integration 1815–1970*, p. 51.
[160] Henderson, *The Zollverein*, p. 146.
[161] Roussakis, *Friedrich List*, p. 81

ture of cars and construction of fixed facilities; moreover, the railway needed these goods in a wide variety of finished forms, ranging from relatively simple items like rails and wheels to complicated engines and machines, all of which gave a special push to the metalworking and engineering trades.[162]

In short, the integrating effect of the railway is beyond doubt. Wilhelm Raabe summarized the importance of the railway well when he wrote that "the German Empire was founded with the construction of the first railway between Nürnberg and Fürth."[163] Railway shares were thought of as "bills drawn upon Germany's future unity."[164] The effect of the railway and similar innovations was to "shrink" distances and thus increase the opportunity cost of transacting in segmented markets. Sooner or later, political leaders had to yield to business pressure and trade away a measure of independence for new institutional arrangements enabling German merchants and producers to reach levels of competitiveness equal to those of their British and French counterparts.

The enlargement issue

Willingness by the political leaders of the various German kingdoms, electorates, duchies, and free cities to accede to demands for integration was never automatic. Henderson writes:

The notion that ... [the Zollverein] was set up as the result of the rise of a German national consciousness and was a touching example of brotherly co-operation on the part of the various states will not bear examination for a moment ... The states concerned fought for their own narrow interests and many of them joined the Zollverein only when economic depression ... made further resistance to Prussia impossible.[165]

Benaerts likewise observes that the formation of the Zollverein was not the spontaneous national movement which legendary German history ascribed to it.[166] He points out that, on the contrary, the rulers of the many kingdoms, electorates, and duchies exhibited the most narrow-minded spirit of *Kleinstaaterei*, clinging to their sovereign rights and obstructing proposals for economic unification till empty treasuries

---

[162] David Landes, *The Unbound Prometheus: Technological Change and Industrial Development in Western Europe from 1750 to the Present* (Cambridge: Cambridge University Press, 1969), p. 153.

[163] Quoted in Ludwig Pohle, *Das Deutsche Wirtschaftsleben seit Beginn des 19. Jahrhunderts* (Leipzig und Berlin: Verlag B. G. Teubner, 6th edn, 1930), p. 11.

[164] In the original: "Wechsel ausgestellt auf Deutschlands Einheit." Quote by the poet Karl Beck in Heinrich von Treitschke, *Deutsche Geschichte im neunzehnten Jahrhundert* (Leipzig: S. Hirzel, 4th edn, 1887), vol. IV, p. 597.

[165] Henderson, *The Zollverein*, p. 95.

[166] Benaerts, *Les Origines de la Grande Industrie Allemande*, p. 63.

forced them to seek membership in the Zollvereins.[167] (See summary table 4.4).[168]

Economic deterioration in the various territories was in most cases a direct consequence of the construction of a single Prussian market. Prussia's external tariff contributed to the economic weakening of neighboring territories by raising the prices of imported manufactured goods on which they heavily depended and by limiting the access of their exports to the large Prussian market. Thus isolated and destitute, these small countries faced the unenviable choice of remaining poor and autonomous or trading some of their sovereignty for market access and prosperity.

Hesse-Darmstadt was the first state to wake up to the inevitable. Its linen industry and viticulture were badly injured by the loss of Prussian markets. Cheap foreign manufactured articles grew scarce.[169] The introduction in 1824 of a boundary tariff system failed to stem the economic decline. Owing to the length of the frontier, the cost of maintaining the new customs line absorbed most of the collected revenues. Smuggling began to flourish and seriously compete with legitimate trade.[170] Hesse-Darmstadt approached Prussia in 1825 for an economic agreement. Three years later, a treaty was signed establishing a joint customs union.[171] It greatly benefitted Hesse-Darmstadt's state finances through increased customs revenues and provided a much-needed boost to its economy.

The creation of the Prussia–Hesse-Darmstadt union was received with great apprehension in neighboring states. The British envoy Mil-

---

[167] *Ibid.*, pp. 63–72. For similar conclusions, see also Price, *The Evolution of the Zollverein*, pp. 252–255; and Roussakis, *Friedrich List*, p. 16.

[168] A comparison between the economic situation of states prior to membership and after joining the Zollverein cannot be made by looking at economic growth rates, since no such data exist for the period. The examination thus relies on historical accounts. The information given in parentheses in table 4.4 refers to the page numbers of four major studies on the Zollverein. H refers to Henderson, *The Zollverein*; B refers to Benaerts, *Les Origines de la Grande Industrie Allemande*; P refers to Price, *The Evolution of the Zollverein*; and HH refers to Hans-Werner Hahn, *Geschichte des Deutschen Zollvereins* (Göttingen: Vandenhoeck & Ruprecht, 1984).

[169] Henderson, *The Zollverein*, p. 50.

[170] Price, *The Evolution of the Zollverein*, p. 203.

[171] The best discussion of the causes and consequences of the adhesion of Hesse-Darmstadt and the remaining Middle German states to the Prussian Zollverein is Hans-Werner Hahn, *Wirtschaftliche Integration im 19. Jahrhundert: Die hessischen Staaten und der Deutsche Zollverein* (Göttingen: Vandenhoeck & Ruprecht, 1982), especially pp. 145–246. See also H. Schmitt, *Die Begründung des Preussisch-Hessischen Zollvereins vom 14. Februar 1828* (Giessen: Philosophische Fakultät der hessischen Ludwigs Universität, 1926); and Christian Eckert, "Zur Vorgeschichte des deutschen Zollvereins. Die preussisch-hessische Zollunion vom 14. Februar 1828," in Gustav Schmoller (ed.), *Jahrbuch für Gesetzgebung, Verwaltung and Volkswirtschaft im Deutschen Reich* 26 (Leipzig: Dunker & Humblot, 1902), pp. 51–102.

Table 4.4. *The timing of application for membership of the Zollverein*

State	Year of accession to Prussian Customs Union	Economic situation just prior to membership of the Zollverein	Economic situation after joining the Zollverein
Hesse-Darmstadt	1828	Economic decline; severe financial crisis. (H:50, B:35, P:203, HH:44)	Great improvement of economic conditions and state finances. (P:224, HH:47–48)
Hesse-Cassel	1831	Economic distress leading to revolution of 1830. (H:81, P:175)	Recovery. (B:58, 170)
Thuringian States	1834	Deplorable economic and financial situation; occasionally social and political unrest. (H:81, B:53, P:250, 252, HH:58–68)	Extended markets permit expansion of local industries and development of new ones. Big increase in customs and excise revenues. (H:141, 180, P:170, 190)
Kingdom of Saxony	1834	Economic hardship; social unrest. (P:176, 250, HH:58–68)	(See Thuringian States)
Bavaria and Württemberg	1834	Inefficient customs union; economic difficulties. (H:58, P:79, HH:74)	Expansion of trade into northern Germany; expansion of industry. Steep increase in customs revenues. (H:138, 141, 186, 213, 227, B:194, HH:77)
Baden	1835	Economic hardship. (H:105)	Agriculture and commerce revive; sugar refining introduced. (H:110, B:170)
Nassau	1835	Economic decline. (H:111, HH:85)	Economic recovery. (H:111)
Frankfurt-am-Main	1836	Trade depression. (H:111, HH:85)	Booming trade. (H:121, HH:87)
Luxemburg	1842	Weak financial position. (H:150)	Financial gains; new markets for ore, hides, and agricultural products. (Remains member of Zollverein till 1919.) (H:150)
Hanover and Oldenburg	1854	Severe financial difficulties. (H:214, B:180)	–

banke wrote to the Earl of Dudley from Frankfurt-am-Main on March 14, 1828:

The news of this negotiation [between Prussia and Hesse-Darmstadt] has created ... no small alarm among the merchants and others connected with the trade in this part of Germany who will undoubtedly suffer considerably by it, as the Prussian custom house establishment is conducted with the utmost severity and the adoption of that system in the duchy of Hesse-Darmstadt will have the effect of raising the duties upon a great number of articles of commerce.[172]

Unsurprisingly, the sequence of events by which most other German states acceded to the Prussian Customs Union followed the pattern of the Hesse-Darmstadt case: first, loss of easy access to the large market, then economic deterioration (at times combined with social unrest) and, finally, resignation to the inevitable, that is, economic merger with Prussia. In some cases, however, unwillingness to pay the price of membership of the Prussian union led affected outsiders to search for substitute export markets or to organize rival commercial unions (the second integrative response). Only after these efforts had failed did these outsiders approach Prussia. Three such temporary unions were established, a customs union between Bavaria and Württemberg, the Middle German Commercial Union, and the Tax Union (Steuerverein).

The first came into force in July of 1828 in response to the new Prussian commercial policy. Bavaria and Württemberg were, however, too small and their economies too much alike to form a powerful and efficient union. The customs revenues per head of population were only 9.5 silver groschen; Prussia collected 24 silver groschen. Administrative costs absorbed 44 percent of receipts which compared poorly to Prussia's 14 percent.[173]

The Middle German Commercial Union (Mitteldeutscher Handelsverein) was set up in September of 1828, only a few months after the Bavaria–Württemberg union. It comprised Hanover, Saxony, Hesse-Cassel, Nassau, Brunswick, Oldenburg, Frankfurt-am-Main, Bremen, the Saxon duchies, the Reuss principalities, Hesse-Homburg, Schwarzburg-Rudolfstadt, and the Upper Lordship (*Oberherrschaft*) of Schwarzburg-Sonderhausen. The oppositional or anti-Prussian character of this union was unmistakable. The union prohibited its members from concluding individual customs or trade agreements with non-members and sought to keep open the north–south main trade routes from Hamburg and Bremen to Frankfurt-am-Main and Leipzig, but to restrict the traffic on the west–east routes in so far as they ran through Prussian lands.[174]

[172] Henderson, *The Zollverein*, p. 53.
[173] Benaerts, *Les Origines de la Grande Industrie Allemande*, p. 46.
[174] Henderson, *The Zollverein*, p. 68.

Efforts to turn this counter-union into a true common market foundered, as did attempts to use the union as a collective bargaining agency in negotiations with neighbouring states.[175] The economies of their members exhibited little complementarity, and lack of clear leadership rendered consensus elusive. Furthermore, the economic conditions in the member states of the Middle German Commercial Union deteriorated rapidly and gave rise to widespread revolts in 1830. The Union's demise had begun. Sachse-Weimar was the first to defect, followed by Hesse-Cassel which joined the Prussian Customs Union in 1831 on essentially the same terms as Hesse-Darmstadt.[176] Most of the remaining states now considered themselves at liberty to approach Prussia. Prussia signed treaties in 1833 with the Thüringen States,[177] Saxony, Bavaria, and Württemberg. These all came into force on January 1, 1834 and on that day the German Zollverein was born. Thirty years after its foundation, Gustav Fischer wrote that

the elder generation can still remember how joyfully the opening hour of the year 1834 was welcomed by the trading world. Long trains of wagons stood on the high roads, which till then had been cut up by tax barriers. At the stroke of midnight every turnpike was thrown open, and amid cheers the wagons hastened over the boundaries, which they could thenceforward cross in perfect freedom. Everyone felt that a great object had been attained.[178]

Baden, an agricultural state that traditionally exported wine, tobacco, hemp, hops, and cattle, joined the Zollverein in 1835 when it became clear that substitute trade with Switzerland and Holland was no adequate compensation for the loss of German markets.[179] It was shortly followed by Nassau and the Free City of Frankfurt-am-Main where commercial isolation was threatening utter ruin.[180]

---

[175] Hans-Werner Hahn, *Geschichte des Deutschen Zollvereins*, pp. 43–51.

[176] Hesse-Cassel agreed, in addition, to introduce the same excise duties as those imposed in Prussia on wine, cider, and tobacco.

[177] The Thüringen States included Sachse-Weimar, the smaller Saxon duchies, the Reuss principalities, the Prussian district of Erfurt, Schleusingen, and Ziegenrück and the Hesse-Cassel district of Schmalkalden.

[178] Gustav Fischer, "Über das Wesen und Bedingungen eines Zollvereins," in *Hildebrands Jahrbuch für Nationalökonomie und Statistik* (1865), p. 375; quoted in Henderson, *The Zollverein*, p. 94.

[179] Ferdinand Wallschmitt, *Der Eintritt Badens in den Zollverein* (Hanau: Waisenhaus Buchdruckerei, 1904), pp. 1–75.

[180] Henderson, *The Zollverein*, pp. 110–121. A dispatch to the British Foreign Office from the British envoy to the German Diet of December 1834 reads: "[H]emmed in by a line of Customs Houses all round the gates of the town ... [Frankfurt's] commercial intercourse with the interior of Germany was greatly harassed and restricted ... [I]ts commerce and trade had already fallen off considerably, and ... great apprehensions were entertained that its fairs would be irretrievably injured unless the union with Prussia was speedily effected; ... the British houses ... finding their old customers

The only states to demur further were Hanover and Brunswick. They formed the Tax Union (Steuerverein) in 1834, which Oldenburg joined in 1836. Unlike the Middle German Commercial Union, this Steuerverein was a genuine customs union with a common tariff, a joint customs administration, and common excise duties. In its early years it obtained a revenue of a thaler per head of population from these duties, which was a third more than was raised by the Zollverein.[181] With no domestic manufacturing industry to protect, the Steuerverein pursued a policy of free trade to obtain English clothes, colonial goods, and wines as cheaply as possible in exchange for its agricultural goods. It also turned a blind eye on the smuggling of foreign merchandise into the Zollverein.[182] By 1840, the revenue differential between the Zollverein and the Tax Union had disappeared.[183] In 1841, Brunswick announced its decision to leave the Tax Union for the Zollverein.[184] Exasperated at Brunswick's desertion, Hanover entered into negotiations with the Zollverein but failed to reach an agreement because Prussia was not prepared to grant the far-reaching concessions demanded by Hanover. A few years later, plagued by severe financial troubles, Hanover reopened talks and agreed to Prussia's terms.[185] It duly signed a treaty with the Zollverein in 1851. Oldenburg joined in 1852.

How did the states fare as members of the German customs union? In a nutshell, overwhelmingly well. Bavaria, for example, had drawn about 2.1 million florins from the revenues of its customs union with Württemberg in 1831. It obtained 3.86 million florins in its first year of membership of the Zollverein.[186] Frankfurt-am-Main reported excellent business at the first fair after its adhesion to the Zollverein, and watched with satisfaction the decline of its arch-rival Offenbach.[187] Agriculture

deterred from frequenting the fairs and their buyers diminish, had themselves become the advocates of the union with Prussia." Quoted in Viner, *The Customs Union Issue*, p. 62.

[181] Henderson, *The Zollverein*, p. 88.

[182] See Hilde Arning, *Hannovers Stellung zum Zollverein* (Hanover: Culemannsche Buchdruckerei, 1930).

[183] Henderson, *The Zollverein*, p. 88.

[184] According to Hilde Arning, Brunswick refused to renew its membership of the Steuerverein after Hanover turned down a request by Brunswick to discontinue the construction of a road from Uelzen to Salzwedel connecting Prussia and Hanover. Brunswick feared that this road would compete with its own trade road to Hamburg. (See Arning, *Hannovers Stellung zum Zollverein*, pp. 42–43.) The prospects of sharing the rapidly growing revenues of the Zollverein arguably also played an important role in Brunswick's decision.

[185] The extent of Hanover's financial and economic difficulties is detailed in Arning's *Hannovers Stellung zum Zollverein*, pp. 74–78. See also Benaerts, *Les Origines de la Grande Industrie Allemande*, p. 180.

[186] Henderson, *The Zollverein*, p. 141.

[187] *Ibid.*, p. 121.

Table 4.5. *Customs revenues of the Zollverein*

Year	Customs revenues of the Zollverein (in millions of thalers)	Revenue per capita (in thalers)
1834	14.8	19
1836	18.5	22
1843	25.4	27.6

Source: Benaerts, *Les Origines de la Grande Industrie Allemande*, p. 58

revived in Baden and sugar refining was introduced under the protection of the Zollverein. Similar examples abound (see table 4.4 above). In general, the extension of the market, along with improved communications by road, inland waterways, and railways, permitted the expansion of existing manufacturers and the development of new ones. Tax collection costs fell from an overall German average of 44 percent of total receipts prior to the Zollverein to 9 percent in the late 1830s. Tax revenues increased by 71 percent between 1834 and 1843 while population increased by only 21.7 percent (see table 4.5).

The supply of integration

The Zollverein brought Germany a broad institutional framework in which technological improvements of the industrial revolution could flourish. A large German market with a growing number of common institutional arrangements created the right environment for confidence in long-term investment, which, in turn, stimulated economic exchange and produced sustained economic growth.[188] These institutional arrangements, and Prussia's role in providing them, are worthy of study in exemplifying the behavior of a regional leader in a successful integration scheme.

The executive body of the Zollverein was the "annual" General Congress, which met each time in the capital of a different member state.[189] It was composed of official delegates who carried out the instructions of their governments. The Congress solved problems

---

[188] German mercantile tonnage doubled between 1835 and 1855; in 1870 it was three and a half times the level of 1835. See Walther Hoffmann, "The Take-off in Germany," in Walt Rostow (ed.), *The Economics of Take-off into Sustained Growth* (London: Macmillan, 1963), pp. 104–105.

[189] Only fifteen General Congresses were held between 1834 and 1863.

arising from the common administration of the Zollverein, settled the accounts, and acted as legislative body.[190]

Prussia was bound to play a leading role in the Zollverein, for two reasons. First, Prussia was by far the largest and wealthiest state in the customs union.[191] Second, Prussia always served as recipient of requests for union membership. This gave it considerable freedom in defining the terms and conditions under which a new state became a member. For example, in the first enlargement of the Prussian market in 1828, Hesse-Darmstadt agreed to adopt the Prussian customs law, tariffs, and auditing procedures. It was allowed to administer the collection of customs duties in its own territory but only according to Prussian pattern. Inspections were designed to assure uniformity. Secret articles further limited Hesse-Darmstadt's sovereign rights: its participation in future changes of the common legislation was restricted, and the Prussian customs inspectors at Darmstadt were given wider powers than those laid down in the principal treaty.[192] In addition, Prussia undertook all important negotiations with foreign countries on behalf of the union, and it distributed the customs revenues. There remains little doubt that "the Prussia–Hesse-Darmstadt Union, though nominally an arrangement between two independent sovereign states, was, in fact, *the absorption of the smaller country into the customs system of the larger.*"[193] The terms on which other German states later joined the union were the same as those which Hesse-Darmstadt had accepted.

Despite its political preponderance, however, Prussia cannot be said to have abused its position. Its fellow-members joined the union voluntarily and were free to leave as they pleased. No state ever left; all remained members and had strong material incentives to do so. Bowden, Karpovich, and Usher write: "[Their] financial return made an end of any hostility that might [have been] felt towards Prussia. The gains in revenue soothed the pain of losing complete independence."[194]

Prussia distributed the proceeds of the customs in proportion to the population of the various states. This was highly favorable to nearly all states because their per capita consumption was considerably smaller

---

[190] After the Seven Weeks' War of 1866, the old General Congress was replaced by a federal customs council. In addition, a popularly elected customs parliament was introduced which was called in session when business required it or when one-third of the customs council demanded a meeting.

[191] Henderson, *The Zollverein*, p. 318.

[192] The secret articles are reprinted in Oncken and Saemisch (eds.), *Vorgeschichte und Begründung des Deutschen Zollvereins 1815–1834*, vol. II, pp. 207–211.

[193] Henderson, *The Zollverein*, p. 68; my italics.

[194] Witt Bowden, Michael Karpovich, and Abbott Payson Usher, *An Economic History of Europe since 1750* (New York: AMS Press, 1970), p. 338.

than the Prussian average. At times, this arrangement imposed important financial costs on Prussia. For example, Prussia experienced a decline in receipts following the establishment of the Zollverein, while the other member states registered strong gains. Its revenue per capita was 20 silver groschens in 1833. It then declined to 15.5 groschens and reached the 1833 level again only in 1838.[195] Nevertheless, Prussia remained the region's paymaster throughout the existence of the Zollverein, despite occasional misgivings by Prussian officials,[196] and despite some changes to the system of revenue distribution over the years.

Prussia also played an important role as institutional focal point and coordinator in the deepening process of integration. It drafted a new German commercial code, for example, that by the mid-1860s had been adopted by nearly all German states. Prussia played a similar leading role in the harmonization of German mining laws and in the adoption of a common Bills-of-Exchange Law, a single weight system, common railway tariffs, and a common judicial system.[197] Its role in monetary coordination deserves special mention: in the early 1830s, each German state issued its own money; as a result, a bewildering variety of coins and notes circulated in Germany. When the Zollverein was established in 1834, the contracting parties agreed to work towards a unification of the monetary systems. In August 1837, the South German states signed a convention creating the South German florin. Almost one year later, the Zollverein member states met in Dresden and signed a monetary convention that secured a fixed exchange rate between the florin and the Prussian thaler which circulated widely in the North German states. Finally, in January 1857, a monetary convention was held at which the German states agreed to introduce a new currency with circulation throughout Germany. The "union thaler" (*Vereinsthaler*), as the new currency was named, was equivalent in value to the Prussian silver thaler. Benaerts notes: "In sum, the new federal money was no other currency than the Prussian thaler."[198] Prussia's currency served as the

---

[195] Henderson, *The Zollverein*, pp. 141–142.

[196] In a memorandum of December 22, 1839, for example, the Prussian government complained that: "Although Prussia fully recognizes that its subjects have shared in the general advantageous results of the customs union ... the position is quite different when viewed from the financial standpoint ... Prussia ... has good reasons for having considerable misgivings if it is to hold no other prospect save that of new financial sacrifices in the future while all other members of the union look forward to a permanent increase of customs revenue." Quoted in Henderson, *The Zollverein*, p. 142.

[197] Benaerts, *Les Origines de la Grande Industrie Allemande*, pp. 409–410, 536, 627. See also Henderson, *The Zollverein*, p. 343.

[198] Benaerts, *Les Origines de la Grande Industrie Allemande*, p. 287.

base of a new monetary system based on a silver standard, which endured until the 1870s. On July 9, 1873, the silver standard was replaced by a new gold standard with a monetary unit named the mark. The thaler was slowly withdrawn from circulation but remained legal tender until 1907.[199]

It is worth pondering why Prussia took it upon itself to build a single market, assume the role of regional paymaster, and offer institutional leadership. The economic gains of a unified German market were considerably smaller to Prussia than they were to most other German states who much depended on access to the Prussian market. A possible explanation is that Prussia's interest in accepting new members was similar to its motivation to create a single Prussian market in the first place, namely, to increase its international bargaining position for both political and economic gains. After the collapse of the continental system with the defeat of Napoleon in 1815, most of Prussia's neighbors reverted to narrow economic nationalism. The Silesian linen industry in the eastern provinces of Prussia was hurt by Russia's policy of national self-sufficiency and Austria's new prohibitive import duties. Industrialists of the Rhineland and Westphalia, who during the war exported most of their production into France and the Netherlands, now found themselves excluded from those markets.[200] Especially damaging to Prussia's economy was Britain's new policy of high tariff protection. The large eastern provinces of Prussia – particularly east and west Prussia, Posen, and Pomerania, whose grain and timber production was mainly intended for British markets – experienced sharp reductions in their exports due to new British duties on those commodities. The effect of the Corn Law of 1815 was to eliminate the importation of wheat except in years of bad harvest. The new charges on European timber reduced the number of ships engaged in carrying timber from the Memel to Britain from approximately 980 to about 250.[201]

---

[199] Bowden, Karpovich, and Usher, *An Economic History of Europe since 1750*, p. 571.

[200] Wilhelm Treue, *Wirtschaftszustände und Wirtschaftspolitik in Preussen, 1815–25* (Stuttgart and Berlin: Verlag von W. Kohlhammer, 1937), especially pp. 6–113. The difficulties of German industries were aggravated by the arrival of inexpensive cotton and woolen textiles and iron goods produced on a large scale by Britain's superior mechanized industry. In response to increased protectionism and competition, German manufacturers themselves advocated protectionist policies. See, for example, the following petitions: "Die Reichenbacher Baumwollfabrikanten an Hardenberg (April 8, 1815)," or "Die Fabrikinhaber in den Gemeinden Rheydt, Süchtels, Gladbach, Viersen und Kaltenkirchen an König Friedrich Wilhelm II (April 27, 1818)," or "Fabrikanten aus Düren and Hardenberg (November 1, 1818)," in Oncken and Saemisch (eds.), *Vorgeschichte und Begründung des Deutschen Zollvereins 1815–1834*, vol. I, pp. 23–25, 69–71, 82 respectively.

[201] Henderson, *The Zollverein*, p. 32.

To revive its industry and commerce, Prussia repeatedly approached its neighbors to negotiate preferential market access agreements. These efforts, however, were in vain. Prussia was economically too weak to influence commercial policies abroad and administratively too disorganized to be considered an attractive negotiation partner.[202] It thus moved, first, to reform its customs system by abolishing internal duties and creating a single Prussian market, and then proceeded to enlarge its economic space by taking smaller German states into its customs union. This sequential enlargement of the single market improved Prussia's international bargaining and retaliation power, enabling it to wring important concessions from neighboring protectionist states in a series of commercial and navigation treaties.

Prussia's neighbors watched these events with growing apprehension. They feared that the extension of the Prussian customs system would lead to a reduction of their trade (both legitimate trade and smuggling) with the German states. In Britain, manufacturers blamed the monopolies accorded to the landed aristocrats for encouraging the formation of an increasingly protected German market. Benaerts provides various revealing statements by British deputies who saw a direct link between British protectionist policies and the enlargement of the German Zollverein. One deputy, Mr. Ewans, is quoted as saying: "This German commercial confederation is the product of our own destructive policy. Haven't we refused access to German timber and grain exports?" Lord Palmerston concurs: "One of the reasons why Prussia seeks to attract the other German states into its union is to force Britain to reduce its duties on grain and timber."[203] The detrimental effect of the Prussian strategy on British industry is strikingly illustrated in a dispatch by Cartwright to the Duke of Wellington dated December 1, 1834:

Before 1819 British cotton manufactured goods were only subjected to a very trifling duty on their introduction into Bavaria. By ... 1819 that duty was fixed at twenty florins (Gulden) the Bavarian hundredweight ... In 1828 ... the duty was further increased to sixty florins, which was considered very high; and now, under the regulations of the Prussian Union, it stands at nearly ninety-five florins. [This is] ... a most rapid and immense augmentation, to the detriment

---

[202] Carl Brinkmann, *Die Preussische Handelspolitik vor dem Zollverein und der Wiederaufbau vor Hundert Jahren* (Berlin and Leipzig: Walter de Gruyter & Co., 1922), pp. 159–160.

[203] Quoted in Benaerts, *Les Origines de la Grande Industrie Allemande*, pp. 74–75. Similarly, John Bowring of the British Board of Trade argued in a testimony before the Select Committee on Import Duties in 1840: "I believe we have created an unnecessary rivalry by our vicious legislation." Quoted in Charles Kindleberger, "The Rise and Fall of Free Trade in Western Europe, 1820–1875," *Journal of Economic History* 35 (March 1975), 34.

of British trade; and if these high duties are persisted in, it is feared that the demand for British goods must decrease every year.[204]

Metternich's Austria also frowned at the ever-growing Zollverein not only because it feared the security implications of a powerful Zollverein, but also because it was concerned about a unified German market's unfavorable commercial repercussions on its industries.

Little by little, under the active direction of Prussia and in light of the common interest which must inevitably emerge, the states composing this union will form a ... coherent bloc ... And when one considers that ... th[e] power [to define external commercial policies] lies in the hands of ... Prussia, ... one must expect that the influence it has just acquired over our communications with and through Germany will be extremely harmful for the industry of the Empire.[205]

In short, Prussia's large neighbors were no longer in a position to take advantage of Germany's internal divisions. Prussia adeptly used its newly gained economic weight to secure better terms for its exports. As early as 1824, it obtained concessions from Britain in a shipping convention which was later copied in treaties with Sweden, the Hanse towns, the United States of America, and Brazil.[206] Next, Prussia tackled the vexed question of freedom of navigation on the Rhine. In 1815, the Congress of Vienna had adopted the principle of free navigation in international rivers. Holland, however, made every effort to evade the provisions of the Vienna agreement not only by imposing extra duties but also by prohibiting through-traffic in various commodities. Determined to break Holland's monopolistic position at the mouth of the Rhine, Prussia demanded satisfaction. It negotiated a series of navigation and commercial treaties in which the Dutch made important concessions.[207] An Anglo-Prussian convention was signed in March 1841. Its terms, as modified in 1847, lasted until 1865. In 1836, Britain

---

[204] Quoted in Henderson, *The Zollverein*, pp. 97–98.

[205] Metternich's thoughts on the Zollverein are reprinted in Alfons von Klinkowström (ed.), *Aus Metternichs nachgelassenen Papieren* (Vienna: Wilhelm Braumüller, 1882), vol. V, pp. 507–508.

[206] Pollard, *European Economic Integration*, p. 115.

[207] The new Rhine Navigation Act was signed in March 1831. A navigation act between Prussia and Holland was signed in June, 1837, followed two years later by a commercial treaty. And in December 1851 the two countries signed a new commercial and navigation treaty. See Johanna Kortmann, *Die Niederlande in den handelspolitischen Verhandlungen mit Preussen vom Wiener Kongress bis zum Schiffahrtsvertrag von 1837* (Münster: Fahle, 1929). Kortmann provides a lucid account of how Holland sought by all means to foil the steady expansion of the Zollverein, for it was well aware that a stronger Prussia was bound to contest its monopolistic position on the lower portion of the Rhine. See, in particular, chapter 4 entitled "Die Stellung der Niederlande zur Bildung des Zollvereins" (Holland's position with regard to the formation of the Zollverein). See also P. J. Bouman, "Der Untergang des holländischen Handels- und Schiffahrtsmonopols auf dem Niederrhein, 1831–51," *Vierteljahresschrift für Sozial- und Wirtschaftsgeschichte* 26 (1933), 244–269; and Christian Eckert, "Rheinschiffahrt

offered to abolish its timber duties imposed on Prussia in exchange for lower tariffs on British textiles, but Prussia held out for a reduction of the Corn Laws.[208] Between 1846 and 1849 Britain abolished its navigation code and reduced its import duties on timber.[209] In 1843 France offered to lower various duties if the Zollverein came to terms. Prussia, however, considered that the proposed concessions were inadequate and decided not to enter into negotiations with France. A Franco-Prussian treaty reducing import duties on raw materials and manufactured articles was only signed in 1862.[210] In 1842 Russia announced its intention to reduce its prohibitive duties on certain Prussian exports; and an agreement was reached between Russia and Prussia in 1844.[211] The Austro-Prussian commercial treaty of February 1853 reduced import duties to 25 percent *ad valorem* and stipulated that new tariff concessions made by one of the contracting parties to a third state would automatically be enjoyed by the other party.[212] In 1857, Prussia tackled a long-standing irritation in its Baltic trade: stream and sound dues. These dues were monopolistic rents that Denmark had been extracting for over four hundred years from ships and cargoes passing its many islands. Under Prussian pressure, Denmark agreed to abolish these tolls and dues in return for a compensatory payment. North German trade also benefitted from a substantial reduction of Danish transit dues on roads, railways, and canals in Jutland, Schleswig, Holstein, and Lauenburg.[213]

In sum, Prussia was successful in enhancing its international bargaining position by increasing the size of the market under its command.

---

im 19. Jahrhundert," *Staats- und Socialwirtschaftliche Forschungen* 18 (Leipzig: Von Duncker & Humblot, 1900), 1–450.

[208] Douglas Irwin, "Multilateral and Bilateral Trade Policies in the World Trading System: An Historical Perspective," in Jaime de Melo and Arvind Panagariya (eds.), *New Dimensions in Regional Integration* (Cambridge: Cambridge University Press, 1993), p. 94.

[209] Britain also repealed its Corn Laws in 1846. The repeal is attributed, in part, to the harvest failure in Ireland. But it may also have been influenced by Prussian pressure.

[210] The most significant reductions in the French tariff were those on the importations of iron and textiles. Prussia's chief concessions to France were reductions in import duties on wines and silks. The treaty contained the Most-Favored-Nation clause.

[211] Henderson, *The Zollverein*, p. 176.

[212] Karl Mamroth, *Die Entwicklung der österreichisch-deutschen Handelsbeziehungen: Vom Entstehen der Zolleinigungsbestrebungen bis zum Ende der ausschliesslichen Zollbegünstigungen (1849–1865)* (Berlin: Carl Heymanns Verlag, 1887); Adolf Beer, *Österreichische Handelspolitik im neunzehnten Jahrhundert* (Vienna: Manz, 1891); chapters 6 and 7 (pp. 136–205) provide a detailed discussion of the 1853 treaty between Prussia and Austria.

[213] Charles Hill, *The Sound Dues and the Command of the Baltic* (Durham: Duke University Press, 1926), especially pp. 254–268.

It may be assumed that this was a large part of its motivation to extend integration through the incremental enlargement of the Zollverein.[214]

4   Failed European integration schemes

Chapter 3 argued that states that are negatively affected by regional integration schemes to which they do not belong will respond either by seeking to merge with the area generating external effects (first integrative response), or – if that option is deemed impossible or too costly – by creating their own regional group (second integrative response). However, like any integration project, such a counter-union is likely to fail when a region lacks an undisputed leader and when the potential for gains from integration is limited either because regional economies lack complementarity or because the small size of regional markets does not offer significant economies of scale.

Several examples of such failed European counter-unions have been mentioned above. One was the European Free Trade Association (EFTA) of 1960. Its members traded primarily with the Community rather than with each other. The group was neither compact nor contiguous. Its members were strewn in a loose circle around the Community. Further, EFTA's cohesion was repeatedly weakened by successive defections of EFTA members to the Community, most notably when the UK, the group's potential leader, left in 1973. Regional groups founded in the wake of the Prussian customs union, such as the union between Bavaria and Württemberg, the Middle German Commercial Union, and the Tax Union, failed because the economies of their members were too small or too much alike and because none of the groups had a clear leader capable of defining a coherent commercial policy *vis-à-vis* Prussia.

The remainder of this chapter presents one final episode of failed European integration: projects for a European commercial union in the 1890s. They were triggered, like many other integration schemes, by negative externalities. These were (1) rising American protectionism and (2) competitive pressure from giant American industrial conglomerates, the so-called trusts. The rise of such externalities were related, in part, to the widening and deepening of the single American market. Several European countries responded by creating a European commer-

---

[214] Over the years Prussia, on behalf of the Zollverein, concluded commercial treaties with countries other than Great Britain, France, Russia, and Austria. These included: Portugal (1844), Sardinia (1845), Mexico (1855), Uruguay, Argentina, Paraguay (all three between 1856 and 1859), Italy (1865), Spain (1865), Japan (1869), Switzerland (1869). Many of these treaties included the Most-Favored-Nation clause. See Sartorius von Waltershausen, *Deutsche Wirtschaftsgeschichte, 1815–1914*.

cial treaty system. Hopes that this system would develop into a broader and deeper scheme, a European Zollverein or even a "United States of Europe," proved vain. This failure can be attributed, in part, to lack of an undisputed leading state in Europe capable of defining a common European commercial policy, and absence of support by business groups for a European commercial union.

This neglected episode in European commercial history is particularly striking given that the logic of integration operated against a backdrop of power politics at its crudest. Since 1871 France had been diplomatically isolated. Upon Bismarck's fall in 1890, the German Emperor William II terminated the secret treaty between Germany and Russia, thus opening the door to a new constellation of military alliances in Europe. In 1894, for example, an alliance was concluded between France and Russia by whose terms each partner promised to aid the other in case of attack by Germany or Germany's allies. Another central feature throughout the 1890s was recurrent rivalry among European colonial powers in Africa and the Far East. Nevertheless, there was much thought given to the idea of building a European Commercial Union. The following discussion examines the origins of such a seemingly eccentric idea and considers the causes of its failure.

Rising American protectionism

Throughout the nineteenth century the United States exported mainly agricultural products and raw materials, such as cotton, wheat flour, and meat products. American manufacturers began to sell significant quantities of goods abroad only in the 1890s, much later than Britain, France, and Germany (see table 4.6). America's strength in international trade of manufactures was in machinery, metals, electrical equipment, and processed food.[215] This surge of American exports coincided with a period of accentuated protectionism in the United States, aimed both at defending infant industries and obtaining better terms of trade.[216]

Under the Republican presidency of Benjamin Harrison, Congress adopted the 1890 McKinley Tariff Act. This Act embraced two principles: protection and reciprocity. First, it sought to impose duties on

[215] See Mary Locke Eysenbach, *American Manufactured Exports, 1879–1914: A Study of Growth and Comparative Advantage* (New York: Arno Press, 1976), pp. 1–31; G. G. Huebner, "The Foreign Trade from the Civil War to the Close of the Nineteenth Century," in Emory Johnson, T. W. Van Metre, G. G. Huebner, and D. S. Hanchett (eds.), *History of Domestic and Foreign Commerce of the United States* (Washington: Carnegie Institution of Washington, 1915, reprint 1922), vol. II, pp. 64–85.

[216] Sidney Dell, *Trade Blocs and Common Markets* (New York: Alfred Knopf, 1963), p. 9.

Table 4.6. *Share of world trade in manufactures (%)*

	1890	1899	1913
United States	3.9	9.8	11.0
United Kingdom	35.8	28.4	25.4
Germany	17.2	19.5	23.0
France	14.5	12.6	10.6
Belgium	5.1	4.9	4.3

Source: William Arthur Lewis, "International Competition in Manufactures," *American Economic Review* 47 (May 1957), 579.

articles that were produced in the United States and to admit free of duty those goods that Americans did not produce at all or could only produce in insufficient quantities to meet domestic demand.[217] Second, the McKinley Tariff envisaged a series of bilateral reciprocity agreements between the United States and Latin American countries. Sugar, molasses, coffee, tea, and raw hides were freely admitted in return for preferential duties on specific American agricultural and manufactured goods. The aim of these agreements was to redirect the trade of Latin American countries – previously dominated by Great Britain – away from Europe and toward the United States.[218]

This was not the first American attempt to undermine commercial relations between Latin America and Europe. One year prior to the adoption of the McKinley Tariff, Secretary of State James Blaine convoked a conference in Washington to discuss the feasibility of a Pan-American customs union, which was attended by nineteen Latin American states.[219] Baltimore's daily, *The Sun*, described the American intention behind that conference as follows:

[217] David Lake, *Power, Protectionism, and Free Trade: International Sources of US Commercial Strategy, 1887–1939* (Ithaca: Cornell University Press, 1988), p. 100; Frank Taussig, *The Tariff History of the United States* (New York: Putnam's, 1905, 6th edn), pp. 251–283.

[218] Lake, *Power, Protectionism, and Free Trade*, p. 98; Huebner, "Tariff Provisions Concerning the Shipping and Foreign Trade of the United States," in Johnson, Van Metre, Huebner, and Hanchett, *History of Domestic and Foreign Commerce of the United States*, pp. 335–351.

[219] See Louis Bosc, *Unions Douanières et Projets d'Unions Douanières* (Paris: Librairie Nouvelle de Droit et de Jurisprudence, 1904), pp. 254–264; Paul Leroy-Beaulieu, "Un Zollverein Américain," *Economiste Français* (May 25, 1889), 641–644; Gustave de Molinari, "Le Congrès des Trois Amériques et l'Union Douanière des Trois Amériques," *Journal des Economistes* 48 (Paris: Librairie Guillaumine, October 1889), 3–6; Alexandre Peez, "Le Congrès des Trois Amériques," *Revue d'Economie Politique* 4 (Paris: Larose et Forcel, 1890), 272–286; Amédée Prince, *Le Congrès des Trois Amériques, 1889–90* (Paris: Librairie Guillaumine, 1891). Discussions at the

[The motives of the organizers] are ... the widening of the area over which our high-tariff laws shall prevail, the idea being that, by reciprocal tariff arrangements, we can *exclude European manufacturers from the trade of the countries that enter into the proposed customs union.* We are to monopolize, if possible, the commerce of Central and South America, but not by the cheapness and excellence of our wares, but by including those regions within our present high tariff wall. We are to have exclusive rights to enter the ports of the signatories on a free-trade basis, while our European competitors are kept out by suitable protective laws.[220]

The daily press in Europe followed the Washington conference with the greatest attention. The tone was mostly alarmist. A major Viennese daily, for example, wrote:

The government of the United States has invited all the states of the New World to participate in a conference in Washington. Its objective is to forge a PanAmerican Union against Europe. Europe ships a large part of its manufactured goods to South America ... If the [South American] ports are closed to us because of high external tariffs similar to those currently in force in the United States, then a great many of our workers and many more still in France, Germany and Great Britain would be at risk of losing their jobs. [221]

This and subsequent efforts by the United States to create a Pan-American commercial union foundered in the end, primarily because of growing resistance to American hegemony in Latin America. Nevertheless, they sent tremor waves to Europe in the early 1890s and provided added incentive for Europeans to respond in kind.

Another protectionist measure taken by the Americans was the Wilson–Gorman Tariff of 1894, passed under the Democratic administration of Grover Cleveland. It continued the special trading relationship with Latin America by lowering duties on a selected and limited number of raw materials. It also reimposed a duty on raw sugar, thereby abrogating the reciprocity treaties negotiated under the McKinley Tariff, and introduced countervailing duties against countries that subsidized their sugar exports to the United States. These provisions were particularly damaging to German sugar exporters.[222] Between 1897 and 1912 the United States continued highly protectionist policies. Republican President William McKinley called Congress into a special session soon after taking office in 1897 to revise the tariff once again. Congress responded by passing the Dingley Tariff Act, which eliminated many

Washington conference touched not only on customs union issues but included deliberations on harmonization of standards, monetary union, common transportation policies, and regional arbitration procedures.

[220] *The Sun* 105 (Wednesday, May 29, 1889), supplement, p. 1, my italics.
[221] Quoted in Prince, *Le Congrès des Trois Amériques*, p. 87.
[222] David Lake, *Power, Protection, and Free Trade*, p. 96; Taussig, *The Tariff History of the United States*, pp. 284–230.

items from the list of freely importable goods and raised general import duties to the highest level they had yet reached.[223]

The trusts

A second development that the Europeans watched with alarm was the creation of giant American industrial conglomerates, the so-called trusts that emerged in the widening American internal market. A trust was a new type of large-scale industrial organization in which the voting rights of a controlling number of shares of competing firms were entrusted to a small group of men who thus were able to manage competition among their companies while rationalizing productive processes. Early examples of such "big business" were the Standard Oil Trust, the American Tobacco Company, and the American Sugar Refining Company.[224] The trend towards industrial concentration accelerated particularly during the presidency of McKinley, when government was securely in the hands of friends of big business.[225]

This restructuring of American industry was of concern to Europeans for two reasons. First, the largest proportion of manufactured exports to Europe came from industries with very high levels of concentration. The three industry groups that accounted for about two-thirds of manufactured exports – metals; machinery; and food, drink, and tobacco – were made up of 48 of the 100 largest corporations.[226] American restructuring therefore meant keener competition for European producers. Second, gains in the domestic market from economies of scale and monopolistic rents obtained through increased concentration permitted these giant firms to undersell competitors abroad.[227]

[223] Taussig, *The Tariff History of the United States*, pp. 321–360.
[224] In 1890 the Republican administration of Benjamin Harrison adopted the Sherman Anti-Trust Act. The Act did not curb the development of industrial monopolies and remained essentially unenforced for twelve years. Ironically, it was invoked by the federal government in 1894 to obtain an injunction against a striking railroad union. The Supreme Court upheld the use of the injunction. It was argued that unions were combinations in restraint of trade within the meaning of the law. On trusts in this period, see Alfred Chandler, "The Beginning of Big Business in American Industry," *Business History Review* 33 (Spring 1959), 1–31; Alfred Eichner, *The Emergence of Oligopoly* (Baltimore: The Johns Hopkins Press, 1969); Ralph Hidy and Muriel Hidy, *Pioneering in Big Business, 1882–1911* (New York: Harper, 1955).
[225] William Becker, *The Dynamics of Business–Government Relations: Industry and Exports, 1893–1921* (Chicago: The University of Chicago Press, 1982), p. 36; Alfred Chandler, *Strategy and Structure: Chapters in the History of American Industrial Enterprise* (Cambridge, Mass.: MIT Press, 1990), pp. 19–51.
[226] Becker, *The Dynamics of Business–Government Relations*, p. 12.
[227] William Stead, for example, writes in his *The Americanization of the World* (New York and London: Horace Markley, 1902): "The Industrial Commission, which has just concluded its inquiry into the whole question, found from the replies received from

The European response

The combination of rising American protectionism and "unfair" competition were perceived in Europe as the "American menace."[228]

German Chancellor Von Caprivi explained the essence of the problem as follows:

What we import from foreign countries we need; to a great extent it consists of indispensable means of subsistence, raw materials and a few half-finished products which are indispensable for our industry. We must be in a position to pay for these things, and in order to be able to pay for them, we have in general but one means, and that is to send our manufactured articles to the countries from which we have received these raw materials and these means of subsistence.[229]

But how was this to be achieved in the face of prohibitive tariffs and increasing competition? An anonymous pamphlet appeared in Berlin in 1890 entitled *Die Zukunft der Völker von Mitteleuropa*.[230] Its presumed author belonged to the entourage of Chancellor von Caprivi. The pamphlet stressed the pernicious effect of the McKinley Act on European trade and pointed to the danger for the Old World of rising American protectionism and competition. Europe's prosperity and its very civilization were at risk. The pamphlet concluded that only a tariff union between France and Germany would be an effective remedy against the "American menace."

The idea of a European customs union spread quickly throughout Europe. The French journal *Le Temps* regarded it as likely that the triumph of the prohibitive tendencies in the United States would lead to

over one hundred manufacturers that American manufactures are often sold at lower prices abroad than in the United States" (p. 377). See also Bosc, *Unions Douanières et Projets d'Unions Douanières*, pp. 472–482; and Mira Wilkins, *The Emergence of Multinational Enterprise: American Business Abroad from the Colonial Era to 1914* (Cambridge, Mass.: Harvard University Press, 1970), especially pp. 70–110.

228 Variations on the theme of "American menace" can be found in Jules Domergue, "Le Péril Américain," *La Réforme Economique* 21 (May 26, 1901), 691–693; Fred McKenzie, *The American Invaders* (New York: Street and Smith, 1901); Louis Leger, "L'Américanisation du Monde," *Le Correspondant* (April 25, 1902), 221; Edouard Reyer, "L'Américanisation de l'Europe," *Revue Bleue* 17 (April 19, 1902), 484–488; Matthew Simon and David Novack, "Some Dimensions of the American Commercial Invasion of Europe, 1871–1914," *Journal of Economic History* 24 (December 1964), 591–605; William Stead, *The Americanization of the World*, especially pp. 342–380; B. H. Thwaite, *The American Invasion* (London: Swan Sonnenschein, 1902); Frank Vanderlip, "The American 'Commercial Invasion' of Europe," *Scribner's Magazine* 31 (January, 1902), 3–22, (February, 1902), 194–213, (March, 1902), 287–306.

229 Quoted in Henry Farnam, "German Tariff Policy, Past and Present," *The Yale Review* 1 (May 1892/February 1893), 22.

230 *Die Zukunft der Völker von Mitteleuropa* [The Future of the People of Central Europe] (Berlin: Druck und Verlag Georg Reimer, 1890), pp. 1–70.

the abolition of the tariff barriers between European countries "as Colbert had abolished the customs barriers between the [French] provinces."[231] In Germany, the Agrarian Party leader Count Kanitz argued in the Reichstag: "If we are to arrive at some effective measures it will be desirable to go hand-in-hand, if possible, with other European powers, and I am happy to say there is some prospect that this may be done. In all of the European states there is a strong reaction against the new advancement of the American tariff-policy."[232]

In France, Count Paul de Leusse feared that American commercial policies would lead to European agricultural ruin, industrial decadence, depopulation, and bankruptcy.[233] De Leusse advocated the establishment of a customs union in agriculture between Germany and France, with a common tariff bureau in Frankfurt. This union would gradually include Belgium, Switzerland, Holland, Austria-Hungary, Italy, and Spain. In Austria, Alexander Peez forged plans for a Middle European Zollverein. The entrance of France into the Union was for him a *sine qua non*. He appeared particularly irritated by the McKinley Act but also lamented protectionist tendencies in Britain.[234] A European Zollverein, he claimed, would enable its members to obtain concessions which they could never obtain individually, in particular from the United States.[235] Many more proposals for European union by politicians, economists, and journalists made the rounds of European capitals.[236] But no one

[231] Quoted in George Fisk, "Continental Opinion Regarding a Proposed Middle European Tariff-Union," *Johns Hopkins University Studies in Historical and Political Science*, nos. 11–12 (November/December, 1902), 27.

[232] *Ibid.*, p. 34.

[233] See Paul de Leusse, "L'Union Douanière Européenne," *Revue d'Economie Politique* (Paris, 1890), 393–401.

[234] In 1887 Britain passed the Merchandise Marks Act restricting imports of manufactured goods, while the Society of Fair Trade of 1881 and the Imperial Federation League, founded in 1884, advocated the creation of a customs union for Britain and all its colonies.

[235] Alexandre Peez, "A Propos de la Situation Douanière en Europe," *Revue d'Economie Politique* 5 (February, 1891), 121–139, especially 138–139; see also his *Zur neuesten Handelspolitik* (Vienna: Commissionsverlag v. G. Szelinski, 1895).

[236] See, for example, Paul Leroy-Beaulieu, "De la Nécessité de Préparer une Fédération Européenne," *L'Economiste Français* (September, 1898), 305–307; Gustave De Molinari, "A Zollverein in Central Europe," *Gunton's Magazine* 12 (January 1897), 38–46; Gustav Schmoller, "Die Wandlungen in der Europäischen Handelspolitik des 19. Jahrhunderts," *Jahrbuch für Gesetzgebung, Verwaltung und Volkswirtschaft im Deutschen Reich* 24 (1900), 373–382; Sartorius von Waltershausen, *Deutschland und die Handelspolitik der Vereinigten Staaten von Amerika* (Berlin: Siemenroth & Troschel, 1898); Handelskammersekretär Wermert, "Einige Betrachtungen über einen Mitteleuropäischen Zollverein," *Annalen des Deutschen Reichs für Gesetzgebung, Verwaltung und Statistik* 12 (1888), 943–954. The best overview article on projects for European integration in the 1890s is Ernst Francke, "Zollpolitische Einigungsbestrebungen in Mitteleuropa während des Letzten Jahrzehnts," *Schriften des Vereins für Socialpolitik* 1 (1900), 187–272.

urged Europeans to stand up to the "American parvenu" as passionately as Count Goluchowski, the Minister of Foreign Affairs of Austria-Hungary. In an address to the Hungarian Committee on Foreign Relations on November 20, 1897, he recommended concerted European action against "the countries beyond the sea," meaning primarily the United States. His speech, which excited world opinion, is worth quoting at some length:

The disastrous competition which ... we have to submit to from over the seas, and which we will also have to encounter in the future, must be resisted if the vital interests of Europe are not to suffer, and if Europe is not to fall into gradual decay ... Religious warfare filled the Sixteenth and Seventeenth Centuries; during the Eighteenth century liberal ideas took root; the Nineteenth Century has been an epoch of struggle between nations; but the Twentieth Century will be a century of struggle for existence in the domain of economics. *The nations of Europe must unite in order to defend their very means of existence.* May that be understood by all, and may we make use of those days of peaceful development to which we look forward with confidence, to unite our best energies.[237]

The importance of Goluchowski's statement is highlighted in a comment on his speech published in 1897 by the American weekly *The Commercial and Financial Chronicle*: "The speeches of Austrian foreign ministers have always been regarded in Europe with special interest. It has often happened in previous years that [their] public utterances ... to the delegations have been received as the highest official statement of the policy, not only of the Dreibund [Triple Alliance], but of European diplomacy in general."[238]

The American response to these grand plans for European union varied. Most observers thought them utopian. They felt secure in their belief that such schemes would quickly founder on the proven rocks of intra-European distrust, animosity, and hatred. Occasionally, however, concern was voiced. Former Assistant Treasury Secretary Frank Vanderlip, for example, feared that a European Zollverein was bound to trigger "the most gigantic commercial war in the history of humanity."[239] Later he added: "The [European] governments are preparing for a trade war against America ... [T]he air is full of it. One cannot talk with officials there five minutes before the all-pervading impression is secured that Europe is jealous of America."[240]

In the end, the American skeptics were proved to be right. Germany, Austria-Hungary, Italy, Belgium, and Switzerland signed in 1891–1892

---

[237] Quoted in Alfred Fried, *The German Emperor and the Peace of the World* (New York: Hodder and Stoughton, 1912), pp. 19–20, my italics.
[238] *The Commercial and Financial Chronicle* 65 (December 1897), 1147–1148.
[239] Quoted in *Revue Bleue*, 17, 484.
[240] Quoted in *The Economist* (July 6, 1901), 1016.

a central European commercial treaty system.[241] France, though not a signatory to the commercial treaties, benefitted indirectly from them by virtue of Article 11 of the Franco-German peace treaty signed in Frankfurt in 1871. This clause obliged Germany to give France Most-Favored-Nation (MFN) privileges.[242] However, hopes that the system would develop into a deeper and broader European Commercial Union never materialized.

What prevented the central European Commercial Treaty system from growing into a genuine European Union? A central factor was the absence of an undisputed leader. The dividing forces of deeply ingrained animosity and resentment, particularly between the French and the Germans, foiled any attempt at defining a common European commercial policy. The Alsace-Lorraine question rendered it emotionally trying and politically delicate for France to seek a rapprochement with Germany. This in turn prompted Germany to blame "France's irremediable hatred" against it for the failure of concerted European action. "Germany and France together would have been in a position to prevent the McKinley [and Dingley] Tariff[s] which [are] so detrimental to all European states ... [Instead], France went its own way to obtain special favors [at the expense of the Community]."[243]

A second reason for failure is the virtual absence of sustained demand by business for integration. The American economist H. H. Powers sent a circular letter in 1898 to the secretaries of several chambers of commerce in Europe asking their opinion on plans for a European Zollverein. The typical response expressed little interest in such a union. A common concern was raised by the secretary of the chamber of commerce at Leipzig, who believed that "owing to present protective tendencies and inter-state mistrust and envy," the realization of such a union was a question of the far distant future. "This opinion," he added, "is also shared ... by our trading classes."[244] The British journal *The Economist* similarly dismissed the idea of a European commercial union as "peculiarly absurd and impossible." It added:

How are you to define "European" interests? Take the coal mines and iron

---

[241] On the central European commercial treaty system, see Francke, "Zollpolitische Einigungsbestrebungen in Mitteleuropa während des letzten Jahrzehnts," 195–206; Werner Sombart, "Die Neuen Handelsverträge, Insbesondere Deutschlands," *Jahrbuch für Gesetzgebung, Verwaltung und Volkswirtschaft im Deutschen Reich* 16 (Leipzig, 1892), 215–279.

[242] See Henry Farnam, "German Tariff Policy, Past and Present," 29–30.

[243] Schmoller, "Die Wandlungen in der europäischen Handelspolitik des 19. Jahrhunderts," 381; see also Francke, "Zollpolitische Einigungsbestrebungen in Mitteleuropa während des letzten Jahrzehnts," 194.

[244] Fisk, "Continental Opinion Regarding a Proposed Middle European Tariff-Union," 40–41.

furnaces in North-Eastern France and those over the border in Germany. They are rivals to one another all over the world just as truly as either is a rival of the coal and iron industries of Pennsylvania. The French ironmaster, to say the least, is no more likely to ally himself with the German against the American than with the American against the German. Why should he? Does competition wear a less serious aspect when just over the border than when it acts three thousand miles over the sea? We should say, rather, that it becomes more keen and intense, especially when it is inflamed by old national feuds.[245]

Europe remained divided. European countries now resorted to self-help measures to deal with the "American menace." Many increased their tariff barriers and began to discriminate against American products. France increased protection considerably with its Meline Tariff. The Tariff also instituted minimum and maximum schedules. The maximum schedule applied, notably, to the United States whose McKinley Tariff hurt the bulk of French exports, namely luxury goods such as wines, silks, china, gloves, woolens, and works of art. Most European countries secured the minimum schedule. The preferred rates of the minimum schedule were eventually extended in whole or in part to Colombia, Ecuador, Mexico, Paraguay, Uruguay, Venezuela, Egypt, and Japan – all countries with which the United States desired closer commercial relations. Canada and Argentina, whose agricultural products competed with American exports in the French market, also received the minimum schedule.[246] Germany followed France in the direction of discriminatory trade practices and increased protection against the United States by raising tariffs and passing stringent patent laws.

Taking advantage of Europe's division, however, Americans managed to overcome the new barriers with ease. Rather than unilaterally lowering its own duties and adopting an unconditional interpretation of the Most-Favored-Nation clause, the United States obtained concessions by pursuing an active bilateral trade strategy. This was rendered possible with the reinstatement of reciprocity as an instrument of export expansion in the Dingley Tariff Act of 1897. Kasson, the special reciprocity commissioner of President McKinley, negotiated four treaties with European countries. An agreement was reached with France in 1898 whereby concessions authorized by the Dingley Tariff Act were granted in return for the French minimum rates on various goods.[247] In 1900 Germany granted minimum rates to the United States which were similar to those conceded earlier to some of its neighbors. Two more

[245] "Europe and America," *The Economist* 58 (December 29, 1900), 1855.
[246] Lake, *Power, Protection and Free Trade*, p. 122; see also Ashley, *Modern Tariff History*, pp. 331–346.
[247] Taussig, *The Tariff History of the United States*, pp. 352–354.

reciprocity agreements were negotiated, with Portugal in 1899 and Italy in 1900. They all accomplished the same objective: to penetrate the walls of tariff protection that were rising in Europe against products from overseas.

In the end, there was no sign of abatement of American business in Europe. Europe had failed to put itself on a par with the United States. Instead of a Union capable of confronting the "American menace," Europeans preferred the comfort of the old routine: division, delusion, and mutual distrust.[248]

---

[248] In his preface to a book by Edmond Théry entitled *Europe et Etats-Unis d'Amérique* (Paris: Ernest Flammarion, 1899), Marcel Dubois contrasts the experience of the United States of America with the "spectacle lamentable des *'Etats-Désunis' d'Europe*" (pitiable spectacle of the "Disunited States" of Europe), p. 12, my italics.

5 Integration outside Europe

1 Introduction

In this chapter, the success or failure of various integration schemes outside the continent of Europe is discussed as a further test of the validity of the analytical framework elaborated in chapter 3. Section 2 takes up regional integration projects in Latin America in the 1960s and then in the wave of integration in the 1990s. The argument is made that these projects can be understood as examples of the "second integrative response." The formation of the European Community was critical in triggering integration projects in the 1960s, while the recent deepening and enlargement of the European Union has been a key factor in triggering the latest wave of integration. Another external catalyst was the creation of the North American Free Trade Area in the early 1990s. All but one of the Latin American integration schemes of the first wave eventually failed. Two factors explain this outcome: lack of sustained demand for integration and failing regional leadership. The outcome of the latest wave is less certain. Latin America has changed in many ways since the 1960s. Most notably, the structure of the economies has changed. Industrialization has broadened the scope for mutually beneficial exchange at the regional level, giving rise to demand for regional institutional arrangements. However, weak leadership and an absence of "commitment mechanisms" have already derailed several integration objectives.

Section 3 addresses integration in Asia. Using the analytical categories of chapter 3, it examines the motives behind old and new integration projects in the region, assesses the performance of early schemes and ponders the prospects of the latest wave, including plans for a free trade area comprising the members of the Association of Southeast Asian Nations and regional integration within the Asia Pacific Economic Cooperation forum. Section 4 concludes the chapter with an examination of the factors motivating integration in North America and a prediction of the likely fate of the North American Free Trade Area.

2   Integration in Latin America

The first wave of integration

Commercial unions have been established in Latin America as collective responses to external shocks that threatened to inflict severe damage on the economies of the region. One such external event was the creation of the European Community. The EC's common external tariff and protectionist agricultural policy sent shockwaves through Latin America, a continent that heavily depended on free access to the markets of industrialist countries for its primary commodity exports. Another discriminating feature was the EC's extension of the preferential arrangements of individual colonial powers to the whole Community. As a result, the dependent territories of France, Belgium, Italy, and the Netherlands in Africa and Asia had preferential market access to all the member states of the Community after 1958.[1] Thus, for example, cocoa and coffee exported from the French colonies in Africa were admitted duty free to the entire common market after the creation of the EC, while cocoa supplied by Honduras or coffee supplied by Brazil now faced a uniform external tariff.

This threat of trade diversion caught Latin America at a particularly inopportune moment. Latin America's trade gap with industrialized countries had been rapidly widening and its terms of trade deteriorating.[2] Furthermore, the average annual growth rate of Latin American economies had fallen from approximately 5 percent between 1950 and 1955 to only 1.7 percent between 1956 and 1959. The President of Uruguay captured the general sense of panic well when he noted that "the formation of a European Common Market ... constitutes a state of near-war against Latin American exports. Therefore, *we must reply to one integration with another one*, to one increase of acquisitive power by internal enrichment by another, to inter-European cooperation by inter-Latin American cooperation."[3] Successful economic integration, it was hoped, would improve Latin America's bargaining power and thus raise the price of its exports.[4] It would also contribute to import

[1] Sidney Dell, *Trade Blocs and Common Markets* (New York: Alfred Knopf, 1963), p. 187.
[2] The terms of trade of developing countries declined from 1950 to 1962 by 12 percent; Latin America's terms of trade dropped 21 percent in the same period, due in great part to adverse movements in coffee prices. See Sidney Dell, *A Latin American Common Market?* (London: Oxford University Press, 1966), p. 9.
[3] *The Observer* (London, July 30, 1961), 1; cited in Dell, *Trade Blocs and Common Markets*, p. 210, my italics.
[4] Some countries urged the formation of a Latin American economic bloc not only to face the European threat more effectively, but also to have greater leverage in dealings with the United States. Grunwald, Wionczek, and Carnoy, for example, noted: "Very few

substitution industrialization at the regional level by forcing national economies to specialize within the framework of the expanded and protected regional market.[5]

A first Latin American response to the European common market was the creation of the Latin American Free Trade Association (LAFTA). It was established by the Treaty of Montevideo, which was signed in February 1960 by Argentina, Brazil, Chile, Mexico, Paraguay, Peru, and Uruguay. Ecuador and Colombia joined LAFTA in 1961, Venezuela in 1966, and Bolivia in 1967. The signatory governments expressed their determination "to establish, gradually and progressively, a Latin American common market" and "to pool their efforts to achieve the progressive complementarity and integration of their economies on the basis of an effective reciprocity of benefits."[6] In pursuit of these goals, the treaty provided for the establishment of a free-trade area. Tariff reductions were to be effected according to two schedules. The Common Schedule listed products whose tariff rates were to be eliminated by 1973. The National Schedules, on the other hand, included products on which individual member states granted concessions in annual bilateral negotiation sessions. The treaty permitted temporary trade restrictions in case of payment imbalances or if import competition damaged an industry of strategic importance to a member's economy. Special provisions were made to assist the development of the more backward members of the Association. The

Latin American leaders were ready to speak openly, but the feelings of many were echoed by Chile's President Eduardo Frei in 1964, when he called for 'the twenty poor and disunited [Latin American] nations [to] form a powerful and progressive union which can deal with the United States as an equal'." See Joseph Grunwald, Miguel Wionczek, and Martin Carnoy, *Latin American Economic Integration and US Policy* (Washington, D.C.: Brookings Institution, 1972), pp. 8–9.

[5] Miguel Wionczek, "The Rise and the Decline of Latin American Economic Integration," *Journal of Common Market Studies* 9 (September 1970), 49–66. The idea of import-substitution industrialization at the regional level was most forcefully propagated by Raúl Prebisch, the executive secretary of the United Nations Economic Commission for Latin America. Policies of import substitution at the national level had already been implemented after the Second World War in countries such as Argentina, Brazil and Chile. See Raúl Prebisch, *The Economic Development of Latin America and its Principal Problems* (New York: United Nations Economic Commission for Latin America, 1950).

[6] The text of the Treaty of Montevideo is reprinted in Dell, *A Latin American Common Market?*, pp. 228–256. Dell's book is an excellent early description and analysis of LAFTA. See also Miguel Wionczek (ed.), *Latin American Economic Integration* (New York: Praeger, 1966); Ernst Haas and Philippe Schmitter, *The Politics of Economics in Latin American Regionalism*, Monograph Series in World Affairs (Denver: University of Denver, 1965); Edward Gale, *Latin American Free Trade Association: Progress, Problems, Prospects* (Washington: Office of External Research, US Department of State, 1969); Edward Milenky, *The Politics of Regional Organization in Latin America: The Latin American Free Trade Association* (New York: Praeger, 1973).

LAFTA agreement also encouraged closer coordination of industrial policies.[7]

The implementation of the treaty provisions, however, was arduous and remained unfinished. Chile's President, Eduardo Frei, complained in early 1965: "The advance towards economic integration has become slow and cumbersome. The possibilities of making further headway ... seem to be exhausted."[8] Trade expansion failed to materialize: while the average share of intraregional trade in the total trade of LAFTA countries was 8.7 percent from 1952 to 1960, the average from 1961 to 1964 was only 7.9 percent, despite a slight increase in total trade from 1960. Intraregional trade ceased to grow in 1967 while extraregional trade continued to boom. Attempts to revive the process of integration by creating a LAFTA Council of Ministers proved unsuccessful. Failure was publicly acknowledged at LAFTA's 1969 Annual Conference. The ensuing Caracas protocol postponed the deadline for free trade from 1973 to 1980, suspended the Common Schedule, and made only token reference to the idea of a common market. For all practical purposes, LAFTA was shelved.[9] In 1980, LAFTA was replaced by the Latin American Integration Association (LAIA), a considerably more flexible trade-liberalization arrangement that granted tariff preferences to only about 10 percent of all goods traded.[10]

Besides LAFTA, there was another major integration scheme launched in the early 1960s, the Central American Common Market (CACM). It was established by the Treaty of Managua signed in December 1960 by El Salvador, Guatemala, Honduras, and Nicaragua.[11] Costa Rica joined CACM in 1963. The treaty provided for immediate free trade in all products originating in the region except for those listed. Trade in the excluded products, which comprised approxi-

---

[7] See the Treaty of Montevideo in Dell, *A Latin American Common Market?*, chapter 16.

[8] Quoted from a letter by Frei dated January 6, 1965, addressed to Raúl Prebisch, José Antonio Mayobre, Felipe Herrera, and Carlos Sanz de Santa María; reprinted in Dell, *A Latin American Common Market?*, Appendix II, p. 280.

[9] On LAFTA's demise, see Miguel Wionczek, "The Rise and the Decline of Latin American Economic Integration," especially 54–58; "Latin American Integration and United States Economic Policies," in Robert Gregg (ed.), *International Organization in the Western Hemisphere* (Syracuse: Syracuse University Press, 1968), pp. 91–156, especially pp. 105–125; Keith Griffin and Ricardo French-Davis, "Customs Unions and Latin American Integration," *Journal of Common Market Studies* 4 (October 1965), 1–21; and Bela Balassa, "Regional Integration and Trade Liberalization in Latin America," *Journal of Common Market Studies* 10 (September 1971), 58–77.

[10] Organization for Economic Cooperation and Development, *Regional Integration and Developing Countries* (Paris: OECD, 1993), p. 59.

[11] The text of the Treaty can be found in Dell, *A Latin American Common Market?*, pp. 256–269.

mately 50 percent of intra-regional trade, was to be freed by 1966. The signatories also agreed to adopt a common external tariff (without specifying a deadline), to establish a Central American Bank for Economic Integration to serve "as an instrument for the financing and promotion of ... regionally balanced ... economic growth," and to "ensure as soon as possible a reasonable equilization of the relevant laws and regulations in force ... [with a] view to establishing uniform tax incentives [towards] ... industrial development."[12]

CACM was triggered, like LAFTA, by external events: fear of a protectionist common market in Europe and deteriorating terms of trade. Another event of importance was Fidel Castro's victorious revolution in Cuba. Schmitter notes that "the pervasive fear of Castroide subversion after 1959 added a desperate sense of urgency, making elites much more willing to experiment with policy innovations."[13] Unlike LAFTA, CACM proved highly successful during its first decade. It quickly set up a Permanent Secretariat, directed by a Secretary-General, and other bodies including the Central American Economic Council, an Executive Council, the Central American Integration Bank, a Monetary Clearing House, and an advisory Central American Monetary Council. By 1966, tariffs were removed on 94 percent of intraregional trade, and 80 percent of extraregional imports were covered by a common external tariff.[14] The dramatic change in intraregional trade between 1958 and 1968 is detailed in tables 5.1 and 5.2 and summarized in table 5.3.

Intraregional trade among CACM countries represented 5.9 percent

---

[12] See chapters 7 and 8 of the Treaty of Managua.

[13] Philippe Schmitter, *Autonomy or Dependence as Regional Integration Outcomes: Central America* (Berkeley: Institute of International Studies, University of California [Berkeley], 1972), p. 18. Studies on CACM include Roger Hansen, *Central America: Regional Integration and Economic Development*, Studies in Development Progress, no. 1 (Washington: National Planning Association, 1967); James Cochrane, *The Politics of Regional Integration: The Central American Case* (New Orleans: Tulane Studies in Political Science, 1969); Alberto Fuentes Mohr, *La Creación de un Mercado Común: Apuntes históricos sobre la experiencia de Centroamérica* (Buenos Aires: Instituto Para La Integración de América Latina [INTAL], 1972); Stuart Fagan, *Central American Economic Integration: The Politics of Unequal Benefits*, Research Series, no. 15 (Berkeley: Institute of International Studies, University of California [Berkeley], 1970); Carlos Castillo, *Growth and Integration in Central America* (New York: Praeger, 1966); Joseph Nye, "Central American Regional Integration," *International Conciliation* 562 (March 1967), 1–66. The studies by Hansen, Cochrane, Castillo, and Nye were reviewed in Gary Wynia, "Central American Integration: The Paradox of Success," *International Organization* 24 (Spring 1970), 319–334.

[14] OECD, *Regional Integration and Developing Countries*, p. 56. See also Sebastian Edwards and M. Savastano, "Latin America's Intra-regional Trade: Evolution and Future," in David Greenaway, Thomas Hyclak, and Robert Thornton (eds.), *Economic Aspects of Regional Trading Arrangements* (New York: Harvester Wheatsheaf, 1989).

Table 5.1. *CACM intraregional and extraregional trade 1959*
(Sum of exports [X] and imports [M] in millions of US $ [% share of X and M in total trade])

	Costa Rica	Guate-mala	El Salvador	Hondu-ras	Nicara-gua	CACM	United States	Europe
Costa Rica		0.6 (0.3%)	1.3 (0.7%)	— (—)	3.1 (1.7%)	5 (2.8%)	88.8 (49%)	59 (33%)
Guate-mala	— (—)		2.6 (1.1%)	0.9 (0.4%)	— (—)	3.5 (1.5%)	138.3 (58.3%)	66.2 (27.9%)
El Salvador	1.1 (0.5%)	8.5 (4.0%)		10.5 (4.9%)	2.9 (1.4%)	23 (10.8%)	84.8 (40%)	70.8 (33.3%)
Hondu-ras	— (—)	1.6 (1.2%)	9.9 (7.5%)		— (—)	11.5 (8.7%)	69.3 (52.7%)	23.1 (25.2%)
Nicara-gua	3.7 (2.7%)	0.2 (0.01%)	3.2 (2.3%)	1.1 (0.8%)		8.2 (5.9%)	54.4 (39.1%)	41.3 (29.7%)

Source: International Monetary Fund, *Directions of Trade Statistics Yearbook*, various issues.

Table 5.2. *CACM intraregional and extraregional trade 1968*
(Sum of exports [X] and imports [M] in millions of US $ [% share of X and M in total trade])

	Costa Rica	Guate-mala	El Salvador	Hondu-ras	Nicara-gua	CACM	United States	Europe
Costa Rica		23.9 (6.2%)	24.8 (6.4%)	11.6 (3%)	25.3 (6.6%)	85.6 (22.2%)	222.3 (57.9%)	76.4 (19.9%)
Guate-mala	21.1 (4.4%)		58.8 (12.3%)	18.4 (3.9%)	13.8 (2.9%)	112 (23.5%)	163.9 (34.4%)	100.8 (21.2%)
El Salvador	25.6 (6%)	65.7 (15.5%)		38.5 (9.1%)	21.9 (5.1%)	151.7 (35.7%)	103.2 (24.3%)	94.9 (22.3%)
Hondu-ras	11.7 (3.2%)	11.3 (3.1%)	37 (10.1%)		8.9 (2.4%)	68.9 (18.9%)	163.3 (44.9%)	76.7 (21.1%)
Nicara-gua	25.2 (7.4%)	16.5 (4.8%)	20.6 (6%)	8.5 (2.5%)		70.8 (20.7%)	116.8 (34.2%)	67.1 (19.6%)

Source: International Monetary Fund, *Directions of Trade Statistics Yearbook*, various issues.

Table 5.3. *Summary of CACM Trade Changes*
(% Change in intraregional and extraregional Trade [share of X and M in total trade] between 1959 and 1968)

	1959	1968	% change
Intra-CACM trade	5.9	24.2	+18.3
Trade between CACM and Latin America (other than CACM)	4.8	4.4	−0.4
Trade between CACM and the United States	47.8	39.1	−8.7
Trade between CACM and Europe	29.8	20.8	−9

Source: International Monetary Fund, *Directions of Trade Statistics Yearbook*, various issues.

of total trade in 1958. In the span of only ten years the number had increased to 24.2 percent, a stunning 18.3 percent leap. In the same period, the relative importance of CACM's two major trading partners declined. Trade with the United States decreased by 8.7 percent, from 47.8 percent to 39.1 percent, in 1968, and trade with Europe fell from 29.8 percent to 20.8 percent. Equally significant was the change in the composition of intraregional trade. In the late 1950s, most trade was in food products and raw materials. A decade later, two-thirds of regional trade consisted of manufactured (mainly consumer) goods and chemicals.[15]

CACM's success story came to an abrupt end when the El Salvadorean army attacked neighboring Honduras on July 14, 1969. This attack cannot plausibly be attributed to the integration process but appears to be the result of other and more complex causes.[16] The

[15] See W. T. Wilford and G. Christou, "A Sectoral Analysis of Disaggregated Trade Flows in the Central American Common Market, 1962–1970," *Journal of Common Market Studies* 12 (December 1973), 159–175.

[16] I thank Philippe Schmitter for clarifying this point. For a good account of the causes of the Soccer War, see William Durham, *Scarcity and Survival in Central America: Ecological Origins of the Soccer War* (Stanford: Stanford University Press, 1979), p. 1. According to Durham, the critical issue leading to the hostilities was the presence in Honduras of some 300,000 Salvadorean immigrants. In June 1969, Honduras reversed its policy of tolerating the immigration and began expelling these Salvadoreans from their rural homesteads. The expulsions began shortly before the soccer teams of the two countries met in the World Cup semi-final matches. With the defeat of the Honduran team in San Salvador in June 1969, many of the Honduran spectators were set upon and mauled by the crowd. The immediate reaction in Honduras was to step up the expulsion of Salvadorean immigrants. This prompted El Salvador to close its borders in the hope that such action would force Honduras to relocate the *campesinos*.

ensuing "Soccer War" lasted only 100 hours but left several thousand dead on both sides, turned 100,000 people into refugees, and destroyed half of El Salvador's oil refining and storage facilities. Attempts to renew economic integration in the following years were thwarted by lingering hostilities. The share of intraregional trade in total trade of CACM countries represented only 11.9 percent in 1988, a sharp decline from the 24.2 percent twenty years earlier.[17]

Explaining outcomes of the first wave

The failure of LAFTA can be attributed to the absence of the integration conditions discussed in chapter 3, notably lack of sustained demand for integration and failing regional leadership.

The damage which EC protection caused to Latin American exports was reversed surprisingly quickly. Several factors played a role in this. Growing prosperity in the EC member states, successive reductions of the Community's external tariff in the Dillon, Kennedy, and Tokyo Rounds of the General Agreement on Tariffs and Trade (GATT) negotiations, and the EC's grant of preferential market access to an ever-increasing number of countries, including several members of LAFTA, triggered an unprecedented export boom in Latin America, pulling the region out of relative economic decline. Paradoxically, Latin American exports to the Community fared better than those from associated countries, growing by 97 percent between 1958 and 1964 while exports from associated countries rose by only 33 percent.[18] This export boom and ensuing economic prosperity in Latin America quickly eased the pressure for integration. As Wionczek notes, once the atmosphere of external trade crisis that was hanging over Latin America began to dissipate, the objective of integration was conveniently forgotten.[19] Market actors regained access to their traditional export markets and political leaders saw little reason to pay the higher price in terms of forgone national autonomy that deeper integration would have entailed.

This failed, however, and El Salvador launched its attack on Honduras to "defend the human rights of their countrymen" (*ibid.*, p. 2 and pp. 163–164).

[17] For a detailed study of CACM's evolution in the 1980s, see Juan Alberto Fuentes, *Desafíos de la Integración Centroamericana* (San José, Costa Rica: Instituto Centroamericano de Administratión Pública [ICAP], 1989).

[18] Sidney Wells, "The EEC and Trade with Developing Countries," *Journal of Common Market Studies* 4 (December 1965), 158.

[19] Miguel Wionczek, "The Rise and the Decline of Latin American Economic Integration," 61. Dell makes a similar point in his *A Latin American Common Market?*, p. 75.

Another reason for failure was absence of leadership. As argued in chapter 3, absence of leadership raises the costs of haggling over redistribution issues and complicates the coordination of institutional arrangements. Many of these obstacles were present in the LAFTA case. LAFTA was composed of three groups: the semi-industrial "giants" Brazil, Argentina, and Mexico, a middle group led by Chile, Colombia, and Venezuela, and the group of least-developed economies that included Bolivia, Ecuador, and Paraguay. Integration of these different economies risked benefitting the more developed larger countries at the expense of the less developed smaller economies. The drafters of the treaty were sensitive to the issue of equitable distribution of benefits from integration and therefore inserted a provision giving the weaker economies special privileges, such as concessions on tariff reductions, escape clauses based on balance-of-payment difficulties, and technical assistance. Nevertheless, Paraguay and Ecuador complained almost from the onset that they were not benefitting from their special rights and that gains from trade liberalization, however modest, were accruing disproportionately to Brazil, Argentina, and Mexico.[20] None of these big countries, however, were willing either to address the redistribution issue or to show leadership in coordinating regional policies. Writing in 1965, Griffin and French-Davis noted: "So far ... no attempt has been made to ... ensure that the benefits of integration are equitably distributed ... No institutional mechanism [exists] to translate [LAFTA's] aspirations into reality."[21]

Displeased with the *laissez-faire* attitude of the three "giants," the countries on the western coast of South America began in 1967 to contemplate the creation of their own commercial group. By uniting, they would also increase their voice in Latin American affairs.[22] Two years later, Bolivia, Chile, Colombia, Peru, and Ecuador signed the Cartagena Agreement establishing the Andean Common Market (also

---

[20] See William Avery and James Cochrane, "Innovation in Latin American Regionalism: The Andean Common Market," *International Organization* 27 (Spring 1972), 181–223, figure 1 on page 185; Kevin Kearns, "The Andean Common Market: A New Thrust at Economic Integration in Latin America," *Journal of Interamerican Studies* 14 (May 1972), 225–249. See also Shoshana Tancer, *Economic Nationalism in Latin America: The Quest for Economic Independence* (New York: Praeger, 1976), pp. 55–56.

[21] Keith Griffin and Ricardo French-Davis, "Customs Unions and Latin American Integration," *Journal of Common Market Studies* 4 (October 1965), 1–21.

[22] The bargaining power motive is highlighted in Grunwald, Wionczek, and Carnoy, *Latin American Economic Integration and US Policy*, p. 56. Avery and Cochrane also acknowledge its importance but note that it was "not ... emphasized in the public statements of the [Andean Pact] member-governments" (Avery and Cochrane, "Innovation in Latin American Regionalism," p. 183).

called the Andean Pact).[23] Venezuela joined in 1973.[24] The creation of the Andean Pact does not follow the logic of the "second integrative response" and thus must be viewed as an exception to the framework of chapter 3. It is a response to the internal failings of LAFTA, not a response to negative externalities of integration elsewhere. Nevertheless, the analytical framework remains relevant in explaining the failure of the Andean Pact.

The Cartagena Agreement called for free trade, a common external tariff by 1980, joint planning and execution of industrial projects, harmonization of economic and social policies, improvement of regional transportation, and a regional foreign investment code. The founding countries were intent on avoiding LAFTA's mistakes and shortcomings – particularly with regard to the thorny issues of redistribution and coordination. To this purpose, they set up the Andean Development Corporation (Corporación Andina de Fomento).

Despite good intentions, Andean integration came to naught. The pact was afflicted by structural weaknesses similar to those of LAFTA. Andean countries were not natural trading partners, and thus the potential for gain from integration was relatively limited. The bulk of their exports consisted of agricultural and mineral products such as bananas, sugar, coffee, copper, and iron ore. Eighty percent of these exports went in approximately equal shares to the United States and Europe.[25] Most of their imports, in turn, originated in the US and Europe and consisted overwhelmingly of machinery equipment, manu-factured goods, and chemicals. The share of intraregional trade in the total trade of Andean countries amounted to a very modest 1.2 percent in 1970. By 1988, the share had grown to only 2.5 percent.[26]

Naturally high transaction costs in the region were another reason

---

[23] For studies on the Andean Pact, see the analysis by Kearns, Avery, and Cochrane mentioned above, and Edward Milenky, "From Integration to Development Nationalism: The Andean Group 1965–1971," *Inter-American Economic Affairs* 25 (Winter 1971), 77–91; Kenneth Switzer, "The Andean Group: A Reappraisal," *Inter-American Economic Affairs* 26 (Spring 1973), 69–81; José Luis Gálvez and Augusto Llosa, *Dinámica de la Integracion Andina* (Lima: Ediciones Banco Popular del Perú, 1974); Rafael Vargas-Hidalgo, "The Crisis of the Andean Pact: Lessons for Integration Among Developing Countries," *Journal of Common Market Studies* 27 (March 1979), 213–226; Elisabeth Ferris, "Foreign Investment as an Influence on Foreign Policy Behavior: The Andean Pact," *Inter-American Economic Affairs* 33 (Autumn 1979), 45–67; and George Koopmann, "Ten Years Andean Pact: A Re-examination," *Intereconomics* (May/June 1979), 116–122.

[24] For an analysis of Venezuela's entry into the Andean Pact, see William Avery, "Oil, Politics, and Economic Policy Making: Venezuela and the Andean Common Market," *International Organization* 30 (Autumn 1976), 541–571.

[25] The source of the data is International Monetary Fund, *Directions of Trade, Yearbook 1960/70* (Washington, D.C.: IMF).

[26] OECD, *Regional Integration and Developing Countries*, p. 46, table 5.

why the potential for mutual gains, and thus the demand for integration, were weak. Geographer Kevin Kearns wrote:

In theory... integration ... and free flow of trade work well, but in practice it is somewhat more difficult – and especially so in the Andean region. Nowhere can the resistance to subregional cohesion be seen more lucidly than in the physical realm. The utterly discordant physiography of Western South America is among the most astringent and restrictive on earth. The land is fraught with barriers. The high ranges of the Andean cordillera, heavily forested selva plains, and broad and treacherous rivers work at keeping people and resources apart rather than joined.[27]

Andean integration also failed to satisfy supply conditions. Most notably, it lacked a regional leader. This led to insurmountable problems of policy coordination.[28] A case in point is the failure to agree on a common external tariff. Peru favored an effective protection rate no higher than 40 percent, Colombia proposed a 60 percent tariff. Ecuador and Venezuela, however, insisted on a rate no lower than 80 percent.[29] No country was willing to compromise or able to bribe the others into acquiescence. As a result, the Protocol of Arequipa was signed on April 21, 1978, postponing the deadline for completing the customs union until December 31, 1989. Another example is the Andean Pact's Sectoral Programs of Industrial Development (SPIDs). Governments could not agree on who was to produce what, and they were unwilling to close down existing plants, fearful of drawing the ire of entrenched local interests or worried about the political consequences of rising unemployment.[30] A final factor contributing to the coordination difficulties of Andean countries was the great instability of the political regimes in the

---

[27] Kevin Kearns, "The Andean Common Market," 239.

[28] See Rafael Vargas-Hidalgo, "The Crisis of the Andean Pact," 213–226; and Kevin Middlebrook, "Regional Organization and Andean Economic Integration, 1967–75," *Journal of Common Market Studies* 17 (September 1978), 62–82.

[29] David Hojman, "The Andean Pact: Failure of a Model of Economic Integration?," *Journal of Common Market Studies* 20 (December 1981), 147.

[30] On the difficulties of SPIDs for chemicals, pharmaceuticals, fertilizers, electronics, and cars, see for example "Andean Group: Summary of the Current Situation," *Bank of London & South America Review* 12 (December 1978), 669–674. In light of these problems, it may seem surprising that the member governments of the Andean Pact were able to agree on a regional investment code. "Decision 24" – as the code was called – provided for the transformation of foreign subsidiaries into mixed companies and national firms according to a fixed timetable. New foreign investment projects had to give local partners an equity share of at least 51 percent and participation in the management of new firms. Stringent restrictions were placed on profit remittances and reinvestment. But the success of the investment code proved ephemeral. Individual countries relaxed the restrictions on foreign investment when foreign capital became scarce. The region's share of foreign investment in Latin America dropped from 34 percent to 20 percent between 1967 and 1975. See Elizabeth Ferris, "Foreign Investment as an Influence on Foreign Policy Behavior: The Andean Pact," 67.

area. Newly formed governments frequently reversed the policies of the previous administration, thereby jeopardizing regional consensus.

Prima facie, the success of CACM during the 1960s appears anomalous. The economies of CACM countries were similarly endowed and therefore exhibited little complementarity. Their exports consisted mainly of coffee, bananas, cotton, and extractive resources. Half of them went to the United States and about 30 percent to Europe. No single Central American country stood out as natural leader of the group and problems of equitable distribution of the gains from integration emerged repeatedly in the process of trade liberalization. Nevertheless, there was a critical difference between LAFTA and the Andean Pact on the one hand and CACM on the other. In CACM, unlike in the other two integration schemes, the United States came to play the role of an adopted regional leader, easing distributional problems and assisting policy coordination. In turn, CACM countries accepted the rules of integration as defined by the United States.

Historically, the US was opposed to regionalism in the Americas, preferring instead to deal bilaterally with individual countries.[31] The creation of the European Community, however, motivated a rethinking of the conventional policy. "If the EC builds Eurafrica . . ., why should not the United States . . . draw the obvious conclusions regarding its own position in the Western Hemisphere?"[32] In the early 1960s, Nelson Rockefeller evoked in public speeches the idea of "free flow of men and goods and money from Point Barrow [Alaska] to Tierra del Fuego."[33] Big business seconded his views.[34] And Senator Hubert Humphrey wrote in 1964: "The emergence of a powerful Western Europe – likely to pursue a more independent foreign policy – makes hemisphere cooperation more urgent if the nations of this hemisphere are not only to solve their immediate internal problems but to play a proper role in world affairs in future decades."[35]

Most Latin American leaders were not eager, however, to open their markets to American competition or to give their powerful northern neighbor a say in their affairs. Eduardo Frei, the President of Chile and

---

[31] Philippe Schmitter, *Autonomy or Dependence as Regional Integration Outcomes: Central America*, p. 21; see also Lorenzo Harrison, "Central American Dilemma: National Sovereignty or Unification," *International Review of History and Political Science* 2 (December 1965), 100–110; and Arthur Whitaker, *The Western Hemisphere Idea: Its Rise and Decline* (Ithaca: Cornell University Press, 1954).

[32] Sidney Dell, *A Latin American Common Market?*, p. 30.   [33] *Ibid.*

[34] On US corporate interest in LAFTA see Robert Edwin Denham, "The Role of the US as an External Actor in the Integration of Latin America," *Journal of Common Market Studies* 7, no. 3 (March 1969), 215–216.

[35] Hubert Humphrey, "US Policy in Latin America," *Foreign Affairs* 42 (July 1964), 586, quoted in Dell, *A Latin American Common Market?*, p. 32.

a champion of Latin American integration, wrote in *Foreign Affairs* that the objective of integration was to establish a Latin American common market for Latin Americans. He added, without mentioning the United States: "It is inadmissible that the mere fact of making available financial aid gives any nation the right to demand that another implement specific types of structural changes ... This would constitute an intolerable infringement of national sovereignty."[36] The President of Mexico, Gustavo Díaz Ordaz, echoed this theme in a speech at Punta del Este by insisting that "Latin American integration is, and we should make every effort so that it continues to be, an exclusively Latin American process."[37]

Central American attitudes to US involvement in regional integration were quite different. In March 1963 the presidents of Central America met with President Kennedy in San José, Costa Rica, to discuss the integration issue. The meeting ended with the leaders of the region pledging unity in their efforts to accelerate the establishment of a customs and monetary union and the adoption of common fiscal, economic, and social policies. President Kennedy, in turn, promised generous technical, logistic, and financial assistance.[38] For Kennedy, successful regional integration in Central America offered not only new business opportunities for American firms but also a way of containing the spread of communism from Cuba. American support played a critical role in fostering integration in Central America. In Joseph Nye's words, "economic issues tend to become easier to resolve when a large slice of pie may be gained from taking a long-run view of one's interests, and the United States aid ... contributed to the expectation that the pie will grow."[39] The US established the Regional Office for Central America and Panama (ROCAP) to provide a coordinating point for the planning and administration of regional programs supported by the Agency for International Development. By 1969, ROCAP had distributed some $112.5 million for industrial projects as well as for research and feasibility studies.[40]

Additional US funds were disbursed through the Organization of American States (OAS) and the Interamerican Development Bank

---

[36] Eduardo Frei Montalva, "The Alliance that Lost its Way," *Foreign Affairs* 45 (April 1967), 447.
[37] Quoted in Miguel Wionczek, "Latin American Integration and US Economic Policies," in Robert Gregg, *International Organization in the Western Hemisphere* (Syracuse: Syracuse University Press, 1968), p. 151. Díaz's speech was reproduced in full by the Mexican daily press on April 13, 1967.
[38] Dell, *A Latin American Common Market?*, p. 60.
[39] Nye, "Central American Regional Integration," 54.
[40] Schmitter, *Autonomy and Dependence*, pp. 22–23.

(IDB). Credits of $16 million established the Central American Integration Bank (CABEI). By 1968, $55 million of the bank's $65 million capitalization came from the United States.[41] The US also helped other regional organizations. For example, it covered 22 percent of the operating budget of CACM's Permanent Secretariat and many special projects within it.[42] An important effect of this financial assistance was to ease tensions that arose in the process of integration because of perceived distributional inequities. Honduras and Nicaragua charged at times that their regional terms of trade were deteriorating because their markets were being flooded by imports from Guatemala and El Salvador while their exports stagnated. In response, the US increased its contributions to these two countries. Schmitter notes: "[T]he … prospect of losing [access to US funds] may have inhibited withdrawal (especially in the case of Honduras and Nicaragua)."[43]

The latest wave of integration

The second wave of integration in Latin America was triggered, like the first one, by external events that threatened to inflict severe damage on the economies of the region. It thus represents another example of the "second integrative response" logic.

The new round of enlargement and deepening of the European Union coincided with the collapse of communism in Eastern and Central Europe. It appeared that a period of sustained introspection was dawning in Europe, and Latin America was afraid of being relegated to the bottom of Europe's priorities. There was also concern that Germany, preoccupied and burdened by the demands of reunification, would no longer be able to play its central role in economic relations between Europe and Latin America.[44]

More specifically, Latin America feared damage in three areas: trade, investment, and aid. In the late 1980s, it shipped about 20 percent of its

---

[41] CABEI loans assisted local industrialists in modernizing their factories in order to serve the enlarged market better. See Aron Segal, "The Integration of Developing Countries: Some Thoughts on East Africa and Central America," *Journal of Common Market Studies* 5 (March 1967), 270.

[42] See Nye, "Central American Regional Integration," table 2, 35.

[43] Schmitter, *Autonomy or Dependence*, p. 31.

[44] Dieter Benecke, "Relaciones entre América Latina y Alemania a la luz de los cambios en Europa Oriental," *Contribuciones* 4 (Buenos Aires, 1990), 113–119; Violanda Botet, "Die deutsch-lateinamerikanischen Beziehungen in den neunziger Jahren," *Aussenpolitik* 44 (1993), 44–54; and Andrew Hurrell, "Regionalism in the Americas," in Abraham Lowenthal and Gregory Treverton (eds.), *Latin America in a New World* (Boulder: Westview Press, 1994), pp. 167–190.

Table 5.4. *Foreign investment stock in selected Latin American countries*
(% of total stock in selected countries held by Europe, the United States, and Japan
between 1988 and 1989)

Brazil	Mexico	Argentina	Chile	Venezuela	Colombia
Europe 49.6	United States 63.0	Europe 48.0	United States 45.3	United States 45.5	United States 70.6
United States 28.2	Europe 25.2	United States 41.8	Europe 19.1	Europe 28.5	Europe 17.1
Japan 9.2	Japan 4.8	Japan 1.2	Japan 3.2	Japan 4.3	Japan 1.2

Source: Susan Kaufman Purcell and Françoise Simon (eds.), *Europe and Latin America in the World Economy* (Boulder: Lynne Rienne Publishers, 1995), p. 25.

exports to Europe.[45] The likely imposition of new trade barriers in "sensitive" industries such as textiles, clothing, footwear, steel, and certain minerals threatened to reduce that share significantly.[46] Investment diversion to Eastern Europe was another worry. In the past, Europe had played a very significant investment role in Latin America. In 1988, for example, its investment stock in Brazil, Argentina, Paraguay, and Uruguay was larger than the US stock (see table 5.4).

Aid diversion was also a concern to Latin American countries. European official development assistance to the region had steadily increased in the 1980s and reached $2.7 billion in 1990 – almost twice the amount provided by the United States.[47] With growing instability in Eastern Europe and the Mediterranean Basin, aid diversion seemed inevitable.[48]

Another external catalyst for integration in Latin America was the "defection" of Mexico when President Salinas proposed a free-trade agreement with the United States. The proposal sent shockwaves throughout Central and South America for two reasons. First, Latin

---

[45] 41 percent went to the United States and 5.9 percent to Japan. (Data is from the IMF, *International Financial Statistics*, various issues.)

[46] See Comisión Economica para América Latina y el Caribe (CEPAL), *Las Barreras No Arancelarias a las Exportaciones Latinoamericanas en la Comunidad Económica Europea* (Santiago, Chile: March 22, 1991); *La Política Comercial de la Comunidad Económica Europea después de 1992: Implicaciones para América Latina* (Santiago, Chile, April 28, 1992); Instituto de Relaciones Europeo-Latinoamericanas (IRELA), *El Mercado Único Europeo y Su Impacto En América Latina* (Madrid: IRELA, 1993).

[47] Blake Friscia and Françoise Simon, "The Economic Relationship Between Europe and Latin America," in Susan Kaufman Purcell and Françoise Simon (eds.), *Europe and Latin America in the World Economy* (Boulder: Lynne Rienne Publishers, 1995), p. 32.

[48] Christopher Stevens, "The Single Market: All-European Integration and the Developing Countries – The Potential for Aid Diversion," *Journal of Development Planning* 22 (1992), 19–35.

Americans had grown accustomed to Mexico vetoing United States initiatives and asserting its separateness and independence.[49] The "defection" had the consequence of weakening Latin American resistance to US hegemony. Second, the establishment of NAFTA threatened Mexico's Southern neighbors with substantial economic costs. Free access to the US market improved the competitive position of Mexican exporters over those located in other Latin American countries, thus raising the issue of trade diversion.[50] Investment diversion was another economic threat. American firms would now give investment priority to Mexico in order to create regional production networks throughout NAFTA, and European and Japanese investors would be drawn to Mexico to serve the US market.[51]

As in the late 1950s, these external events coincided with a period of general economic decline in Latin America. Years of underinvestment, mounting external debt, protectionism, and technical backwardness had resulted in economic marginalization, and the prices of many export commodities (such as oil, sugar, coffee, and tin) had plummeted.[52] As a result, Latin American countries became "obsessed by the fear of 'falling off' the map of the world economy."[53] Statistics bore out these

[49] Robert Pastor, "The North American Free Trade Agreement: Hemispheric and Geopolitical Implications," in *Trade Liberalization in the Western Hemisphere* (Washington, D.C.: Interamerican Development Bank and Economic Commission for Latin America and the Caribbean, 1995), 54.

[50] On trade diversion caused by NAFTA, see Nora Lustig, "NAFTA: Potential Impact on Mexico's Economy and Beyond," in Roberto Bouzas and Jaime Ros (eds.), *Economic Integration in the Western Hemisphere* (Notre Dame: University of Notre Dame Press, 1994), pp. 46–80; Carlos Alberto Primo Braga, "NAFTA and the Rest of the World," in Nora Lustig, Barry Bosworth, and Robert Lawrence (eds.), *North American Free Trade: Assessing the Impact* (Washington, D.C.: Brookings Institution, 1992), pp. 210–234; and Refik Erzan and Alexander Yeats, "US–Latin American Free Trade Areas: Some Empirical Evidence," in Sylvia Soborio (ed.) *The Premise and the Promise of Free Trade in the Americas* (New Brunswick: Transaction Publishers, 1992), pp. 117–146.

[51] There is now evidence that these concerns were legitimate. Blecker and Spiggs, for example, report that US foreign direct investment in manufacturing in Latin America (without Mexico) fell sharply in 1990 and 1991 while FDI in Mexico continued to grow. See Robert Blecker and William Spiggs, "Beyond NAFTA: Employment, Growth, and Income Distribution Effects of a Western Hemisphere Free Trade Area," in *Trade Liberalization in the Western Hemisphere*, pp. 123–164, table 17, p. 158. On European investment attracted to Mexico because of NAFTA, see Blake Friscia and Françoise Simon, "The Economic Relationship Between Europe and Latin America," p. 25, and Alberto van Klaveren, "Europe and Latin America in the 1990s," in Abraham Lowenthal and Gregory Treverton (eds.), *Latin America in a New World* (Boulder: Westview Press, 1994), pp. 81–104.

[52] Moises Naim, "Latin America: Post-Adjustment Blues," *Foreign Policy* 92 (Fall 1993), 133–150.

[53] Alberto van Klaveren, "Why Integration Now? Options for Latin America," in Peter Smith, *The Challenge of Integration: Europe and the Americas* (New Brunswick: Transaction Publishers, 1993), p. 118.

feelings of isolation. The region's share of world exports had dropped from a high of 12 percent in 1950 to 3.6 percent in 1992, the lowest in this century.[54] The investment picture looked equally bleak. Latin America's share of total US direct investment in developing countries, for example, had dropped from 73 percent in 1980 to 68 percent in 1989, while the Asia Pacific region's share had increased in the same period from 15 percent to 22 percent. European and Japanese investments in Latin America followed the same trend.

In sum, the new regionalism in Latin America can be understood as an effort to reverse a decade of economic decline and to fend off the negative externalities of bloc formation elsewhere. Many countries in the region have tried to attract foreign investment by unilaterally implementing market reforms and adopting market-oriented policies. The response of international investors, however, has been disappointing. Regional integration, it is hoped, will serve the function of improving Latin America's appeal to international investors who seek large markets endowed with credible institutional guarantees. It may also help Latin America enhance its bargaining position *vis-à-vis* NAFTA and the EU.[55]

The integration projects

At the core of the latest wave of regionalism in Latin America is the Mercado Común del Sur, MERCOSUR (in Portuguese MERCOSUL). It was established by the Treaty of Asunción signed by Brazil, Argentina, Uruguay, and Paraguay in March 1991. Its original objective was to create a single market in goods, capital, and people by January 1995, but inability to coordinate economic policies and to agree on common trade and industrial policies forced the signatories to adopt a less ambitious objective. Thus the Treaty was amended by the Protocol of Ouro Preto in December 1994, with the member states agreeing on an imperfect customs union by January 1995.[56] When and whether to proceed to a full common market is to be decided before 2001.

The Protocol scheduled 90 percent of goods to be freely traded and 85 percent of MERCOSUR's 9,000 products categories to be covered by a Common External Tariff (CET). The CET ranges from zero to 20

---

[54] Naim, "Latin America: Post-Adjustment Blues," 145.

[55] The bargaining power argument is made in Stephan Haggard, *Developing Nations and the Politics of Global Integration* (Washington, D.C.: Brookings Institution, 1995), pp. 97–98, and "Thinking About Regionalism," p. 60.

[56] See Winston Fritsch and Alexandre Tambini, "The MERCOSUL: An Overview," in Bouzas and Ros (eds.), *Economic Integration in the Western Hemisphere*, pp. 81–99. The data in this section are drawn from a special survey on MERCOSUR, *Financial Times* (January 25, 1995), 12–14.

percent, averaging 14 percent,[57] but each government was permitted to exempt 300 products from the CET temporarily.[58] Executive power within MERCOSUR is with the governments rather than with a European-style Commission. Chapter 1 of the Protocol of Ouro Preto describes the structure and role of the various MERCOSUR institutions. The highest decision-making body is the MERCOSUR Council, made up of the foreign and finance ministers of the four countries. Each country holds the presidency of the Council for six months on a rotating basis. The Council meets at least once every six months with the four presidents present. There are two decision-making bodies beneath the Council: the MERCOSUR Group – the main executive body composed of officials from the four governments, and a trade commission to review trade policy and examine complaints. Other institutions are a parliamentary commission to represent the four countries' legislatures, a consultative forum for private sector businesses and trade unions, and a purely administrative MERCOSUR secretariat based in Montevideo. An annex to the Protocol sets out the trade commission's complaint procedure: the four partners will attempt to solve complaints and trade disputes through consensus. If there is no consensus, or a decision is not upheld, the complainant can initiate proceedings under the 1991 Protocol of Brasília. Cases are then decided by a tribunal with one judge from each of the countries in dispute, and a third independent judge. This adjudication procedure remains untested, however.

In December 1995, MERCOSUR agreed to a five-year program under which it hopes to perfect the customs union. This involves standardizing many trade-related rules and procedures and moving towards harmonizing its members' economic policies.

Besides MERCOSUR, two other major integration schemes have been either launched or revived. In 1990, for example, the Andean Pact leaders agreed to consolidate their free-trade zone within two years and to establish a customs union by December 1993 (1995 for Bolivia and Ecuador).[59] Bolivia, Colombia, Ecuador, and Venezuela achieved

---

[57] Tariffs on 10 percent of goods exempted from free trade will be cut progressively to zero by January 1, 1999 for Argentina and Brazil, and one year later for Paraguay and Uruguay. The most important exempted goods are cars and sugar; these are subject to special arrangement.

[58] Argentina chose to exempt 232 products (including steel, chemicals, paper, and shoes), Uruguay exempted 212 goods (milk products, chemicals, paper, and shoes), Paraguay 210 (chemicals and agricultural products), and Brazil 175 (chemicals and petroleum derivatives). The tariff on exempted goods will converge, through annual increases or decreases, at the CET by January 2001 (2006 for Paraguay). Tariffs on imported capital goods are to converge by 2001 at a CET of 14 percent and computer and telecommunications equipment at 16 percent by 2006.

[59] See José Antonio Ocampo and Pilar Esguerra, "The Andean Group and Latin

the goal of free trade in 1992, but negotiations towards a customs union became bogged down because of major differences regarding the design of a common tariff, harmonization of export incentives, and the rules for negotiating free-trade agreements with third countries. The process was further disrupted when Peru's President Fujimori assumed dictatorial powers in April 1992. Venezuela responded by suspending diplomatic relations with Peru. Fujimori retaliated by temporarily withdrawing from the Andean Pact, arguing that the subsidies Venezuela and Columbia were granting to their exporters put Peruvian companies at a competitive disadvantage. Talks resumed in May 1994, after Peru announced its willingness gradually to rejoin the free trade zone. Within a few weeks, the five members of the Andean Pact agreed to launch a customs union with a four-tier common external tariff on January 1, 1995.[60]

The Central American Common Market is the other once-moribund regional organization that was infused with new life in the early 1990s. In December 1990 its member states signed the Puntarenas Declaration, committing themselves to the goal of a common customs and tariff policy. Six months later, they pledged to eliminate duties on regional trade in agriculture by June 1992 and to erect a common external tariff with a ceiling of 20 percent by December 1992.[61] In October 1993, CACM countries and Panama signed the Central American Economic Integration Treaty which replaced the General Treaty on Central American Economic Integration of 1960.[62]

A feature that distinguishes this latest wave of trade liberalization in Latin America is the extent to which regional integration efforts are being supplemented by multilateral trade diplomacy to create preferential trade relations between insiders and outsiders. In January 1994, for example, the Central American countries and Mexico agreed to forge a free trade area by 1996. A similar free-trade agreement was reached in

American Integration," in Bousaz and Ros (eds.), *Economic Integration in the Western Hemisphere*, pp. 122–145.

[60] Venezuela, Colombia, and Ecuador agreed to an external tariff structure of 5, 10, 15, and 20 percent. Ecuador negotiated a list of 600 exceptions for which it is allowed, during four years, to set a tariff within a 10 percent band around the tariff agreed by other countries. Bolivia maintains its two-tier level of 5 and 10 percent. See Stephen Fidler, "Andean Pact Nations in Tariff Accord," *Financial Times* (May 31, 1994), 6, and "Andean Pact Keeps on Growing," *Latin American Monitor – Andean Group* 11 (May 1994), 12.

[61] Gary Clyde Hufbauer and Jeffrey Schott, *Western Hemisphere Economic Integration* (Washington, D.C.: Institute for International Economics, 1994), p. 120. See also Ennio Rodríguez, "Central America: Common Market, Trade Liberalization, and Trade Agreements," in Bouzas and Ros (eds.), *Economic Integration in the Western Hemisphere*, pp. 146–170.

[62] See *Latin America Monitor – Central America* 10 (December 1993), 1228.

February 1993 between CACM and Colombia and Venezuela.[63] Colombia and Venezuela had already established a customs union in 1992;
they then teamed up with Mexico to form the G3 group in 1994. Its aim
is to erase all tariffs and quotas over ten years, starting in January
1995.[64] A Chile–Mexico free-trade treaty was signed in 1991 which
called for the phasing out of all trade barriers by 1998. Chile signed
similar agreements with Venezuela and Colombia in 1993. A year later,
it started seeking closer commercial links with MERCOSUR.[65] A model
free-trade accord between Mexico and Costa Rica came into effect in
January 1995. Its objective is to remove tariff and non-tariff barriers to
trade in goods and services, to offer national treatment to investors from
each country, to set rules on intellectual property rights, to ease the
movement of workers between the two countries, and to provide for a
dispute resolution panel.[66] Finally, the leaders of nineteen Latin American and Caribbean nations met in Cartagena, Colombia, in June 1994,
to discuss how this patchwork of agreements might be merged. One
proposal, suggested by Brazil, is to establish "a South American Free
Trade Area that would unite, in a common market, the countries that
comprise Mercosul, the Andean Group ... and ... Chile."[67]

Prospects for the latest wave

Latin America has changed in many ways since the 1960s. Democratic
processes in most countries have been reinforced by economic reforms,
particularly in the last decade. The structure of the economies in Latin
America has changed as well. Industrialization has broadened the scope
for mutually beneficial exchange of goods at the regional level.[68] This is
perhaps most evident in the case of MERCOSUR. Brazil experienced
swift industrialization in the 1970s; today it is home to Latin America's
most productive light and heavy industry sectors, particularly cars, car
parts, chemicals, machinery, and sophisticated technology. Argentina,
in turn, has a strong comparative advantage in food (processed meats,

---

[63] See Hufbauer and Schott, *Western Hemisphere Economic Integration*, p. 114; and
"Embracing Free Trade," *Latin America Monitor – Central America* 10 (March 1993), 1.

[64] "Group of Three Agrees Programme," *Latin America – Weekly Report* (December 16,
1993), 579.

[65] See "Chile wants 'Four-Plus-One' Agreement with Mercosur by End of this Year,"
Latin American Regional Reports – Southern Cone Report (October 20, 1994), 1.

[66] See Damian Fraser, "Central America's 'Model' Accord," *Financial Times* (March 9,
1994), 6.

[67] James Brooke, "In Latin America, A Free Trade Rush," *New York Times* (June 13,
1994), C1 and C5.

[68] See Primo Braga, Raed Safadi, and Alexander Yeats, "Regional Integration in the
Americas: Déjà Vu All Over Again?," *The World Economy* (June 1994), 577–601.

wheat, dairy products) and energy production. However, not all regional trade is based on comparative advantage; a growing share stems from economies of scale and is characterized by firms within an industry swapping products or components. In 1995, for example, almost half of Argentina's $5.6 billion of exports to Brazil and about 85 percent of the $4 billion of goods that Brazil sent to Argentina fit into the intra-industry trade category. Intra-industry trade has been fuelled by the massive inflow of foreign direct investment, especially into the car, chemical, and food industries. FDI totalled around $6 billion in both 1994 and 1995.[69]

A measure of the expanded scope for mutually beneficial exchange is reflected by the following numbers: intraregional trade has grown at an average 27 percent a year from 1990 to 1995; in the same period MERCOSUR's trade with the rest of the world expanded at an annual 7.5 percent. One-fifth of the four countries' foreign trade is now conducted with the other members, compared with 9 percent in 1990.[70] Argentina's exports to Brazil quadrupled between 1990 and 1994 and reached more than $4 billion in 1996, that is, twice the amount for 1994. Brazil saw its exports to MERCOSUR rise from 4 percent to some 16 percent in 1996. Paraguay and Uruguay have registered similarly sharp increases in intraregional trade.

The growing potential for gains from regional exchange has created a powerful lobby in the private sector for deeper integration.[71] Big business has been complaining about several inefficiencies in the functioning of MERCOSUR and has demanded that they be eliminated. For example, goods for which the common external tariff (CET) has already been paid are not automatically exempted from having to pay the CET again if reshipped to another member state. The reason is that no supranational institution exists to collect the proceeds and redistribute them among the members. Besides improving customs procedures, business groups have also been lobbying for the liberalization of trade in services, and the coordination of rules in areas such as economic policy, exchange rate, intellectual property, antitrust, antidumping, tax standards, public procurement, and the environment. Finally, demands for deeper integration also include an institutionalized formal dispute-resolution mechanism. As Michael Reid put it, "[u]ntil a tested and

[69] Michael Reid, "A Survey of Mercosur: The End of the Beginning," *The Economist* (Oct. 12, 1996), 3–6.
[70] Stephen Fidler, "Trade Pact sets the Pace for Integration," *Financial Times* survey on Mercosur (February 4 1997), 16.
[71] On the importance of corporate interests in Mercosur integration, see Luigi Manzetti, "The Political Economy of Mercosur," *Journal of Interamerican Studies and World Affairs* 34 (Winter 1993–1994), 101–141.

politically-neutral dispute settlement mechanism is in place, investors thinking of setting up in, say, Uruguay cannot be certain of guaranteed and barrier-free access to the Brazilian market."[72]

Progress towards deeper integration, however, has been painfully slow. Most attempts have failed. The crux of the problem can be traced to coordination and distribution dilemmas. For example, in 1993 Argentina boasted a growing economy with inflation running at an annual rate of 7.4 percent. Brazil, however, was plagued by annual inflation of 2,500 percent and an undervalued currency. As a result, the trade gap quickly widened in Brazil's favor and the ensuing tensions between the two countries brought trade negotiations to the brink of collapse. Another stubborn problem emerged over industrial policy. Brazil wanted higher common external tariffs, in order to protect its high-technology and capital-goods industries. Argentina, which is less industrialized, insisted on low tariffs.[73] Distributional concerns have been voiced particularly in the context of investment. As capital flows into the richer and larger Brazilian economy, smaller and less-developed members will demand assistance to cope with dislocation and payment imbalances.[74]

Chapter 3 argued that the chances for successful integration improve considerably if there is a regional leader capable of serving as institutional focal point and willing to act as regional paymaster. Within MERCOSUR Brazil is the dominant economy. It accounts for approximately 75 percent of total MERCOSUR GDP and for 80 percent of its industrial manufacturers. Nevertheless, Brazil has been reluctant to use its economic and political position to assume active regional leadership. Whenever short-term national interests have been at stake, Brazil has relegated MERCOSUR to second place. For example, it has decreed investment incentives with little regard to their effects on the other members, and has unilaterally imposed tariff and non-tariff barriers on imports whenever domestic developments demanded such actions. In addition, Brazil has staunchly opposed plans to establish an EU-styled Commission or a supranational court. Similarly, it has refused to pay heed to calls for regional redistribution schemes, which may be of little surprise in a country that is used to one of the world's least equitable distributions of domestic wealth.

[72] Michael Reid, "A Survey of Mercosur: The Road to a Single Market," *The Economist* 20, 24–27.

[73] John Barham and Agnes Foster, "Teething Troubles Continue to Nag at Mercosur Market," *Financial Times* (January 7, 1994), 6; see also "Mercosur Deadline Slips By," *Latin American Monitor – Southern Cone* 11 (January 2, 1994), 2.

[74] Canute James, "Americas Free Trade Area Easier Said than Done," *Financial Times* (December 21, 1994), 3.

Brazil may well change its approach and embrace an agenda for deeper integration as both external and corporate pressures make themselves more strongly felt on its leaders and as domestic reforms bring greater stability to the country. In the absence of active Brazilian leadership, MERCOSUR is unlikely to develop much beyond today's imperfect customs union.

Coordination and distribution problems have also hindered the other recent Latin American integration projects, in much the same way as they disrupted similar schemes thirty years ago. In Central America starkly different views on economic policies have pushed the countries in different directions, "against their governments' wishful rhetoric about the need for integration."[75] Unilateral liberalizing policies in El Salvador and fiscal problems in Costa Rica have provoked them to break ranks on the regions' common external tariff, which nominally ranges from a 20 percent ceiling to a 5 percent floor. Honduras and Nicaragua, the region's least-developed countries, have again voiced concerns about unfair distribution of the gains from integration. Thus far, these concerns have fallen on deaf ears in the region. There have also been differences over other issues, notably bananas, an important export for all of the countries except El Salvador. Costa Rica and Nicaragua have agreed to a quota with the EU, while Guatemala and Honduras opposed the deal.[76]

In the Andean region, efforts to relaunch integration have run into similar problems. The latest attempt to breathe life into the process of integration came in March 1996 when the five leaders of the Andean pact countries announced the creation of an "Andean Community" at their weekend summit in Trujillo. The new organization, modelled on the European Community, replaced the old bureaucracy with a secretariat based in Lima. A council of foreign ministers elects a Secretary-General, intended to carry real executive power and resolve disputes, with the post rotating between member countries. Within five years, according to the Act of Trujillo, the Andean Community is supposed to have a directly elected parliament. Good intentions notwithstanding, it is difficult to see how this new community will come about and manage to solve the critical issues of policy coordination and regional redistribution that have bedevilled earlier attempts at Andean integration. Without a clear plan of how these problems will be tackled, the Andean Community is unlikely to fare any better than its predecessor schemes.[77]

[75] Edward Orlebar, "Quandary for Central America," *Financial Times* (May 10, 1995), 7.
[76] *Ibid.*
[77] For recent evidence, see Sally Bowen, "Andean Pact Begins to Crumble," *Financial Times* (April 23, 1997), 5.

Could North America provide the leadership to act as policy coordinator and regional paymaster? The United States has undoubtedly played an important role as policy model in the last few years. Most Latin American countries have jettisoned economic models of import substitution, price controls, regulation, and state intervention in favor of free-market policies or what John Williamson calls the "Washington Consensus."[78] But does the US have an interest in assuming a more active role and pushing hemispheric integration? The US is rhetorically committed to a Free Trade Area of the Americas (FTAA). In June 1990 President Bush launched the Enterprise of the Americas, and at the Miami summit of December 1994, the US and thirty-three Latin American countries agreed to aim for a free trade pact by 2005. However, political and economic events have since taken their toll and many fundamental questions about the creation of FTAA still have to be answered.

From the point of view of corporate America, there is an increasingly strong argument for the US to extend integration beyond Mexico. With 430 million people and opening markets, Latin America is naturally appealing to US multinational corporations. Integration on North American terms would provide investors in the region with strong institutional safeguards against various hazards. However, it would require Latin American countries to accept the stringent economic terms and conditions of the NAFTA accord. These include comprehensive provisions on copyrights and patents and the dispute-settlement mechanism that is the major means of enforcing not only trade and investment-related laws but also environmental and labor provisions. In the words of a senior US official, "NAFTA is the floor, in all respects . . . [w]e build from there."[79]

During the first wave of integration some thirty years ago, most Latin American leaders vigorously denounced attempts by the US to attach conditions to the provision of financial assistance as an intolerable infringement on national sovereignty. Resistance to American hegemony has eased of late. But there are no foregone conclusions. Mexico accepted the stringent NAFTA terms because it had no other option

[78] The "Washington Consensus" includes reducing fiscal deficits, shifting expenditure priorities, tax reform, interest-rate reform, exchange-rate adjustment, trade liberalization, liberalization of rules governing foreign direct investment, privatization, deregulation, and protection of property rights. See John Williamson, "What Washington Means by Policy Reform," in John Williamson (ed.), *Latin American Adjustment: How Much Has Happened?* (Washington, D.C.: Institute for International Economics, 1990), pp. 7–20; cited in Haggard, *Developing Nations and the Politics of Global Integration*, p. 78.

[79] Quoted in Stephen Fidler and George Graham, "Pledging a Market Partnership," 4.

(see pp. 181–184 below). Economically and financially, it depended overwhelmingly on its neighbor to the north. Most of South America, however, has important ties to Europe; and Europe has an obvious interest in keeping American commercial ambitions in Latin America in check. Furthermore, for some Latin American countries the cost of integration on NAFTA terms is simply too high. This is most evident in the Brazilian case. Why would Brazil want to give up its position of dominance within MERCOSUR for membership of a union dominated by the United States? After all, regional integration in South America has produced tangible economic benefits, despite recent problems. Unimpeded access to an increasingly integrated vast North American market may sway Brazilian leaders and others as well, but possibly not before a Latin American free trade zone is in place. Such a zone would permit Latin American leaders to negotiate on a more equal footing with the US than an approach based on individual requests for accession to NAFTA.

3   Integration in Asia

Early integration schemes

The early history of the Asia-Pacific region confirms that many proposals for integration are triggered by external events that threaten to undermine economic prosperity in the region. One such attempt was Japan's proposal in the 1960s for a free trade pact with the developed economies of the Pacific rim, namely the United States, Canada, Australia and New Zealand. The project was motivated by the fear that the fledgling European Community and American ideas for "an Atlantic Community" would shut Japan out of the export markets it needed in order to rebuild its war-wrecked economy.[80] The project foundered on American opposition.

The most notable example of regional grouping in Asia is the Association of Southeast Asian Nations (ASEAN). Unlike most other integration attempts in Asia, particularly those of the latest wave, it is not an example of the second integrative response and thus points to a limitation of our analytical framework, that is, it cannot be explained as an integration effort triggered by negative externalities that arise from community-building elsewhere. Nevertheless, the framework remains useful for understanding the fate of ASEAN.

ASEAN's creation was triggered by a war in neighboring Indochina

[80] See Kiyoshi Kojima, *Japan and a Pacific Free Trade Area* (London: Macmillan, 1971); Pekka Korhonen, *Japan and the Pacific Free Trade Area* (New York: Routledge, 1994).

that threatened the stability in the area. The group was founded in 1967 by Indonesia, Malaysia, the Philippines, Singapore, and Thailand.[81] ASEAN defined its main tasks as ensuring the members' stability and security from any external interference and laying down "the foundation for a prosperous and peaceful community of South-East Asian nations."[82] Concrete steps to promote intra-ASEAN cooperation were only taken, however, some eight years later, when the Americans were defeated in the Vietnam War. The security threat posed by Vietnam and the threat of communist insurgency confronting all ASEAN members galvanized the group into action.[83] Economic prosperity through closer commercial links was seen as the most promising way to deal with the new challenge to regional stability.[84] At their first summit conference, held in Bali in 1976, the ASEAN leaders therefore decided to accelerate the process toward regional cooperation in the economic and political domains. To this end, they approved ASEAN Preferential Trading Arrangements (PTAs) one year later, under which ASEAN member states agreed to exchange tariff preferences on approved imports. The Bali summit also brought about the ASEAN Industrial Projects (AIPs),[85] large-scale, capital-intensive public–private sector projects in which all ASEAN members hold equity stakes. The outputs of these projects enjoy tariff preferences within ASEAN.[86] Other projects for regional industrial cooperation adopted over the years include the ASEAN Industrial Complementation (AIC) and the ASEAN Industrial Joint Ventures (AIJV) schemes. AIC sought to promote complementary trade in selected manufactured products within ASEAN.[87] AIJVs were introduced in 1983 to provide tariff reductions of up to 90 percent for products from joint ventures in which ASEAN firms hold at least a 40

---

[81] The oil-rich Sultanate of Brunei joined ASEAN in 1984; Vietnam joined in 1995; Burma and Laos joined in 1997

[82] See Bangkok Declaration (1967) in Hans-Christoph Rieger, *ASEAN Economic Co-operation Handbook* (Singapore: Institute of Southeast Asian Studies, 1991), pp. 101–102.

[83] Security concerns heightened when Vietnam invaded Cambodia in December 1978.

[84] Bilson Kurus, "Agreeing to Disagree: The Political Reality of ASEAN Economic Cooperation," *Asian Affairs* 20 (Spring 1993), 32.

[85] See Majorie Suriyamongkol, *Politics of ASEAN Economic Cooperation: The Case of ASEAN Industrial Projects* (Singapore: Oxford University Press, 1988); and Srikanta Chatterjee, "ASEAN Economic Cooperation in the 1980s and 1990s," in Alison Broinowski (ed.), *ASEAN into the 1990s* (New York: St. Martin's Press, 1990).

[86] Under the original plan, each of the five ASEAN members was to host one AIP: urea projects in Indonesia and Malaysia, a phosphate project in the Philippines, a diesel-engine project in Singapore, and a soda-ash project in Thailand. Each host country was asked to contribute 60 percent of the necessary capital for an AIP with the other four member states each contributing 10 percent.

[87] One example is discussed in Kevin Ruston, "Auto Parts Complementation in ASEAN," *Southeast Asia Business* 23 (Spring/Summer 1990).

percent share and representative firms from at least one other ASEAN country hold a 5 percent share.[88]

Most of these initiatives, however, have made very little progress.[89] ASEAN's Preferential Trading Arrangements have had a minimal impact on intra-ASEAN trade because most member states exclude products deemed "sensitive" from the PTA list.[90] Agreements to extend PTA coverage to a broader range of goods remain a dead letter. In the early 1990s PTA products accounted for less than 1 percent of total intra-ASEAN trade.[91] Likewise, of the five initial ASEAN Industrial Projects only two have become fully operational, and much of their success is due to Japanese financing and technology.[92] The AIC has so far succeeded only for automotive parts and components under a brand-to-brand complementation scheme approved in 1988.[93] As for the AIJVs, only twenty-three projects had been approved by the end of 1994.[94]

A more general indication of ASEAN's failure to foster closer economic ties is provided by statistics on intra-ASEAN trade. Excluding Singapore, intra-ASEAN exports amounted to approximately 5 percent of total ASEAN trade in 1990. This number actually represents a slight

[88] See *Revised Basic Agreement on Industrial Joint Ventures* (Manila, December 15, 1987) in Hans-Christoph Rieger, *ASEAN Economic Cooperation Handbook*, pp. 145–150.

[89] Three good general assessments of ASEAN are Mari Pangestu, Hadi Soesastro, and Mubariq Ahmad, "A New Look at Intra-ASEAN Economic Cooperation," *ASEAN Economic Bulletin* 8 (March 1992), 333–352; Rolf Langhammer, "ASEAN Economic Cooperation: A Stock-Taking from a Political Economy Point of View," *ASEAN Economic Bulletin* 8 (November 1991), 137–150; and Hans Christoph Rieger, "Regional Economic Cooperation in the Asia-Pacific Region," *Asian-Pacific Economic Literature* 3 (1989), 5–33.

[90] Janamitra Devan, "The ASEAN Preferential Trading Arrangement: Some Problems, Ex Ante Results, and a Multipronged Approach to Future Intra-ASEAN Trade Development," *ASEAN Economic Bulletin* 4 (November 1987), 197–209.

[91] For example, at their third summit, held in Manila in 1987, the ASEAN Heads of State signed a five-year agreement to extend PTA coverage to 90 percent of total goods traded. The project failed. See also Lim, "The Role of the Private Sector in ASEAN Regional Economic Cooperation," 5.

[92] These are the two urea projects in Indonesia and Malaysia. The Philippines and Singapore have switched their AIPs to a copper fabrication and a hepatitis B vaccine project, respectively. The AIP for Thailand has been abandoned. See Kurus, "Agreeing to Disagree: The Political Reality of ASEAN Economic Cooperation," 32–33.

[93] The brand-to-brand complementation scheme promotes the trading of auto parts among companies operating in ASEAN member states by granting tariff reductions of up to 50 percent for those parts as well as credit toward local content in member states. See Charles Smith, "Part Exchange," *Far Eastern Economic Review* (September 21, 1989), 73; and Richard Doner, "Japanese Automotive Production Networks in Asia," working paper, Department of Political Science, Emory University, Atlanta, Ga. (September 1994).

[94] Pangestu, Soesastro, and Ahmad, "A New Look at Intra-ASEAN Economic Cooperation," 337; and John Ravenhill, "Economic Cooperation in Southeast Asia: Changing Incentives," *Asian Survey* 35 (September 1995), 853.

decline since the late 1960s.[95] Similarly, intraregional investment accounts for only a very small fraction of total foreign direct investment in ASEAN countries. Apart from Malaysia, intra-ASEAN investment amounts to less than 10 percent of total foreign investments, with over 90 percent of this coming from Singapore alone.[96]

The latest wave of integration

The second wave of integration projects in Asia-Pacific was triggered, like the first, by external events that threatened economic prosperity in the area. The adoption of the Single European Act in 1987 and speedy progress towards the "Europe 1992" goal raised fears of a "Fortress Europe" throughout Asia.[97] The malaise worsened with the steady enlargement of the European Community and ratification of the Maastricht Treaty on European Monetary and Political Union. Equally worrisome were the passage of the North American Free Trade Agreement and the slow pace of the Uruguay Round negotiations.

Ensuing concerns about trade and investment diversion were a primary motivation for Asian integration plans. The Japanese Ambassador to the United States, Murata Ryohei, voiced such a concern in a speech delivered in Los Angeles in July 1991: "I'd like to tell you that there is an apprehension in Asia that the EC and a North American free-trade area might form introverted, less open economic entities ... This ... could conceivably result in the advocacy of economic regionalism in Asia."[98]

[95] If Singapore is included, intra-ASEAN trade increases to about 18 percent. This is due to Singapore's important role as regional trade entrepôt. In 1970, the corresponding numbers were 6 percent (without Singapore) and 21 percent (with Singapore). See Seiji Naya and Michael Plummer, "ASEAN Economic Cooperation in the New International Economic Environment," *ASEAN Economic Bulletin* 7 (March 1991), 266; Pearl Imada, Manuel Montes, and Seiji Naya, *A Free Trade Area: Implications for ASEAN* (Singapore: Institute of Southeast Asian Studies, 1991); and Ippei Yamazawa, "On Pacific Economic Integration," *The Economic Journal* 102 (November 1992), 1519–1529, especially table 3, 1521.

[96] ASEAN investment in Malaysia accounted for about 30 percent of total investment in manufacturing in 1989. See Lim, "The Role of the Private Sector in ASEAN Regional Economic Cooperation," 26.

[97] See, for example, the lengthy cover story entitled "United Europe: The Threat to Asia" in *Asian Business* 25 (June, 1989), 34–41.

[98] Murata Ryohei, "Apprehension Over Trading Blocs," *Los Angeles Times* (July 30, 1991), B7; quoted in Chalmers Johnson, "History Restarted: Japanese–American Relations at the End of the Century," in Richard Higgott, Richard Leaver, and John Ravenhill (eds.), *Pacific Economic Relations in the 1990s: Cooperation or Conflict?* (Allen & Unwin: St. Leonards, Australia, 1993), p. 55. On the potential for trade diversion due to NAFTA, see Lorraine Eden and Maureen Appel Molot, "Fortress or Free Market? NAFTA and its Implications for the Pacific Rim," in Higgott, Leaver, and Ravenhill (eds.), *Pacific Economic Relations in the 1990s*, pp. 201–222; Han Joo Kim and Ann Weston, "A North American Free Trade Agreement and East Asian Developing

Indeed, in the wake of the suspension of the Uruguay Round talks in 1989, Malaysia's Prime Minister Mahathir had already proposed that Asian countries form an economic bloc. Such a bloc would strengthen Asia's bargaining power within GATT and counter the emerging blocs in Europe and North America.[99] Mahathir envisaged an East Asian Economic Grouping (EAEG) with Japan, South Korea, Hong Kong, Burma, Taiwan, China, and the ASEAN countries. The United States, New Zealand, Australia, and Canada were explicitly excluded.[100] The American response to the EAEG was predictably cool. The American Ambassador to Japan, Michael Armacost, expressed concerns that the grouping could "encourage economic rivalry" between Japan and the United States.[101] Japan publicly opposed the plan in order not to upset its trade relationship with the United States, but in private some Japanese government officials and senior executives were favorably inclined to the idea of an Asian bloc.[102] ASEAN formally dropped the EAEG proposal in October 1991 in favor of a looser consultative body, the East Asian Economic Caucus (EAEC). But US Secretary of State James Baker repeatedly pressed both Japan and South Korea not to participate even in this group.[103] Hoon and Delf explain that

Japan's flirtation with the EAEC proposal appear[ed] primarily intended to create new leverage *vis-à-vis* Europe and North America by making the threat of a retaliatory East Asian trade bloc more credible. It [was] hoped that this could forestall or minimise steps that would actively damage Asian interests during the formative stages of the North American Free Trade Agreement.[104]

Countries," *ASEAN Economic Bulletin* 9 (March 1993), 287–300; and Mordechai Kreinin and Michael Plummer, "Effects of Economic Integration in Industrial Countries on ASEAN and the Asian NIEs," *World Development* 20 (1992), 1345–1366. This last study estimated that ASEAN would lose 4 percent of the value of its 1988 exports to North America from the trade-diverting effects of NAFTA, and 8 percent of the value of its exports to the European market from trade diversion caused by the conclusion of the single market program.

[99] See Linda Low, "The East Asian Economic Grouping," *The Pacific Review* 4 (1991), 375–382.

[100] David Sanger, "Malaysia Trading Plan Seeks a Unified Voice," *New York Times* (February 12, 1991).

[101] Quoted in Anthony Rowley, "The Malaysian Two-Step," *Far Eastern Economic Review* (April 18, 1991), 70–71.

[102] Peter Petri, "The East Asian Trading Bloc: An Analytical History," in Jeffrey Frankel and Miles Kahler, *Regionalism and Rivalry: Japan and the United States in Pacific Asia* (Chicago: University of Chicago Press, 1993), pp. 21–48, p. 45.

[103] Shim Jae Hoon and Robert Delfs, "Block Politics," *Far Eastern Economic Review* (November 28, 1991), 26–27.

[104] *Ibid.*, 26. In the same article Saburo Okita, chairman of the Institute for Domestic and International Policy Studies in Tokyo and former minister of foreign affairs, is quoted as saying that the "[EAEC] is intended to counterbalance emerging organizations in Europe and North America and to improve the bargaining position of Asian countries."

As the "Europe 1992" deadline approached, ASEAN leaders again felt compelled to act. In January 1992 they convoked a summit – the fourth since the Association's inception 25 years earlier – and agreed to establish an ASEAN Free Trade Area (AFTA). They also decided to strengthen the ASEAN secretariat, to upgrade the ASEAN Secretary-General's position to a ministerial rank, and to institutionalize their summit by meeting every three years.[105] One feature of AFTA is the creation of a Common Effective Preferential Tariff (CEPT) scheme for manufactured products with at least 40 percent ASEAN-wide content.[106] The goal is to reduce current tariffs on manufactures to no more than 20 percent in five to eight years, and to no more than 5 percent by the year 2008. This deadline was pushed forward to 2003 in September 1994.[107]

Another integration project of the second wave is the Asia Pacific Economic Cooperation forum (APEC) of 1989. It started as a consultative body with the aim of effectively weighing the interests of the Asia-Pacific countries against those of the Europeans in the GATT negotiations.[108] Concern about the outcome of the Uruguay Round was an important drive behind APEC. In 1994, Guy de Jonquières noted: "Last year's [APEC] ... summit was prompted by a common desire to kickstart the Uruguay Round negotiations, which were then stalled. Many APEC members believe that by presenting a united front ... and hinting that the grouping could become an alternative to the GATT if the round failed, they prodded the EU into making the concessions needed to conclude the world trade talks."[109]

Over the years, APEC has grown from a discussion forum into a group with a permanent secretariat based in Singapore and a large number of committees. Its founding members are the ASEAN countries, Canada, the United States, Australia, New Zealand, Japan, and South Korea. China, Taiwan, and Hong Kong joined in 1991, under a compromise arrangement that accommodated the ambivalent sovereignty of the latter two. Mexico and Papua New Guinea became

---

[105] For a detailed analysis of the Singapore summit, see Michael Antolik, "ASEAN's Singapore Rendezvous: Just Another Summit?," *Contemporary Southeast Asia* 14 (September 1992), 142–153; and Leszek Busynski, "Southeast Asia in the Post-Cold War Era: Regionalism and Security," *Asian Survey* 32 (September 1992), 830–847.

[106] Unprocessed agricultural goods and service industries are not included.

[107] In 1992 average tariff levels were almost zero for Brunei and Singapore, 15.64 percent for Malaysia, 21.68 percent for Indonesia, 25.96 percent for the Philippines, and 43.83 percent for Thailand.

[108] Richard Higgott, Andrew Fenton Cooper, and Jenelle Bonnor, "Asia-Pacific Economic Co-operation: An Evolving Case-Study in Leadership and Co-operation Building," *International Journal* (Autumn 1990), 823–866; and Haggard, "Thinking About Regionalism," 27.

[109] Guy de Jonquières, "Different Aims, Common Cause," *Financial Times* (November 18, 1994), 14.

members in November 1993. Chile joined the group in 1994. Vietnam has applied for membership and has been a participant in APEC's working groups since 1995.[110] This steady enlargement has contributed to the extraordinary heterogeneity of the group. Today APEC spans four continents, numerous cultures, and a wide range of incomes from Japan's $30,000 per capita output to China's $400. It runs the gamut of policy regimes from Hong Kong's *laissez-faire* system to the reforming socialism of Vietnam and China.

APEC's stated objective, agreed upon during the 1994 summit held in Bogor, Indonesia, is to dismantle all trade barriers in the region by 2020, and by 2010 in advanced APEC countries. Besides trade liberalization, APEC is also trying to launch several other projects. These include a dispute mediation mechanism and agreements on competition policies and on private investment. Discussions have also taken place on monetary and macroeconomic cooperation, as well as on technical cooperation projects for development of human resources, tourism, infrastructure, and energy.[111]

Prospects for Asian integration

The indecision and squabbles that have characterized past economic and industrial cooperation among ASEAN members augur ill for the future of the association. Many of ASEAN's difficulties can be explained with reference to the framework of demand and supply conditions elaborated in chapter 3.

With the exception of Singapore, the economies of ASEAN members are not complementary. Little scope for mutually beneficial exchange exists and demand for integration by market actors is consequently weak. ASEAN companies compete in the same industrial sectors with each other. They export the bulk of their primary commodities and manufactured goods to the same world markets. Indeed, most of their trade is with Japan and the United States rather than with their ASEAN neighbors. Table 5.5 shows that ASEAN countries are not "first best" trading partners, despite recent increases in intraregional trade.[112]

ASEAN also lacks undisputed leadership. Indonesia, its largest

[110] Ten other countries have applied for membership, including Russia, India, Peru, and Columbia.

[111] See Asia Pacific Economic Cooperation, *A Vision For APEC: Towards an Asia Pacific Community. First Report of the Eminent Persons Group* (Singapore: APEC Secretariat, 1993); and Asia Pacific Economic Cooperation, *Achieving the APEC Vision: Free Trade and Open Trade in Asia Pacific. Third Report of the Eminent Persons Group* (Singapore: APEC Secretariat, 1994).

[112] See also Ravenhill, "Economic Cooperation in Southeast Asia: Changing Incentives," 853–857.

Table 5.5. *Trade dependence indices*
(Trade [imports and exports] between ASEAN countries and selected regions as a
percentage of the country's GNP)

Country	Newly industrialized economies[a]	ASEAN[b]	USA	Japan	World
Singapore	34.48	68.46	60.74	48.79	338.64
Brunei[c]	26.24	27.98 (17.50)	4.30	32.39	103.42
Indonesia	8.05	4.04 (2.97)	5.48	15.26	44.37
Malaysia	39.42	33.11 (25.99)	23.34	27.17	137.89
Philippines	7.92	4.19 (1.70)	12.86	9.16	48.25
Thailand	11.42	8.48 (5.33)	10.96	17.81	70.57

Notes: [a] Singapore is included in both NIEs and ASEAN. [b] Singapore figure is shown in parenthesis. [c] For Brunei, figures are from 1989. All other figures are based on data for 1990.
Source: Junichi Goto and Koichi Hamada, "Economic Preconditions for Asian Regional Integration," Yale University, Economic Growth Center, Discussion Paper no. 685 (February 1993), p. 19.

member state, has a population of 189.4 million living in an area of 1,948,000 square miles. Its large domestic market is heavily protected. At the other extreme is Singapore. With 3 million people and an area of 625,000 square miles, it is a tiny state.[113] Its service and industrial sectors, however, are highly competitive. Integration, however limited, inevitably raises the question of how the gainers will compensate the losers. Within ASEAN, there is no obvious "paymaster," no regional leader to ease the distributional problem. Absence of leadership also implies absence of a normative focal point. This, in turn, raises the cost of coordination. Whose standards, tax structure, regulations, and policies could ASEAN members agree upon if they were to deepen integration among themselves?

Finally, "commitment institutions," such as central monitoring or third-party enforcement are absent from ASEAN.[114] The member

[113] Data is from the World Bank, *World Development Report 1992* (Washington, 1992).
[114] At the Bali Summit in 1976, the members agreed to settle disputes through "friendly negotiations." They proposed that dispute resolution be assisted by a "High Council," which would issue non-binding recommendations. However, no such "High Council" was ever established. On the planned dispute-settlement procedure, see chapter 6,

states have been unwilling to transfer any decision-making authority to such regional institutions. Disputes are handled through political rather than administrative or juridical arrangements. The ineffectiveness of such a mechanism has been vividly illustrated by recent friction between Singapore and Malaysia over trade in petrochemical products.[115]

Considering these difficulties, it is not surprising that under the AFTA agreement of 1992 individual countries can and do undermine free-trade principles by excluding numerous products they regard as sensitive from tariff cuts. The recent decision to enlarge the group, by extending membership to Burma, Cambodia, and Laos in 1997, is unlikely to help the group's internal cohesion. In particular, the decision to accept Burma, a regime with a dismal human-rights record, has created additional strains within the organization. Malaysia, Brunei, and Vietnam, led by Indonesia, supported Burma's admission, while Thailand and the Philippines, the region's democracies, expressed serious reservations. Singapore's worries were more muted; but it did signal concern that Burma's membership may come "at no small cost to ASEAN's prestige."[116]

ASEAN's enlargement is difficult to explain in narrow economic terms. Its purpose seems to be primarily political and strategic. The group's single most conspicuous achievement to date has been its effectiveness as a united bargaining bloc and coveted ally in international fora.[117] A bigger ASEAN group, it is hoped, will improve its international leverage and better balance China's growing regional influence.

APEC appears, at first sight, to be a more promising integration scheme than ASEAN. The potential for gain from unrestricted intra-regional trade and investment is considerable within APEC but quite small within ASEAN. To realize this potential, big business has been lobbying vigorously for deeper integration. For example, the so-called Pacific Business Forum, which was formed in 1994 to represent regional business interests, routinely meets before APEC summits to draft "road-maps" designed to guide APEC to the completion of regional free trade. Since 1995, business interests have been directly represented in the APEC Business Advisory Council (ABAC). Business groups have been lobbying for integration measures beyond free trade, including free

"Pacific Settlement of Disputes," 1976 Treaty of Amity and Cooperation, reprinted in Appendix of R. Nagi, *ASEAN 20 Years* (New Dehli: Lancers Books, 1987).

[115] Ravenhill, "Economic Cooperation in Southeast Asia," 860–861.

[116] "Suharto's Regional Swing: ASEAN Expands," *The Economist* (June 7, 1997), 37–38.

[117] See, for example, Rolf Langhammer, "The Economic Rationale of Trade Policy Cooperation between ASEAN and the EC: Has Cooperation Benefitted ASEAN?," *ASEAN Economic Bulletin* (1985), 107–117; and Ippei Yamazawa, "On Pacific Economic Integration," *The Economic Journal* 120 (November 1992), 1525.

movement of people, services, and capital. They have also demanded common product standards, harmonized customs procedures, an APEC business visa, a Pacific investment code, common rules on the protection of intellectual property rights, and an effective monitoring mechanism to ensure that the promises of the integration are kept.[118]

Despite continuing pressure for integration by corporate actors, APEC has made little progress towards regional free trade. In the conceptual language of chapter 3, APEC's problem lies not on the demand side but on the supply side. Within APEC, the United States and Japan are contending leaders. The creation of APEC was possible because the two leaders had a common concern about "Fortress Europe" and the slow progress of GATT talks. However, the use of APEC as a vehicle of integration requires far more than simply forming a united front against a common threat. The United States and Japan have different economic institutions and differing conceptions of the right policies in development, money, trade, labor, and other domains. Martin Feldstein, for example, recently noted: "Now the contrast between US capitalism of independent shareholder-owned firms and Japanese *keiretsu* capitalism appears more sharply. This is a source of conflict . . . in US–Japan trade relations."[119] It is therefore not surprising to hear top Japanese officials denounce the idea that Japan should conform to American rules and say that Japan's system is in many ways better than the American system.[120]

This rivalry portends trouble for APEC. Disputes among APEC members, particularly Japan and the United States, have in fact been at

---

[118] See also Lawrence, *Regionalism, Multilateralism, and Deeper Integration*, pp. 91–92. Christian Parkes, "Business Leaders Set Pace On APEC Agenda" *Financial Times* (September 4, 1995), 4; and Edward Luse, "APEC Urges To End Non-Tariff Barriers," *Financial Times* (October 25, 1996), 6.

[119] Martin Feldstein, "National Security Aspects of United States–Japan Economic Relations in the Pacific Asian Region," in Frankel and Kahler (eds.), *Regionalism and Rivalry*, p. 453. The recent row over development plans for Vietnam is characteristic. Japan opposes the American-style development promoted by the World Bank and the IMF. It believes that price stability would hurt Vietnam's growth and thus undermine popular support for reform. It also opposes rapid privatization. Its own blue-print for development emphasizes the importance of government intervention. See "The Struggle for Vietnam's Soul," *The Economist* (June 24, 1995), 33.

[120] "The Struggle for Vietnam's Soul," p. 33. Chalmers Johnson observes that many Japanese writers and economists are beginning to acknowledge that there are major differences between Japan and the United States. Sakakibara Eisuke characterizes Japan as a "non-capitalist market economy." Noda Masaaki lists seven principles that distinguish Japan's "samurai capitalism" from its Anglo-American counterpart. And Terasawa Yoshio writes that "Japan is not really the pure survival-of-the-fittest American-type of capitalism. It is half socialism . . . and the government is in control . . . On the surface Japan is a capitalist system like that of the United States . . . but on the inside it is different." See Chalmers Johnson, "History Restarted," pp. 51–52.

the heart of almost every major recent confrontation in the international trading system. Optimism that APEC's members should be able to settle these differences in regional negotiations is clearly unfounded when they have signally failed to do so in the GATT.[121] Tellingly, the APEC "free-trade" agreement, signed in Bogor in November 1994, is nonbinding, fails to define the scope of free trade, and mentions neither a review process nor a dispute settlement mechanism. Differences between the policy preferences of the United States and Japan became particularly conspicuous one year later during APEC's Osaka meeting. The United States pressed for binding rules and a specific timetable of trade liberalization, while opposing exceptions to the principle of free trade. However, Japan the host of the conference, insisted that the liberalization process be "flexible"; in other words, each country should be free to propose whatever it likes at APEC summits. *The Economist* observed:

This "unique" formula, as the Japanese claim it to be, is a far cry from the rigid tit-for-tat typical of other trade talks. It hardly suits America's preference for clear rules and targets. But it does resemble the way that Japan's bureaucrats run things at home, building consensus quietly, making sure nobody transgresses unwritten laws by issuing "administrative guidance."[122]

Not surprisingly, little progress was made at Osaka. The Pacific-rim leaders continued to argue over central points such as the meaning of free trade, whether the deadline should be binding, and whether to extend any APEC free-trade measures unconditionally to third countries or to demand matching concessions.

Progress has continued to be glacially slow, if, indeed, there has been any at all. In 1997, Mexico's trade and industry minister Herminio Blanco observed: "If you want to have a very destructive [APEC] meeting, you [ask]: 'What do you mean by free trade?' That is seen as a spoiler. It will create lots of fights. Free trade for lots of countries has . . . very different meaning[s]."[123] The last two APEC meetings underscored yet again the group's difficulty in defining common denominators. The Manila summit of 1996 was the meeting at which the leaders were supposed to start turning their vision of regional free trade by 2020 into reality. Instead they failed to put any significant market-opening measures on the table, or even to endorse less contentious collective

---

[121] "Seeking a Role for APEC," *Financial Times* (September 2, 1994), 15.
[122] "Japan Conquers APEC," *The Economist* (November 11, 1995), 33. See also Andrew Pollack, "Asian Nations and US Plan Freer Trade – But 'Action Agenda' is Full of Loopholes," *New York Times* (November 17, 1995), A.9; and William Dawkins and Guy de Jonquières, "New Splits Emerge over APEC Free Trade Ambition," *Financial Times* (November 18, 1995), 3.
[123] Quoted in Guy de Jonquières, "What Do You Mean By Free Trade?, Mexico Asks APEC," *Financial Times* (February 12, 1997), 4.

trade facilitation proposals, such as a regional business visa.[124] APEC's most recent summit, held in Vancouver in November 1997, similarly failed to produce concrete commitments to open markets and facilitate regional trade and investment. The members endorsed proposals designed to remove trade barriers in fifteen sectors; the plans, however, are vague and commit APEC members to doing no more than hold further talks.

Arguably, APEC serves a purpose beyond trade. For example, it has offered Presidents Clinton and Jiang Zemin opportunities to rebuild the bilateral Sino-US relationship at a personal level. APEC may also serve as a way to keep the US engaged in Asia, thereby enhancing the region's security. The role of APEC as a security forum, however, is limited by the fact that the group includes both Taiwan and China. The ASEAN Regional Forum, a grouping that includes the United States, China, Japan, Russia, the countries of the European Union, and ASEAN may thus be better suited to effectively underpinning regional security.

In sum, APEC and ASEAN may serve some useful ancillary political and security functions, but they do not appear to be viable vehicles of regional economic integration in Asia. Failure of "public" integration, however, has not prevented private (or informal) forms of integration to spread throughout Asia. Private integration falls outside the definition of integration provided in this book, namely the voluntary linking in the economic domain of two or more formerly independent states to the extent that authority over important areas of domestic regulation and policy is shifted to the supranational level. Private integration is market-driven institutional arrangements put in place by individual firms in order to cope with the risks they face in regional trade and investment. This section concludes with a summary of private regional institutional arrangements. Such integration deserves mention, not least because it tends to be overlooked by international-relations scholars, leading some to reach wrong conclusions about the extent of institutionalization of the Asian economic space.[125]

Private integration has been driven, to a large extent, by the rapid increase of foreign direct investment particularly from Japan since the mid-1980s, and later also from Korea, Singapore, Hong Kong, and Taiwan. One major reason for the increase of Japanese foreign direct investment was the appreciation of the Japanese yen after the Plaza

[124] Most APEC members proposed little more than measures already announced or required by the Uruguay Round agreement.

[125] See, for example, Aaron Friedberg, "Ripe For Rivalry: Prospects for Peace in a Multipolar Asia," *International Security* 18 (Winter 1993/1994), 5–33. Based on the assumption that "Asia [is] strikingly underinstitutionalized," he concludes that the chances of economic integration and regional stability in Asia are slim.

Agreement of 1985, and the concomitant need to restructure the Japanese economy.[126] Total Japanese FDI grew from US $12.2 billion in 1985 to $22.3 billion only one year later. By 1990, Japanese FDI had climbed to $56.9 billion.[127] This massive outflow of capital turned Japan into the main provider of FDI in Asia, a position held by the United States until the mid-1980s.[128] Increased Japanese FDI has led Asian affiliates of Japanese manufacturing firms to raise their export sales to total sales ratio from about 36 percent in 1980 to 40 percent in 1990, with the largest portion of these sales, 24.5 percent, being absorbed by Asian markets (11.8 percent by Japan and 12.7 percent by the other Asian countries).[129] North America receives 7.6 percent of the exports. Japanese firms also resort to regional sourcing strategies with increasing frequency.[130]

These increases in regional sales and procurement are largely due to a growing regional division of labor within multinational companies and often take on the form of intra-industry trade.[131] The importance of intra-industry trade in intraregional trade is considerable. Ariff and Chye found that intra-industry trade accounted in 1989 for 60 percent of trade between ASEAN and NIE countries (up from 29 percent in 1970), and 22 percent of trade between ASEAN and Japan (up from 3 percent in 1970).[132]

[126] In 1985, the Japanese yen was valued at 235 to the US dollar. In 1995 its value was approximately 100 to the dollar.

[127] Japanese FDI diminished somewhat in the early 1990s with the onset of the recession.

[128] T. J. Pempel, "The Emerging Asian Regionalism: Toward a Multi-tiered and Open Pattern," manuscript, Department of Political Science, University of Wisconsin (May 1994), p. 11.

[129] Figures are from Shujiro Urata, "Globalization and Regionalization in the Pacific-Asia Region," *Business and the Contemporary World* (Autumn 1993), 26–45. See also Shujiro Urata, "Japanese Foreign Direct Investment and Its Impact on Foreign Trade in Asia," in Takatoshi Ito and Anne Krueger (eds.), *Trade and Protectionism* (Chicago: University of Chicago Press, 1993), pp. 273–299. Related numbers for some countries are very striking. In Indonesia, for example, the proportion of direct investment projects committed to an export ratio of at least 65 percent has almost doubled between 1986 and 1988, rising from 38 percent to 72 percent. In Thailand, the average export ratio of new Japanese investment projects has risen to 80 percent compared with only 10 percent in the seventies. See Alex Borrmann and Rolf Jungnickel, "Foreign Investment as a Factor in Asian Pacific Integration," *Intereconomics* (November/December, 1992), 282–288; and Hal Hill, "Foreign Investment and East Asian Economic Development," *Asian-Pacific Literature* (1990), 35.

[130] See Ministry of International Trade and Industry (MITI), *Survey on the Overseas Activities by the Japanese Companies* (Tokyo: MITI, 1992); cited in Borrmann and Jungnickel, "Foreign Investment as a Factor in Asian Pacific Integration," 286.

[131] Yung Chul Park and Won Am Park, "Changing Japanese Trade and the East Asian NICs," in Paul Krugman (ed.), *Trade with Japan: Has the Door Opened Wider?* (Chicago: University of Chicago Press, 1991), pp. 85–115, especially pp. 103–108.

[132] See Mohamed Ariff and Joseph L. H. Tan, "Asian-Pacific Relations," *ASEAN Economic Bulletin* 8 (March 1992), 258–283.

The result of all these developments was a swift increase in intra-regional Asian trade from US $95 billion in 1980 to $273 billion in 1990, representing a 287 percent change. Remarkably, this rate is higher than the rate of growth of intraregional trade in North America (246 percent) or even in the European Community (233 percent) for the same period.[133]

What private institutional arrangements have Japanese firms put in place to cope with the risks involved in regional trade and investment? One response has been the creation of supplier networks.[134] These are subcontracting or original equipment manufacture linkages between final producers and providers of components, materials, parts, software, and sub-assemblies. Network links are either intra-firm, between affiliates and a parent company or between affiliates owned by the same parent, or intra-group, between affiliates of firms that have long-standing relationships with the parent or its affiliates.

Another example of a private arrangement is supplier cooperation clubs organized by Japanese assemblers. Unlike supplier networks, these clubs often include non-Japanese suppliers. Their purpose is to promote trust and linkages among club members and increase the flow of information in order to enhance organizational and productive efficiencies.[135]

A third notable example of private institutional arrangements is Japanese general trading companies, known as *sogo shosha*. A characterizing trait of the *shosha* is "the intimacy and history of business relationships built up over generations."[136] *Sogo shosha* are large-scale diversified intermediaries between buyers and sellers. In the late nine-teenth-century, they provided smaller textile firms with foreign market

---

[133] See Urata, "Globalization and Regionalization in the Pacific-Asia Region," table 3, 34.

[134] The discussion of supplier networks and cooperation clubs draws on Richard Doner, "Japan in East Asia: Institutions and Regional Leadership," manuscript, Emory University, Atlanta, Ga., Department of Political Science (May 1995), 19.

[135] Doner describes these in another study: "The club's activities are a combination of the social and the professional. The former include various kinds of outings. The latter include the provision of information on issues such as projected model changes and quality problems, the organization of quality circles ... and factory visits among the members. The diffusion of information is certainly a major objective of the club. But equally if not more important is the promotion of trust." See Richard Doner, "Japanese Foreign Investment and the Creation of a Pacific Asian Region," in Frankel and Kahler (eds.), *Regionalism and Rivalry*, p. 196.

[136] Sam Jameson, "Trading Companies Power Tokyo's Economic Expansion," *Los Angeles Times* 200 (June 7, 1994), H2; quoted in James Rauch, "Trade and Search; Social Capital, Sogo Shosha, and Spillovers," manuscript, University of California, San Diego, Department of Economics (1994), 14; see also Mira Wilkins, "Japanese Multinational Enterprise Before 1914," *Business History Review* (Summer 1986), 199–231.

information, developed foreign outlets for their goods, helped them design products, and extended credit.[137] Later, trading companies teamed up in joint ventures with Japanese manufacturing firms to invest in East Asia. Kunio writes: "If investment was to establish a spinning mill, the participating trading company wanted to be its chief supplier of fiber; if it was to set up a fiber plant, the trading company wanted to be its chief supplier of chemical raw materials; if investment was to build an export base, it wanted to market the goods."[138] The *shosha* continue to act today as information clearing houses and insurers against risk. *Shosha*'s continuing importance is beyond doubt. In the late 1980s, for example, Japan's top nine trading companies handled 45 percent of Japan's total exports.[139]

Not all regional private arrangements are of Japanese origin. The "Chinese diaspora," for example, has created one of the largest and most effective ethnic networks. This comprises a number of tightly held, medium-sized family-owned firms that transcend national boundaries and account for up to 70 percent of the private sector in countries such as Malaysia, Thailand, Indonesia, and the Philippines.[140] A remarkable 80 percent of foreign direct investment in mainland China is estimated to have come from these ethnic Chinese networks that link Southeast Asia to Taiwan, Hong Kong, and China.[141] Ethnic or extended family networks are regional institutional arrangements that can be explained as adaptations to uncertainty, risk, and high information cost. Ethnic

[137] Michael Yoshino and Thomas Lifson, *The Invisible Link: Japan's Sogo Shosha and the Organization of Trade* (Cambridge, Mass.: MIT Press, 1986), p. 23.

[138] Yoshihara Kunio, *Japanese Investment in Southeast Asia* (Honolulu: The University Press of Hawaii, 1978), monograph of the Center for Southeast Asian Studies, Kyoto University, pp. 124–125; quoted in Dennis Encarnation, "Bringing East Asia into the US-Japan Rivalry: The Regional Evolution of American and Japanese Multinationals," manuscript, Massachusetts Institute of Technology, Japan Program (1993), 20. See also Ken-ichi Imai, "Evolution of Japan's Corporate and Industrial Networks," in Bo Carlsson (ed.), *Industrial Dynamics: Technological, Organizational, and Structural Changes in Industries and Firms* (Boston: Kluwer Academic, 1989), pp. 123–155.

[139] See James Rauch, "Trade and Search," and Paul Sheard, "The Japanese General Trading Company as an Aspect of Interfirm Risk-Sharing," in Paul Sheard (ed.), *International Adjustment and the Japanese Firm* (Sydney: Allen & Unwin, 1992), p. 12.

[140] Murray Weidenbaum, "Greater China: A New Economic Colossus?," *Washington Quarterly* 16 (1993), 71–81.

[141] Paul Blustein, "Forging 'Greater China': Emigrés Help Build an Economic Power," *Washington Post* (December 1, 1992), A1 and A30, quoted in Peter Katzenstein, "Japan in Asia: Theoretical and Comparative Perspectives," paper prepared for the workshop "Japan in Asia," Cornell University, Center for International Studies and Southeast Asia Program (May 1994), 27; see also John Kao, "The Worldwide Web of Chinese Business," *Harvard Business Review* (March/April 1993), 24–36; Randell Jones, *The Chinese Economic Area: Economic Integration Without a Free Trade Agreement* (Paris: OECD, 1992); and Henny Sender, "Inside the Overseas Chinese Network," *Institutional Investor* (August 1991), 29–43.

and family networks foster a shared culture and language, repeated interactions, issue linkages, and common norms which allow for clear expectations. All of this works to reduce search and information costs and mitigates the risks due to private opportunism. Common norms are particularly noteworthy, and include the concepts of reciprocity, that is, the moral duty to repay loans and the principle that debt never expires, and collective responsibility, a norm which counteracts the lack of public investigatory machinery at the regional level. In addition, Chinese networks are often connected with Japanese networks. Most recently Japanese firms have used these Chinese ethnic networks to reduce the risks of investing in China and Vietnam.[142]

Chapter 3 noted that internalized forms of production, which include informal integration, do not come without a cost. Removing transactions from markets and organizing them within a private-governance structure may sacrifice economies of scale and scope. Internal organization may also experience serious incentive and bureaucratic disabilities. These problems, it was argued, may raise the appeal of external safeguards in the form of an integrated public-governance structure, particularly as both efficiency costs of private contractual arrangements and efficiency gains of external safeguards increase with greater frequency of transaction. If this argument is correct, we may see private institutional arrangements being supplanted or complemented by their public-sector equivalents in the long-term, as intraregional trade and investment increase in Asia. A Japan-centered Asian economic community may then arise, along with an "Asian Commission" and an Asian Court of Justice.[143]

---

[142] Informal institutionalization of the Asian region has also been helped by the adoption of the Japanese "keiretsu" structure of corporate organization in some countries and the emulation of the Japanese model of economic development. Unlike the American model, with its emphasis on deregulation of import controls, price controls, and other restrictions, the Japanese strategy embraces infant industry protection, tax breaks, preferential government loans and subsidies. It has been successfully implemented in Taiwan, South Korea, Singapore, and the ASEAN states. This mimicking process has led to what Doner calls "institutional convergence" in East Asia. See Doner, "Japanese Foreign Investment and the Creation of a Pacific Asian Region," p. 191. Peter Katzenstein speaks similarly of an "extension of distinct institutional forms of Japanese state–society relations across national borders." See Katzenstein, "Japan in Asia," 26. See also William Dawkins, "The Spread of Japanese Economic Ideas: Radical Shift Towards East Asia," *Financial Times*, survey on Japan in Asia (November 15, 1995), 2.

[143] On Japan's potential for regional leadership, see Alan Rix, "Japan and the Region: Leading From Behind," in Higgott, Leaver, and Ravenhill (eds.) *Pacific Economic Relations in the 1990s*, pp. 62–82. See also Gerard Baker, "Benefits of Building a Bloc," *Financial Times* (May 17, 1995), 11; and "Tokyo May Recognize the Benefits of a Bloc," *Financial Times* Survey on Japan in Asia (November 15, 1995), 5.

4   Integration in North America

On December 17, 1992, the United States, Canada, and Mexico signed
the North American Free Trade Agreement (NAFTA), the most comprehensive economic integration project ever negotiated between a
developing country and industrial countries. NAFTA entered into force
on January 1, 1994, creating the world's largest integration area with
nearly 400 million people and an annual $8 trillion production of goods
and services.

NAFTA is an expanded version of the Canada–United States Free
Trade Agreement (CUSTA) of 1988. It provides for the phased elimination of tariff and most non-tariff barriers on regional trade within ten
years; a few import-sensitive products will have a fifteen-year transition
period. In addition, NAFTA extends the dispute settlement procedure
of CUSTA to Mexico, contains far-reaching rights and obligations
regarding services and investment, and addresses labor and cross-border
environmental issues.

This section considers NAFTA's chances of success, that is, it
inquires whether the agreement is likely to attain its stated integration
goals, thereby boosting intraregional trade and investment and promoting economic growth in North America. The answer, in short, is
that NAFTA, unlike most other integration schemes in the western
hemisphere, is likely to succeed because it satisfies both demand and
supply conditions. First, the potential for economic gains from North
American integration is high and has given market players a strong
incentive to lobby for regional institutional arrangements that render the
realization of these gains possible. Second, the presence of the United
States, the undisputed regional leader, facilitates the coordination of
rules, regulations, and policies, and may help diffuse tensions that could
arise from the inequitable distribution of the gains from integration.
Third, NAFTA has established "commitment institutions" in the form
of innovative dispute settlement procedures, rendering cheating or
defection from treaty obligations difficult.

Demand for integration

The commercial ties between the United States, Canada, and Mexico
were already close before the integration agreement was signed. In
1992, for example, both Canada and Mexico sent about 70 percent of
their worldwide exports to the United States. The percentage of US
exports to the two countries was lower, some 29 percent (about 20
percent to Canada and 9 percent to Mexico), but this share was larger

than the 26 percent that the US exported to all of Western Europe.[144] In addition, US foreign direct investment was higher in Canada than in other industrial countries and higher in Mexico than in most other developing countries.[145]

These close ties offered mutual gains but also posed risks and challenges that needed to be addressed. The paramount concerns for Canadian and Mexican exporters were to secure access to the large US market on which they heavily depended and to be able to rely on an institutional mechanism for managing commercial disputes with their powerful neighbor. US and Canadian firms, attracted to Mexico because of location, cheap labor, and a rapidly developing internal market, demanded reduction of Mexican tariffs, which were on average three times as high as US tariffs; elimination of administrative trade barriers, such as import licences, domestic-content mandates, and obligations to export in exchange for permission to invest; protection of intellectual property; permission to have majority equity in foreign direct investment; equal treatment for non-Mexican and Mexican firms providing services in banking, insurance, and surface transportation; and institutional guarantees to safeguard investments against the hazards of opportunism at both the firm and government levels.

These demands were vigorously supported by almost all major umbrella organizations representing big business, including the National Association of Manufacturers, the National Retail Federation, the Business Roundtable, and the United States Council for International Business. Stephan Haggard notes that lobbying efforts were not limited to Fortune 500 companies, but included small and medium-sized businesses. They were joined by free-trade lobbies, such as the National Foreign Trade Council and the Emergency Committee for American Trade, and a variety of business organizations with specific interests in Mexico, such as the American Chamber of Commerce of Mexico, the Coalition for North American Trade and Investment, the Mexico–US Business Committee, and the US–Mexico Chamber of Commerce.[146]

---

[144] The percentages are from the US Department of Commerce; cited in Sidney Weintraub, "NAFTA: For Better or Worse," in Brenda McPhail, *NAFTA Now! The Changing Political Economy of North America* (New York: University Press of America, 1995), p. 6.

[145] *Ibid.*

[146] Stephan Haggard, *Developing Nations and the Politics of Global Integration* (Washington, D.C.: Brookings Institution, 1995), pp. 90–91. See also Helen Milner, "Industries, Governments, and the Creation of Regional Trade Blocs," in Mansfield and Milner (eds.), *The Political Economy of Regionalism*, pp. 77–106.

Supply of integration

NAFTA is the result of the enlargement of an already existing trade pact, the Canada–United States Free Trade Agreement. Thus, the successful completion of NAFTA negotiations depended largely on the willingness of Mexico, the applicant, to accept the terms and conditions of membership as defined by the regional leader, the United States. What explains this willingness? What are the rules, regulations, and compliance procedures of NAFTA? Finally, what interest does the US have in pursuing regional integration? The questions are considered in order.

Mexico's GDP grew annually at about 6 percent for almost fifty years starting in the early 1930s. During this entire period, Mexico preferred relative isolation to regional integration. This policy choice was driven by the fear that greater openness would unduly subject Mexico to North American influence.[147] As long as its economy was growing robustly, Mexico felt no need to compromise national sovereignty. In the early 1980s, however, economic fortunes changed. Mexico experienced the most severe downturn since the revolution. The price of oil collapsed, forcing Mexico to default on its huge foreign debt. The gross domestic product fell by 0.5 percent in 1982 and by 4.7 percent in 1983; industrial output declined by 2.7 percent and 8.3 percent, respectively. Real wages declined by about 40 percent and open unemployment in the three largest metropolitan areas increased to 8 percent in 1982.[148]

This severe crisis triggered a series of reforms that were not limited to trade but included intellectual property reforms and deregulation in finance, road transport, petrochemicals, telecommunications, sugar, mining, and fishing.[149] Foreign direct investment, however, did not respond as had been hoped.[150] To encourage investment in Mexico, Salinas went to Europe in early 1990 but found the Europeans absorbed with problems relating to Eastern Europe and the deepening of the European Union. He then traveled to Japan only to find the Japanese

---

[147] Sidney Weintraub, *Free Trade between Mexico and the United States* (Washington, D.C.: Brookings Institution, 1984), pp. 84–91.

[148] See Peter Gregory, *The Myth of Market Failure: Employment and the Labor Market in Mexico* (Baltimore: Johns Hopkins University Press, 1986).

[149] Robert Kaufman, Carlos Bazdresch, and Blanca Heredia, "Mexico: Radical Reform in a Dominant Party System," in Stephan Haggard and Steven Webb (eds.), *Voting For Reform* (New York: Oxford University Press, 1994), pp. 360–410; Manuel Pastor and Carol Wise, "The Origins and Sustainability of Mexico's Free Trade Policy," *International Organization* (1994), 459–489.

[150] Stephan Haggard, "The Political Economy of Regionalism in Asia and the Americas," in Mansfield and Milner (eds.), *The Political Economy of Regionalism*, p. 38.

focused on Asia and investing heavily in China and Southeast Asia.[151] Investments from the United States had slowed in the late 1980s compared to the mid-1980s amid complaints that Mexican reforms were not far-reaching enough, or that their implementation was unduly delayed or that their enforcement was lax. Salinas came to realize that in order to attract more American capital, he needed to send stronger signals about Mexico's determination to accommodate the demands of foreign investors. Thus he proposed NAFTA. Such an agreement would attract FDI which, in turn, would improve technology, raise productivity rates, help finance the burgeoning current account deficit, lower interest rates and thus stimulate economic growth.[152] Membership in NAFTA may also open the door to the Organization of Economic Cooperation and Development (OECD) which would help Mexico's credit rating and improve the appeal of Mexican government bonds to foreign investors.

However, membership in NAFTA did not come cheap. It exacted a heavy dose of concessions from Mexico even in areas that Mexico considered untouchable at the onset of negotiations. Simply put, Mexico was asked to accept the rules of integration defined by the United States. Specifically, Mexico agreed to improve investment access to its electricity, petrochemical, gas, and energy services and open up procurement of energy-related goods and services.[153] Mexico also promised to improve access for US and Canadian financial service providers, such as banks, security and insurance firms through elimination of all entry restrictions into the financial services market by January 1, 2000. NAFTA is also intended to free up investment in both bus and trucking services, harmonize technical and safety standards, expand the scope of intellectual property rights, and eliminate barriers in the telecommunications sector. A particularly striking concession is Mexico's willingness to open up its highly protected automotive market. As a

---

[151] Robert Pastor, "The North American Free Trade Agreement: Hemisphere and Geopolitical Implications," in Inter-American Development Bank (IDB) and Economic Commission for Latin America and the Caribbean (ECLAC), *Trade Liberalization in the Western Hemisphere* (Washington, D.C.: 1995), pp. 56–84. Between 1989 and 1993, only 18.5 percent and 2.2 percent of total investment flows into Mexico came from Europe and Japan respectively. See Damian Fraser, "Mexico Enjoys Few Alternatives," *Financial Times* (November 17, 1993), 6.

[152] See Nora Lustig, "NAFTA: Potential Impact on Mexico's Economy and Beyond," in Bouzas and Ros (eds.), *Economic Integration in the Western Hemisphere*, pp. 46–80. See also Barry Bosworth and Robert Lawrence (eds.), *Assessing the Impact of North American Free Trade* (Washington, D.C.: Brookings Insitution, 1992); Luís Rubio, *Cómo Va a Afectar a México el Tratado de Libre Comercio?* (Mexico: Fondo de Cultura Económica, 1992); and Robert Pastor, *Integration with Mexico: Options for US Policy* (New York: Twentieth Century Fund, 1993).

[153] This section draws on Gary Clyde Hufbauer and Jeffrey Schott, *NAFTA: An Assessment* (Washington, D.C.: Institute for International Economics, 1993).

result, an integrated auto market is expected to come into existence within a decade.[154]

Equally sweeping concessions were exacted from Mexico with regard to new investment rules. The treaty bans all new export performance, import substitution, and domestic-content requirements affecting US or Canadian investment, forbids restrictions on capital movements, outlaws expropriation, and bars governments from dictating the nationality of corporate senior managers. It further establishes the principle of national treatment to NAFTA investors and a Most-Favored-Nation obligation that ensures that NAFTA investors are treated as well as any other foreign investor in the country. Mexico also agreed to extensive provisions regarding the settlement of investment disputes. Private investors are entitled to seek binding arbitral rulings against a defaulting host government in an international forum, following rules established by the World Bank's International Center for the Settlement of Investment Disputes (ICSID) or the UN Commission on International Trade Law (UNCITRAL).[155] These provisions were included at the insistence of US negotiators, chiefly with the aim of giving aggrieved foreign investors in Mexico an alternative to the domestic legal and administrative system. "These new provisions amount to a repudiation of the Calvo Doctrine, long espoused in Latin America, that all disputes involving foreign investors should be settled solely in local courts."[156] In sum, the agreement offers new investment opportunities and improves the climate of conducting business not only by lifting restrictions but also by providing several institutional guarantees, notably through the provision of a dispute settlement mechanism for investment.[157]

---

[154] Hufbauer and Schott note: "By world standards, the regional [auto] industry should be highly competitive ... [D]rawing on economies of scale and a variety of labor skills, North America could become the world's low-cost producers of autos and tracks, and a major net exporter of these products," *ibid.*, p. 43.

[155] Note, however, that these arbitration panels cannot enforce money damages or compel the return of property. Investors have to take the arbitral awards to a court in any of the three NAFTA countries and seek enforcement under treaties to which all three countries are parties.

[156] Hufbauer and Schott *NAFTA*, p. 81.

[157] Haggard, *Developing Nations and the Politics of Global Integration*, p. 91. Along similar lines, Blecker and Spriggs write: "Although NAFTA is, on the surface, a trade liberalization agreement, in fact it is just as concerned (if not more so) with investment liberalization ... NAFTA contains stringent and unprecedented guarantees for foreign investment ... intended mainly to secure US multinational firms from nationalization or even more moderate restrictions." See Robert Blecker and William Spriggs, "Beyond NAFTA: Employment, Growth, and Income-Distribution Effects of a Western Hemisphere Free Trade Area," in Inter-American Development Bank and Economic Commission for Latin America and the Caribbean, *Trade Liberalization in the Western Hemisphere*, p. 152.

Concessions, however, were not limited to investment-related areas. Mexico ultimately gave in on side-issues such as entry of Chinese or Cuban immigrants to Mexico, local elections, enforcement of a minimum wage, child labor, health, safety, and environmental laws – all of which carry a penalty of fines or sanctions.[158] In addition, Mexico accepted the rules of third-party enforcement as defined in the Canada–United States Free Trade Agreement of 1988. The rules establish a trilateral North American Free Trade Commission, composed of cabinet-level representatives from each country, to administer the agreement and adjudicate disputes over the interpretation or application of NAFTA law. If a dispute arises, a country can call a meeting of the Commission which will try to resolve the dispute using its good offices, mediation or conciliation. In the absence of a mutually satisfactory solution, the Commission will create a panel of private-sector experts which is to issue a first report within ninety days of panel selection and a final version thirty days later. A panel decision is binding and can only be overturned by so-called extraordinary-challenge committees composed of judges. Failure to comply with a ruling gives the complaining country the right to impose trade sanctions for the duration of the dispute.[159] The procedure for review of antidumping (AD) and countervailing duty (CVD) actions is similar to the general dispute-settlement mechanism, including binding panel decisions and the option of calling for an extraordinary challenge committee. In addition, however, a country may request a special committee to determine whether another country's domestic law has undermined the functioning of the panel system. NAFTA allows members to retain their AD/CVD laws, but any changes may be subject to panel review. Moreover, Mexico agreed to adapt its trade policy procedures to the US model by providing full due-process guarantees and judicial review to US exporters for AD/CVD cases. Never before has a developing country accepted a dispute-settlement mechanism that has the power to levy fines and invoke trade sanctions to guarantee compliance with a treaty. Initially Mexico objected that such a mechanism would constitute an unwarranted violation of national sovereignty. In the end it capitulated on this issue, too.[160]

---

[158] Damian Fraser, "Mexico Enjoys Few Alternatives," *Financial Times* (November 17, 1993), 6. The side agreement on the environment established a Commission on Environmental Cooperation, with a Joint Public Advisory Committee of five nongovernmental members from each country. Any organization or individual may issue a complaint, or submission, that a NAFTA member is not enforcing its national laws. The dispute settlement mechanism in the side agreement on labor is broadly similar.

[159] Hufbauer and Schott, *NAFTA: An Assessment*, pp. 142–143.

[160] Stephan Haggard, *Developing Nations and the Politics of Global Integration*, p. 93.

Why did the United States embrace regional integration? A key factor was external, namely growing concern in the late 1980s that the enlargement and deepening of the European Community would endanger vital US commercial interests through the creation of a "Fortress Europe." The importance of this motivation is confirmed in a testimony given by Clayton Yeutter, the US Trade Representative, at the time of the negotiation of the US–Canada Free Trade Agreement:

There is a bit of leverage here, in that it indicated to the rest of the world that we, the United States, can make progress in opening up borders and confronting trade barriers either bilaterally or multilaterally. Our preference is the multilateral route ... but if the multilateral route should prove fruitless for any one of a variety of reasons, this certainly indicates that we can achieve success bilaterally and that we are prepared to pursue these basic objectives on a bilateral basis should that become essential.[161]

In short, integration in North America in the late 1980s was largely triggered, like most other recent integration schemes, by the effects of integration in Europe. It can thus be thought of as an example of the "second integrative response."

NAFTA offers the United States two additional advantages. First, as mentioned above, it improves the efficiency of the North American market and enhances the international competitiveness of regional multinational corporations by facilitating the creation of regional production networks. Second, as argued in chapter 3, integration may serve as a means of keeping externalities at bay. In the 1980s, the most pressing negative externality confronting the United States was illegal migration from Mexico. The fallout from the Mexican crisis was an unprecedented influx of illegal migrants. The number of illegal Mexican aliens was put at approximately 2.3 million in 1984.[162] The annual volume of illegal alien apprehensions along the Mexican–US border grew to 1.8 million by the mid-1980s. This number was almost thirty times larger than the annual number of legal Mexican immigrants.[163]

---

[161] Clayton Yeutter, Testimony before the US Congress, House Committee on Foreign Affairs, Subcommittee on International Economic Policy and Trade, February 25 and March 16, 1988; quoted in Haggard, "The Political Economy of Regionalism in Asia and the Americas," p. 27. John Whalley notes similarly that regional integration expands the US sphere of trade policy influence for subsequent bargaining with other large blocs. See John Whalley, "Regional Trade Arrangements in North America: CUSTA and NAFTA," in Jaime de Melo and Arvind Panagariya, *New Dimensions in Regional Integration* (Cambridge: Cambridge University Press, 1994), p. 370.

[162] George Borjan, Richard Freeman, and Kevin Lang, "Undocumented Mexican-born Workers in the United States: How Many, How Permanent?," in John Abowd and Richard Freeman (eds.), *Immigration, Trade, and the Labor Market* (Chicago: University of Chicago Press, 1991), pp. 77–100.

[163] US Department of Justice, *1989 Statistical Yearbook of the Immigration and Naturalization Service* (Washington, D.C.: US Governmental Printing Office, 1990), pp. xviii–xix

To curb the flow of illegal immigration, Congress passed the Immigration Reform and Control Act (IRCA) in 1986. The Act imposed sanctions on employers who knowingly hire undocumented workers and also assigned larger resources to the US Border Patrol. Most research analyzing the impact of IRCA has found that the Act has had little or no lasting effect on clandestine immigration.[164] A better means of fighting the undesired influx of labor was needed. The Commission for the Study of International Migration and Cooperative Economic Development (CSIMCED) was established by Congress in 1986 to study the relationship between economic development and immigration. After three years of deliberations, it proposed economic integration as an alternative policy option for dealing with illegal migration. It concluded that "expanded access ... [for the] sending countries to the United States ... through increasingly free trade is the most promising stimulus to their future economic growth. The more able they are to sell their products abroad, the less their people will feel the need to seek economic opportunity away from home."[165] The US International Trade Commission concurred: "A FTA [Free Trade Agreement] is likely to decrease ... the gap between real United States wages and Mexican wages of both skilled and unskilled workers combined ... As wage differentials between the United States and Mexico narrow, the incentives for migration from Mexico will decline."[166]

Much subsequent research supports the conclusion that NAFTA is the most promising option for reducing Mexican migration to the United States in the long run. Total Mexican migration to the United States (both legal and illegal) is expected to increase over time in the absence of economic integration with Mexico. In the short term, free

and p. 7; Thomas Espenshade, "Undocumented Migration to the United States: Evidence from a Repeated Trials Model," in Frank Bean, Barry Edmonston, and Jeffrey Passel (eds.), *Undocumented Migration to the United States: IRCA and the Experience of the 1980s* (Washington, D.C.: The Urban Institute Press, 1990), pp. 111–158.

[164] The Immigration and Naturalization Service apprehended a peak of 1.8 million illegal aliens in 1986. After a drop in 1988 and 1989, the trend of apprehensions has been steadily upward. See Thomas Espenshade, "Policy Influences on Undocumented Migration to the United States," *Proceedings of the American Philosophical Society* 136 (1992), 188–207.

[165] Commission for the Study of International Migration and Cooperative Economic Development (CSIMCED), *Unauthorized Migration: An Economic Development Response*, Final Report of the Commission (Washington, D.C.: US Government Printing Office, 1990), p. xxxvi.

[166] US International Trade Commission, *The Likely Impact on the United States of a Free Trade Agreement with Mexico*, Report to the Committee on Ways and Means of the United States House of Representatives and the Committee on Finance of the United States Senate, Investigation no. 322–297, USITC Publication 2353 (Washington, D.C., 1990), p. viii.

trade may also stimulate migration by enhancing people's ability to migrate and by dislocating labor due to economic restructuring. In the long term, however, free trade and concomitant investment will increase the capacity of the Mexican economy to create jobs. This, in turn, is likely to reduce migration.[167]

NAFTA: preliminary results

Three years into a fifteen-year process to eliminate tariffs, it is impossible to reach a final verdict on the working of the accord. Nevertheless, the current evidence suggests that governments are faithfully implementing the provisions of the treaty, and firms are quickly responding to the new market opportunities offered by the Agreement.

In the three years since NAFTA came into force, Mexico has reduced average tariffs on US goods from 10 percent to 2.9 percent. The US reduced its tariffs on Mexican imports from an average of 2.07 percent to 1.4 percent.[168] The Mexican tariff reduction is particularly noteworthy considering the severity of the shocks that hit Mexico in 1994. In the space of three months, Mexico suffered from a peasant uprising in the southern state of Chiapas, the kidnapping of a senior banker, and the assassination of Luis Donaldo Colosio, the presidential candidate of the governing party. Domestic political uncertainty quickly spilled over into the economy, triggering a deep loss in the value of the Mexican peso against all major currencies. The stock market lost nearly half its value, and the shock waves of the crisis spread around the world.

Fearing deleterious effects on its own economy from a prolonged Mexican crisis, the US administration acted quickly and marshaled an unprecedented $50 billion international-aid package to rescue its neighbor's economy. The operation was a success: after a brief recession, Mexico recovered and repaid the US emergency loan in 1997, three years ahead of schedule.

During the crisis, Mexico continued to implement its NAFTA obligations while raising tariffs on imports from other countries. As a result, American exports recovered in eighteen months and were up nearly 37 percent by the end of 1996 relative to pre-NAFTA levels. In the first

---

[167] See Wayne Cornelius and Philip Martin, "The Uncertain Connection: Free Trade and Rural Migration to the United States," *International Migration Review* 27 (Fall 1993), 484–512; Dolores Acevedo and Thomas Espenshade, "Implications of a North American Free Trade Agreement for Mexican Migration to the United States," *Population and Development Review* 18 (December 1992), 729–744; Sidney Weintraub, "North American Free Trade and the European Situation Compared," *International Migration Review* 26 (Summer 1992), 506–524.

[168] President of the United States, *Study on the Operation and Effects of the North American Free Trade Agreement* (Washington, D.C.: The White House, July 1997), p. ii.

four months of 1997, US exports to Mexico were up by 54.5 percent relative to the same period in 1993 and virtually equalled US exports to Japan, even though Mexico's economy is only one-twelfth the size of Japan.[169] Mexican exports to the US rose in the same time by 80 percent. These increases, of course, cannot be attributed solely to NAFTA. Other factors, such as a strong US economy and a cheap Mexican peso, have also played a role in intensifying regional commercial exchange. However, several studies have concluded that, controlling for these other factors, NAFTA's effect remains significant, particularly in industries such as autos, chemicals, textiles, and electronics.[170]

Is NAFTA helping Mexico attract more foreign direct investment? During the negotiation stage of NAFTA, the prospect of an agreement and its impact on expectations helped propel the growth of inward investment. In 1992, investment flows into Mexico from the United States were approximately 50 percent higher than they were in 1990.[171] In the three years before the treaty came into effect, US foreign direct investment flows into Mexico averaged $2.8 billion; in the following three years the average was $3 billion.[172] This increase, even though modest, is remarkable considering that the period includes the episode of the Mexican crisis which adversely affected foreign investment decisions. It suggests that Mexico's respect of its NAFTA obligations as well as its economic adjustment program quickly helped to restore foreign investment confidence.

In sum, despite unexpected adverse conditions in Mexico, NAFTA governments have been able to keep the implementation schedule on track. This feat is in no small measure due to the willingness of the United States to bail out the Mexican economy at the height of the crisis. Some of the NAFTA rules will not be fully phased in for another twelve years, but the available evidence already suggests that the agreement has produced positive economic effects, boosting intraregional trade and investment and helping economic growth.

---

[169] *Ibid.*, p. 2.

[170] Some of these studies are reviewed in the *Study on the Operation and Effects of the North American Free Trade Agreement*, pp. 13–20.

[171] Whalley, "Regional Trade Arrangements in North America," pp. 364–365.

[172] President of the United States, *Study on the Operation and Effects of the North American Free Trade Agreement*, p. 4.

6   Conclusion

Regional integration has re-emerged in the late 1980s as one of the most important developments of world politics. In 1986, Spain and Portugal acceded to the European Community. In the same year, the Single European Act was adopted with the aim of establishing a genuine common market in goods, services, capital, and labor by 1992. Six years later, the EC agreed to yet another revision of the Treaty of Rome with the signing of the Maastricht Treaty on European monetary and political union. It grew again in 1995 with the admission of Austria, Finland, and Sweden. Poland, Hungary, the Czech and Slovak Republics, Turkey, Malta, and Cyprus and others are also seeking to join the EU as full members.

On the American continent, the Canada–United States Free Trade agreement was adopted in 1988. Six years later, Mexico joined the North American free-trade zone. Chile and Argentina have high hopes of acceding to the exclusive NAFTA club. In the meantime, regional integration schemes are mushrooming throughout Latin America. Similar dynamics are detectable in the Far East since the announcement by the Association of Southeast Asian Nations that it plans to create an ASEAN Free Trade Area.

Some thirty years earlier, a similar wave of integration swept parts of the world. In Europe, the European Community and the European Free Trade Association were created. And in Latin America, the Latin American Free Trade Association, the Andean Pact, and the Central American Common Market were launched.

Each integration wave produces a few success stories and many more failures. This book has sought to identify the conditions under which integration is likely to succeed or to fail. Integration agreements do not establish integration; they only signify promises by the political leaders to engage in particular courses of action over a period of time towards the aim of tying the economies of their countries closer together. Such endeavors are neither easy nor automatic. They typically entail a lengthy process of establishing regional rules, regulations, and policies which are

189

either based on specific treaty provisions or derived over time from the general principles and objectives written into integration treaties.

This focus on the provision of regional institutional arrangements is a key difference between my approach to integration and traditional approaches in economics where integration is viewed primarily as an exercise in reducing or eliminating border barriers. The view of integration in this book is thus much broader. Integration is understood as the process of internalizing externalities that cross borders within a group of countries. Externalities affecting cross-border trade and investment arise from economic and political uncertainty, as well as from hazards due to opportunism at both the firm and government levels. The cost of these externalities increases as new technologies raise the potential for gain from market exchange, thus increasing the payoff to regional rules, regulations, and policies.

The pressure for such regional institutional arrangements does not come from the top but from the bottom, that is, the initiators of successive rounds of deeper integration are typically not the political leaders but market actors who stand to reap large gains from transacting in increasingly integrated economies. This demand for regional rules, regulations, and policies is a critical driving force of integration. Where demand is absent, either because regional economies lack complementarity or because the small size of regional markets does not offer important economies of scale, the process of integration will quickly peter out. Demand alone, however, is not enough for integration to succeed. Several supply conditions must be satisfied as well. They include willingness by political actors to accommodate demands for functional integration at each step of the integration process, and the presence of an undisputed regional leader that can serve as a focal point in the coordination of rules, regulations, and policies, and is able to ease distributional tensions by acting as regional paymaster.

In sum, regional groups that meet both demand and supply conditions stand the greatest chance of succeeding, whereas groups that fulfill neither set of conditions are least likely to match their stated integration goals with subsequent achievements.

The discussion of the internal logic of integration was complemented by an account of the external logic, focusing on the effects of community-building on outsiders. The process of regional integration may have discriminatory effects on the economies of outsiders. Affected outsiders may respond in one of two ways. First, they can seek to merge with the area generating the external effects. The enlargement of the European Union and the German Zollverein are prime examples of such mergers. Second, outsiders can respond by creating their own regional group. I have discussed many examples of such counter-unions. Like any integration scheme, counter-unions must satisfy both demand and supply conditions to be successful.

What implications can be drawn from the analysis in this book with regard to the future of the world economy? Will the creation of regional groups result in the splintering of the world economy into self-absorbed and self-sufficient regions or is it more likely to spur inter-regional tariff reductions and usher in a harmonious period of multilateral free trade? This question has been much debated of late in economics. Jagdish Bhagwati, for example, has argued that regional economic integration leads to the proliferation of non-tariff barriers between regions, thus undermining progress towards a nondiscriminatory world economy as envisaged by the General Agreement on Tariffs and Trade. Further, large countries may use their power position within regional groups to pressure smaller member states into making concessions that the powerful members would be unable to obtain in more balanced multi-lateral negotiations.[1] Anne Krueger shares this pessimistic assessment of the impact of integration. She argues that the establishment of FTAs increases the protection that some industries receive when governments adopt rules of origin. The resulting discrimination may turn out to be lasting because rules of origin can give protected firms a vested interest in maintaining protection, thus reducing the ability of the members of a free-trade area to engage in external trade liberalization.[2]

This pessimistic outlook has been questioned, notably by Paul Krugman and Lawrence Summers.[3] They have suggested that the trade-diversion effect of preferential trading areas (PTAs) is minimal because most PTAs are "natural," that is, they are determined by geography; and since countries within geographical areas usually trade a lot with each other anyway, PTAs divert little trade.

---

[1] See Jagdish Bhagwati, *The World Trading System at Risk* (Princeton: Princeton University Press and Harvester Wheatsheaf, 1991); "Regionalism and Multilateralism: An Overview," in Jaime de Melo and Arvind Panagariya (eds.), *New Dimensions in Regional Integration*, pp. 22–51.

[2] Anne Krueger, "Free Trade Agreements Versus Customs Union," *NBER Working Paper* no. 5084 (Cambridge, Mass.: NBER, 1995); Kola Krishna and Anne Krueger, "Implementing Free Trade Areas: Rules of Origin and Hidden Protection," in Alan Deardorff and Robert Stein (eds.), *New Dimensions in Trade Theory* (Ann Arbor: University of Michigan Press, 1993); Anne Krueger, "Rules of Origin as Protectionist Devices," *NBER Working Paper* no. 4352 (Cambridge, Mass.: NBER, 1993).

[3] Paul Krugman, "The Move Toward Free Trade Zones," in *Policy Implication of Trade and Currency Zones* (Symposium Sponsored by the Federal Reserve Bank of Kansas City, Jackson Hole, Wyo., August 1991), pp. 7–42; and Lawrence Summers, "Regionalism and the World Trading System," in *Policy Implication of Trade and Currency Zones*, pp. 46–48.

Jeffrey Frankel has recently conducted a comprehensive empirical examination of these competing views.[4] His findings confirm the importance of geography and other factors, such as common language and common borders, in accounting for regional trade. However, he also finds that membership of a preferential trade group contributes to intraregional trade concentration, even after holding constant geography and other natural determinants of trade. In short, trading blocs tend to become "supernatural," that is, the members of a regional group tend to trade more with each other than can be justified on the basis of geography and related factors. In other words, trade diversion is a corollary of the creation of PTAs.

Frankel's study thus confirms an argument of this book that the creation of regional groups imposes costs on outsiders. However, to assess the general welfare implications of regionalism, the analysis must move beyond this observation and consider the dynamic political-economy aspects of integration.[5] This book, for example, has shown that the cost imposed on outsiders will trigger further integrative processes (the first and second integrative responses) leading to the expansion and propagation of free trade areas. Hence multilateral cooperation is not a *sine qua non* for trade liberalization.[6] Nineteenth century Europe offers many examples of bilateral agreements that sparked wide movements of trade liberalization. When Prussia established the customs union with Hesse-Darmstadt in 1828, Bavaria and Württemberg responded with their own customs union. Other German states formed the Middle German Commerical Union. The members of these counter-unions later joined the Prussian Zollverein. And with the expansion of the Zollverein, Prussia managed to extract trade concessions from its protectionist neighbors. On behalf of the Zollverein, it signed commercial treaties with Holland (1851), Great Britain (1841, 1847), Russia (1844), Austria (1853), and the Baltic States (1857).

Another compelling example of trade liberalization, triggered by a bilateral trade agreement, is the Anglo-French commercial treaty of

[4] Jeffrey Frankel, *Regional Trading Blocs in the World Economic System* (Washington, D.C.: Institute for International Economics, 1997); see also Jeffrey Frankel, Ernesto Stein, and Shan-jin Wei, "Trading Blocs and the Americas: The Natural, the Unnatural, and the Super-Natural," *Journal of Development Economics* 47 (1995), 61–95.

[5] Frankel, *Regional Trading Blocs in the World Economic System*, p. 230.

[6] On the idea of regionalism (or bilateralism or plurilateralism – the terms are used interchangeably in the literature) as a stepping-stone towards multilateralism, see also Robert Lawrence, "Emerging Regional Arrangement: Building Blocks or Stumbling Blocks?" in Richard O'Brien (ed.), *Finance and the International Economy*, The AMEX Bank Review Prize Essays (Oxford: Oxford University Press, 1992).

1860.[7] Britain made its tariff reductions applicable to all nations. However, France lowered its import duties on British goods only. As a result, outsiders were left at a substantial disadvantage in exporting to the large French market. Irwin notes: "As other European states quickly sought agreements with France to secure equal treatment for their own goods, the Anglo-French treaty – which began as a purely bilateral arrangement … – rapidly cascaded into a series of bilateral trade arrangements."[8] France signed commercial treaties with Belgium (1861), the Zollverein (1862, effective in 1865), Italy (1863), Switzerland (1964), Sweden, Norway, Spain, and the Netherlands (all in 1865), and Austria (1866). This gradual expansion of the trading network brought low tariffs to virtually all of Europe.

Kenneth Oye's recent book on economic discrimination contains other examples of bilateralism and regionalism leading to inter-regional trade liberalization.[9] Most strikingly, Oye finds that even in the 1930s bilateralism managed to slow and ultimately reverse movement toward economic closure. For example, the American shift from the relatively nondiscriminatory protectionism of Smoot Hawley to the discriminatory liberalization of the Reciprocal Trade Agreement Act was an inadvertent consequence of the adoption of discriminatory policies by European states in response to Smoot Hawley. The reason is that the latter discrimination disadvantaged US export-oriented interests, mobilizing these interests in the United States in the struggle against protectionism.[10]

The examples demonstrate that trade liberalization can be attained entirely through bilateral agreements. Thus regional trade agreements can serve as building blocks rather than stumbling blocks on the path to global free trade. The reason is that the cost of such agreements to outsiders, namely trade diversion due to discriminatory market access, can trigger a dynamic sequence of bargaining steps that ushers in a period of freer trade.

A very similar dynamic seems to be at work in today's world economy. The adoption of the Single European Act in 1987 and the speedy progress towards the "Europe 1992" goal raised fears of a "Fortress

---

[7] See William Otto Henderson, "A Nineteenth-Century Approach to a West European Common Market," *Kyklos* 10 (1957), 448–457; and Douglas Irwin, "Multilateral and Bilateral Trade Policies in the World Trading System: A Historical Perspective," in De Melo and Panagariya (eds.), *New Dimensions in Regional Integration*, pp. 90–119.

[8] Irwin, "Multilateral and Bilateral Trade Policies in the World Trading System," 97.

[9] Kenneth Oye, *Economic Discrimination and Political Exchange* (Princeton: Princeton University Press, 1992).

[10] Oye also provides examples of economic discrimination with liberalizing effects for the 1980s.

Europe" throughout the world. The malaise worsened with the steady enlargement of the European Community and the ratification of the Maastricht Treaty on European Monetary and Political Union. The Americans responded by creating a Canada–US free trade area and later signing NAFTA. This process of integration in the northern hemisphere, in turn, provoked the creation of counter-unions in the developing world.

Many of these counter-unions serve useful functions as bargaining chips in negotiations with other unions, and thus have a catalyzing effect on the process of general trade liberalization. A striking example comes from the Asia Pacific Economic Cooperation forum (APEC). President Clinton upgraded the APEC Seattle meeting of November 1993 by adding a high-profile leaders' meeting. This move came on the heels of the approval of NAFTA in the US Congress. Frankel notes: "In this way the United States signaled to the Europeans that if they continued to allow French farmers to hold up the Uruguay Round, other countries might proceed with other initiatives without [Europe] ... German policy-makers have reportedly confirmed that [the prospect of exclusion] was part of [the European motive] for concluding the Uruguay Round in December 1993."[11]

Regional groups may also help to accelerate the process of liberalization if there is competitive pressure among them. For example, to counter the effects of American-led regionalism, the European Union announced – a few months before the Miami Summit of the Americas of December 1994 – its readiness to negotiate a free-trade zone with MERCOSUR.[12] A cooperation agreement between the EU and MERCOSUR, intended to prepare the way for a free-trade accord, was signed a year later.

Finally, the most telling piece of evidence of the progressive nature of today's regionalism is the renewed élan in US–European relations. In the early 1990s, the United States complained with increasing frequency about protectionist European policies, particularly in agriculture, the audio-visual sector, and the environment. European labor standards and subsidies to industry were also a source of discontentment. Conversely, the Europeans took offense at American "aggressive unilateralism" in commercial diplomacy. Disputes were not solely limited to trade issues but included deadlocked negotiations over a suitable candidate to lead the new World Trade Organization (WTO), disagreements

---

[11] Frankel, *Regional Trading Blocs in the World Economic System*, p. 221.

[12] Miles Kahler, *Regional Futures and Transatlantic Economic Relations* (New York: Council on Foreign Relations Press, 1995), p. 21. During the Miami summit, the United States and thirty-three Latin American countries agreed to conclude talks for a free-trade pact by 2005.

over how to bail out Mexico, squabbles over the appointment of a new NATO Secretary-General, and European objections to the US-led effort to speed the enlargement of the NATO alliance to the East, which many Western European governments feared could provoke Russia. Writing in 1995, Robert Blackwell – a former senior Bush administration official – observed that "[US–European] relations have not been so bad for decades."[13] But just as the dire predictions of opponents of regionalism seemed confirmed, politicians and business-leaders on both sides of the Atlantic began to explore ways to improve inter-regional relations. Jacques Santer, President of the European Commission, called for a genuine transatlantic treaty, including a transatlantic single market. US Secretary of State Warren Christopher responded by promising that the idea of a Transatlantic Free Trade Area (TAFTA) would be given "the serious study it deserves."[14] However, worries that a large discriminatory trading area in the West would provoke a hostile response, particularly from Asian trading partners, convinced the US and the EU to shift their attention to proposals for a transatlantic "economic area" which, in contrast to TAFTA, would focus on non-tariff barriers to trade and investment. In December 1995, the United States and the European Union signed an ambitious agreement in trade and political cooperation. The agreement commits the two allies to negotiate the phasing out of tariff and trade barriers on all information-technology products, including computers, semi-conductors, and software; to accelerate the liberalization in telecoms and maritime services; and to formulate a policy of mutual recognition of each side's standards, certification, and testing procedures. In addition to collaboration over trade issues, the signatories agreed to coordinate their aid policies, particularly in Central and Eastern Europe; to exchange information on drug trafficking and terrorism; and to increase communications across the Atlantic through educational exchanges, joint action programs for high-level civil servants, and the nascent Transatlantic Business Dialogue (TBD), a grouping of more than fifty top US and European executives from multinational companies that include Ford, Chrysler, Xerox, Glaxo, Nokia, and ABB. The TBD is designed to involve the private sector in dismantling transatlantic business barriers.[15]

---

[13] Quoted in Lionel Barber, "Niggling Trade Disputes Threaten US–EU Relationship," *Financial Times* (March 13, 1995), 2.

[14] See "Charting a Transatlantic Agenda for the 21st Century: Address by Secretary of State Warren Christopher" (Casa de America, Madrid, Spain, June 2, 1995), quoted in Kahler, *Regional Futures and Transatlantic Economic Relations*, p. 81.

[15] See Lionel Barber, "US–EU Accord Aims to Cement Transatlantic Ties," *Financial Times* (December 2/3, 1995), 2; and Sander Thoenes, "Pact Set to Boost Transatlantic trade," *Financial Times* (June 6, 1997), 2.

It is significant that the new transatlantic agenda omits reference to the TAFTA project. This may be an indication of American and European determination to pursue strategies that appear to be compatible with the principles enshrined in the WTO, and hence minimize the risk of confrontations with other regions. Thus the new agenda is a good example of the "building-block" approach towards global trade and investment liberalization. It pursues issues not yet covered, or covered only poorly, by multilateral agreements and leaves the door open to those who are able and willing to make similar commitments. While it may be too early to provide a full assessment of the implications of the new agenda, there is evidence that it augurs well for the future development of the world economy.

Index